ONE HUNDRED YEARS
IN YOSEMITE

HIGH SIERRA CLASSICS SERIES

ONE HUNDRED YEARS IN YOSEMITE

The Story of a Great Park and Its Friends

OMNIBUS EDITION

BY CARL PARCHER RUSSELL

INTRODUCTION AND ANNOTATIONS BY
HANK JOHNSTON

YOSEMITE
ASSOCIATION

Yosemite National Park, California

Yosemite Association
P.O. Box 545
Yosemite National Park, CA 95389

The Yosemite Association is a non-profit, membership
organization dedicated to the support of Yosemite National Park.
Our publishing program is designed to provide an educational service
and to increase the public's understanding of Yosemite's special
qualities and needs. To learn more about our activities and
other publications, or for information about membership, please
write to the address above, or call (209) 379-2646.

This "Omnibus Edition" reprints the last version of the text that
Carl Russell personally authored (1959 edition). Several appendices have
been included from the first edition, including key documents
from Yosemite's early history.

LIBRARY OF CONGRESS CATALOGING-IN-PUBLICATION DATA
Russell, Carl Parcher, 1894-1967.
One Hundred Years in Yosemite: the story of a great park and its friends
/ by Carl Parcher Russell;
introduction and annotations by Hank Johnston.—Omnibus ed.
p. cm—(High Sierra classics series)
"Except for minor typographical corrections, the text is reproduced verbatim
from the 1959 edition"–Introd.
"The chronology . . . comes from the 1959 printing, with entries after 1958
added by the editors . . . Also included are nine rare documents from 1851-52 that
appeared only in the original Stanford University edition . . . The bibliography . . . [combines]
the Cited publications and Additional bibliography from the 1932 Stanford University
edition with the Bibliography from the 1947 University of California edition"–Introd.
Includes bibliogaphical references and index.
ISBN 0-939666-60-X (paper):$9.95
1. Yosemite National Park (Calif.)–History. 2. Yosemite Valley (Calif.)–History.
I. Johnston, Hank. II. Title. III. Series.
F868.Y6R8 1992   92-13678
979.4'47–dc20   CIP

Other books in the "HIGH SIERRA CLASSICS SERIES":

Discovery of the Yosemite
by Lafayette H. Bunnell

A Journal of Ramblings Through the High Sierra of California
by Joseph LeConte

Contents

INTRODUCTION

One Hundred Years in Yosemite, Carl Russell's enduring account of human events in our great national park, was originally published in April, 1932, by Stanford University Press. The title of the 258-page hardcover book referred to the century that had passed since 1833 when recorded history in Yosemite really began. During the fall of that year, the Joseph Walker party, traveling from east to west over the Sierra Nevada, became the first group of non-Indians to cross a portion of what is now Yosemite National Park. Whether or not Walker's group looked down into the "incomparable valley" itself remains a matter of conjecture, but the outside world's knowledge of Yosemite unquestionably begins with the scanty reports left by the Walker expedition.

Dr. Russell was eminently qualified to write the first significant study of Yosemite National Park. A recognized authority on the early Westward Movement, he held advanced degrees in both biology and ecology. In the 1920's, while Chief Park Naturalist, he introduced an innovative curatorial program at the new Yosemite Museum that resulted in the acquisition of many valuable relics and records from the past. Russell's scholarly, fact-filled book, the culmination of nearly a decade of research, was uniformly well-received by historians and lay readers alike.

In 1947, Dr. Russell brought out a revised version of *One Hundred Years in Yosemite*, making use of source material that had come to light since the publication of his original work 15 years before. Published by University of California Press, the new 244-page hardcover edition quickly became a popular favorite with Yosemite visitors.

The Yosemite Natural History Association, a park support group nurtured by Dr. Russell from its inception in the early 1920's, took over publication of *One Hundred Years* in 1957. Since that time the book has gone through four softcover editions, the most recent dated 1976, and now out of print. (A summary of the publishing history of *One Hundred Years in Yosemite* appears elsewhere in these pages.)

The present Yosemite Association reprint might be called a "Best of *One Hundred Years in Yosemite*." Except for minor typographical corrections, the text is reproduced verbatim from the 1959 edition, the last volume with which Dr. Russell was directly involved. Certain items in the story may seem a bit dated today, but the bulk of Russell's historical information remains as valuable as ever. The chronology also comes from the 1959 printing, with entries after 1958 added by the editors.

Also included are nine rare documents from 1851-52 that appeared only in the original Stanford University edition. They provide important background information about the Mariposa Indian War. The bibliography was created by combining citations from the 1932 Stanford University edition with those from the 1947 University of California edition, the last version to offer such a list. It contains excellent references for further reading.

Even as fine a book as *One Hundred Years in Yosemite* suffers a few errors of fact. Most of these became apparent because of later information unavailable to Dr. Russell. In this regard, I have annotated the text where I thought commentary or further exposition was required. These references are indicated by superior letters (not to be confused with Dr. Russell's own numerical footnotes appearing at the bottom of some pages). The explanatory notes are listed in alphabetical order, chapter by chapter, following the main text.

❖   ❖   ❖

Carl Parcher Russell was born on January 18, 1894, at Fall River, Wisconsin. He received an A.B. degree in biology from nearby Ripon College in 1915, and an M.A. in cytology from the University of Michigan in 1917. He later earned Doctorates from both institutions.

After teaching briefly at the College of St. Thomas in St. Paul, Minnesota, Russell joined the U. S. Army during World War I. He served overseas in 1918-19 as a second lieutenant with the 8th Infantry. After the war, Russell taught high school biology at Reno, Nevada, for several years. There he met his future wife, Betty. After a brief romance, the couple married on June 10, 1922.

"We drove to Yosemite as our honeymoon tour," Russell later recalled. "I encountered Ansel Hall in the old Yosemite Museum. During the course of our conversation he indicated an interest in employing me as Ranger-Naturalist during the next summer. On June 10, 1923, I went to work in Yosemite Valley. Before the end of the year, Ansel was made Chief Naturalist in Washington, and I was asked to take the Chief Naturalist job in Yosemite as a regular appointee. I jumped at the opportunity."

Russell served in the Yosemite position until 1929. During his tenure, the Yosemite Museum was developed and many new exhibits prepared. In 1929 Russell became Field Naturalist-Museum Specialist for the Western Region, giving attention to museum needs throughout the western national parks and monuments. He moved up to Chief, Museum Division, of the National Park Service in Washington in 1935. Four years later he was promoted to Chief Naturalist of the entire park system. During his eight-year term as Chief, he instituted imaginative new Service-wide programs in geological research, wildlife management, and park museum administration.

Russell returned to his "first love," as he put it, in December, 1947, when he was appointed Superintendent of Yosemite National Park. He left this position in November, 1952, to accept a two-year Guggenheim Fellowship that allowed him to pursue research on his specialty, the study of fur trade and pioneer life on the Western frontier. Russell returned to the Park Service in 1954 as Coordinator of Research for the Western Region. In 1957 he ended his 34-year N.P.S. career by retiring to Orinda, California.

In the ten years before his death in June, 1967, Russell gave his energy to the pursuit of knowledge in his fields of interest. He also served as a lecturer and consultant for historical museums and facilities throughout the United States. He wrote two books about pioneer life, *Guns on the Early Frontier* (published in 1957) and *Firearms, Traps, and Tools of the Mountain Men* (published posthumously in 1967).

Washington State University purchased Russell's personal library of books, papers, and other material dealing with the Western frontier from his widow in October, 1967. Called "near definitive" in scope, the collection of 24,916 items occupies more than 45 linear feet of shelf space. It is still widely used by scholars seeking further knowledge of a significant period in United States history.

Carl Parcher Russell was an able writer, a skillful lecturer, and a recognized expert in curatorial and interpretive work. Perhaps his greatest attribute, however, was his tenacious research, his never-ending quest to learn all there was to know about something that interested him. It was a trait Russell himself recognized and took pride in.

"My studies have involved thousands of investigations, each to the fifth decimal point," he wrote a friend shortly before his death. "My facts will stand hard scrutiny. I have dealt with the written word, records, documents, artifacts, and all other forms of source information with hardly an hour when not actually with a source item or thinking about it. I have thrived upon that which others have overlooked or regarded as unimportant scraps. There have been no minor matters to me."

Hank Johnston
Yosemite, California

CHAPTER I

DISCOVERY

*T*hat picturesque type known as the American trapper ush-
ered in the opening event of Sierra Nevada history. True,
the Spaniards of the previous century had viewed the "snowy range
of mountains," had applied the name Sierra Nevada, and even had
visited its western base. But penetration of the wild and snowy fast-
ness awaited the coming of Americans.

In the opening decades of the nineteenth century the entire
American West was occupied by scattered bands of trappers. From
the ranks of the "Fur Brigade" came Jedediah Strong Smith, a
youthful fur trader, not yet thirty years old but experienced in his
profession and well educated for his time. In the summer of 1826 he
took his place at the head of a party of men organized to explore the
unknown region lying between Great Salt Lake and the California
coast. Smith's leadership of this party gave him a first place in the
history of the Sierra Nevada. His party left the Salt Lake rendezvous on August 22, 1826. A southwest course was followed
across the deserts of Utah and Nevada, penetrating the Mojave
country and the Cajon Pass. On November 27 they went into camp
near Mission San Gabriel. Smith was thus the first American to
make the transcontinental journey to California, the harbinger of a
great overland human flood.

The Spanish governor of California refused to permit the party
to travel north as Smith had planned. Instead, he instructed that
they should quit California by the route used in entering.
Reinforced with food, clothing, and horses supplied by the friendly
Mission San Gabriel, Smith returned to the neighborhood of the
Cajon Pass. It was not his intention, however, to be easily deterred
in his plan to explore California. He followed the Sierra Madre to

the junction of the Coast Ranges and the Sierra Nevada and entered the San Joaquin Valley.

He found the great interior valley inhabited by large numbers of Indians, who were in no way hostile or dangerous. There were "few beaver and elk, deer and antelope in abundance." Reaching one of the streams flowing from the mountains, he determined to cross the Sierra Nevada and return to Great Salt Lake. Smith called this stream the Wimmelche after a tribe of Indians by that name who inhabited the region thereabouts. C. Hart Merriam has established the fact that Smith's "Wimmelche" is the Kings River, and the time of his arrival there as February of 1827. Since the passes of the Sierra in this region are never open before the advent of summer, it is not surprising that his party failed in this attempted crossing of the range. Authorities have differed in their interpretation of Smith's writing regarding his ultimate success in traversing the Sierra, but there is little doubt that he crossed north of the Yosemite region, perhaps as far north as the American River.

Smith was, then, the first white man known to have crossed the Sierra Nevada. His pathfinding exploits did not take him into the limits of the present Yosemite National Park, but because his manuscript maps were made available to government officials who influenced later expeditions and because he was the first to explore the mountain region of which the Yosemite is an outstanding feature, his expedition provides the opening story in any account of Yosemite affairs.

Smith's explorations paved the way for a notable influx of American trappers to the valleys west of the Sierra Nevada. Smith, in fact, returned to California that same summer. Pattie, Young, Ogden, Wolfskill, Jackson, and Walker all brought parties to the new fields during the first five years following the Smith venture. Fur traders informed the settlers in the western states of the easy life in California and enticed them with stories of the undeveloped resources of the Pacific slope. Pioneers were then occupying much of the country just west of the Missouri, and a gradual tide of westward emigration brought attention first to Oregon and then to California.

The presence of Americans in California greatly annoyed the Mexican officials of the country. The fears of these officials were justified, for the trappers scarcely concealed their desire to overthrow Mexican authority and assume control themselves. To add to the threatened confusion, revolt brewed among the Mexicans who held the land.

In 1832 Captain B. L. E. Bonneville secured leave of absence from the United States Army and launched a private venture in exploring and trapping. One Joseph Reddeford Walker, who had achieved fame as a frontiersman, was engaged by Bonneville to take charge of a portion of his command. Walker's party of explorers was ordered to cross the desert west of Great Salt Lake and visit California. Reliable knowledge of the Sierra Nevada and the first inkling of the existence of Yosemite Valley resulted from this expedition, made in 1833.

Joseph Walker, born in 1798 on the Tennessee River near the present Knoxville, Tennessee, had moved westward with the advancing frontier in 1818 to the extreme western boundary of Missouri. There he and his brothers rented government land near the Indian Factory, Fort Osage. They put in a crop and during slack seasons mingled with the Osages and the Kanzas Indians. Here Walker formed his first ideas of trade with the Indians—ideas which bore fruit during his later experiences on the Santa Fe Trail and with the fur brigades in the Rocky Mountains.

Early in 1831, Walker, en route southward from his home to buy horses, stopped at Fort Gibson in the heart of the Cherokee Nation in the eastern part of the present Oklahoma. Several companies of the 7th U. S. Infantry were stationed here. This circumstance brought about a sequence of events which left permanent marks upon Walker's personal career and upon the history of the American West. Captain B. L. E. Bonneville was in command of B Company of the 7th Infantry. Bonneville confided in Walker that the government was about to place him on detached service in order that he might conduct a private expedition into the Rocky Mountains for furs and geographical data. He asked Walker to join him as guide and counselor. To this proposal Walker acceded enthusiastically and proceeded forthwith to organize the equipment and personnel needed for the venture.

On the first of May, 1832, Bonneville and Walker led westward a caravan of twenty wagons attended by one hundred and ten mounted trappers, hunters, and servants from the Missouri River landing where Fort Osage had once stood. Out upon the Kansas plains they went, up the Platte, to the Sweetwater, and through South Pass. In the valleys of the Green and the Snake they trapped and traded through the winter and spring of 1832-33. After the rendezvous on the Green in July, 1833, Walker was named by Bonneville to be the leader of the now famous Walker expedition to the Pacific.

The reports of Jedediah Smith on his trip of 1826 to California and the much talked about adventures of Smith, as discussed by the mountain men, seem to have been decisive factors which influenced Bonneville to authorize this ambitious undertaking. The fact that a scant 4,000 pounds of beaver was all he had to show for his campaign of the past year also may have contributed to his determination to take another fling at exploration, trapping, and the trade. Walker's California party consisted of fifty men, with four horses each, a year's supply of food, ammunition, and trade goods. Zenas Leonard and George Nidever, two free trappers who had joined the Bonneville crowd at the Green River rendezvous, were selected as members of the Walker party. Both were to become conspicuous in

California history by virtue of their writings.

Because Walker was the first white man to lead a party of explorers to the brink of Yosemite's cliffs, he is given a first place in Yosemite history. It is worthwhile to record here some of the appraisals of Walker, the man, made by his contemporaries and companions.

Zenas Leonard, clerk of the Walker party, wrote, "Mr. Walker was a man well calculated to undertake a business of this kind [the California expedition]. He was well hardened to the hardships of the wilderness — understood the character of the Indians very well . . . was kind and affable to his men, but at the same time at liberty to command without giving offence . . . and to explore unknown regions was his chief delight."

Washington Irving said of Walker, "About six feet high, strong built, dark complexioned, brave in spirit, though mild in manners. He had resided for many years in Missouri, on the frontier; had been among the earliest adventurers to Santa Fe, where he went to trap beaver, and was taken by the Spaniards. Being liberated, he engaged with the Spaniards and Sioux Indians in a war against the Pawnees; then returned to Missouri, and had acted by turns as sheriff, trader, trapper, until he was enlisted as a leader by Captain Bonneville."

Hubert Howe Bancroft, the historian, estimated, "Captain Joe Walker was one of the bravest and most skillful of the mountain men; none was better acquainted than he with the geography or the native tribes of the Great Basin; and he was withal less boastful and pretentious than most of his class."

Walker's biographer, Douglas S. Watson, referring to Bonneville's effort to blame the financial failure of his western enterprises upon a scapegoat, stated, "Whatever may have been Bonneville's purpose in besmirching Walker in which Irving so willingly lent himself, he has hardly succeeded, for where one person today knows the name Bonneville, thousands regard Captain Joseph Reddeford Walker as one of the foremost of western explorers, worthy to be grouped with Jedediah Strong Smith and Ewing Young as the trilogy responsible for the march of this nation to the shores of the Pacific; the true pathfinders."

Walker's perseverance in completing his California journey grew out of a solemn determination to make a personal contribution to the expansion of the United States westward to the Pacific. His cavalcade crossed the Great Basin west of Great Salt Lake via the valley of the Humboldt and, passing south by Carson Lake and the Bridgeport Valley, struck westward into the Sierra Nevada. The exact course they took across the Sierra has been a matter of conjecture; some students have attempted to identify it with the Truckee route, and others have maintained that no ascent was made until the party reached the stream now known as Walker River. It seems probable that they climbed the eastern flank of the Sierra by one of the southern tributaries of the East Walker River. Once over the crest of the range, they traveled west along the divide between the Tuolumne and the Merced rivers directly into the heart of the present Yosemite National Park.

In Leonard's narrative is found the following very significant comment regarding the crossing:

> We travelled a few miles every day, still on top of the mountain, and our course continually obstructed with snow hills and rocks. Here we began to encounter in our path many small streams which would shoot out from under these high snow-banks, and after running a short distance in deep chasms which they have through the ages cut in the rocks, precipitate themselves from one lofty precipice to another, until they are exhausted in rain below. Some of these precipices appeared to us to be more than a mile high. Some of the men thought that if we could succeed in descending one of these precipices to the bottom, we might thus work our way into the valley below—but on making several attempts we found it utterly impossible for a man to descend, to say nothing of our horses. We were then obliged to keep along the top of the dividing ridge between two of these

chasms which seemed to lead pretty near in the direction we were going—which was west, —in passing over the mountain, supposing it to run north and south.

Walker's tombstone, in Martinez, California, bears the inscription, "Camped at Yosemite Nov. 13, 1833." Leonard's description of their route belies the idea of his having camped in Yosemite Valley, and the date is obviously an error as there is reliable evidence that Walker had reached the San Joaquin plain before this date. L. H. Bunnell in his *Discovery of the Yosemite* records the following regarding Walker's route and his Yosemite camp sites:

> The topography of the country over which the Mono Trail ran, and which was followed by Capt. Walker, did not admit of his seeing the valley proper. The depression indicating the valley, and its magnificent surroundings, could alone have been discovered, and in Capt. Walker's conversations with me at various times while encamped between Coulterville and the Yosemite, he was manly enough to say so. Upon one occasion I told Capt. Walker that Ten-ie-ya had said that, "A small party of white men once crossed the mountains on the north side, but were so guided as not to see the Valley proper." With a smile the Captain said, "That was my party, but I was not deceived, for the lay of the land showed there was a valley below; but we had become nearly barefooted, our animals poor, and ourselves on the verge of starvation; so we followed down the ridge to Bull Creek, where, killing a deer, we went into camp."

Francis Farquhar, in his article, "Walker's Discovery of Yosemite," analyzes the problem of Walker's route through the Yosemite region and shows clearly that the Walker party was not guided by Indians. He concludes quite rightly that Bunnell was not justified in depriving Walker of the distinction of discovering Yosemite Valley. Douglas S. Watson, in his volume, *West Wind: The Life of Joseph Reddeford Walker*, offers further evidence to this end.[a]

It requires no great stretch of the imagination to visualize scouts along the flanks of the Walker party coming out upon the brink of Yosemite Valley and looking down in wonder upon the

plunging waters of Yosemite Falls and, perhaps, venturing to the
edge of the Hetch Hetchy. In any case we have in the 1839 account
by Leonard the first authentic printed reference to the Yosemite region. Another passage from this narrative must be quoted here:

> In the last two days travelling we have found some trees of the
> Redwood species, incredibly large—some of which would measure from 16
> to 18 fathom round the trunk at the height of a man's head from the
> ground.

This is the first published mention of the Big Trees of the
Sierra. If we accept Bunnell's contention that the Walker party
camped at Bull Creek (Hazel Green), we will also agree that the
party followed the old Mono Trail of the Indians. This route would
have taken them near the Merced Grove of Big Trees. There is
probably no way of determining definitely whether the Merced
Grove, the Tuolumne Grove, or both, were seen by Walker's men,
but this incident so casually mentioned is clearly the discovery of
the famous Big Trees, and here for the first time is a scholarly
record of observations made in the present Yosemite National Park.
We may accept Leonard's writings as the earliest document in
Yosemite history and the Walker party as the discoverer of both the
Yosemite Valley and the *Sequoia gigantea.*

The next persons other than Indians to view Yosemite Valley
were William Penn Abrams and U. N. Reamer who were mill-
wrights prospecting for a mill site along the Merced River. On
about October 10, 1849, while tracking a grizzly bear from Savage's
Trading Post at the mouth of the South Fork of the Merced River,
they became lost and eventually found their way back over an
Indian trail that led past Yosemite Valley. Abrams' diary describes a
valley enclosed by stupendous cliffs rising 3,000 feet, and other features which without doubt were Bridalveil Falls, Cathedral Rocks
and Half Dome.

CHAPTER II

MARIPOSA HILLS

*F*ollowing the significant work of the early overland fur
traders there came a decade of immigration of bona fide
California settlers. The same forces that led the pioneer across the
Alleghenies, thence to the Mississippi, and from the Mississippi into
Texas, explain the coming of American settlers into California.
Hard times in the East stimulated land hunger, and California publicity agents spread their propaganda at an opportune time. Long
before railroads, commercial clubs, and real estate interests began to
advertise the charms of California, its advantages were widely her-
alded by the venturesome Americans who had visited and sensed the
possibilities of the province. The press of the nation took up the
story, and the people of the United States were taught to look upon
California as a land of infinite promise, abounding in agricultural
and commercial possibilities, full of game, rich in timber, possessed
of perfect climate, and feebly held by an effeminate people quite
lacking in enterprise and disorganized among themselves.

The tide of emigration resulting from this painting of word pictures began its surge in 1841 with the organization of the Bidwell-
Bartleson party. Other parties followed in quick succession, and
many of the pioneer fur hunters of the preceding decade found
themselves in demand as guides. The settlers came on horseback, in
ox wagon, or on foot, and with the men came wives and children.
They entered the state by way of the Gila and the Colorado, the
Sacramento, the Walker, the Malheur and the Pit, and the Truckee.
Some journeyed to the Mono region east of Yosemite and either
struggled over difficult Sonora Pass just north of the present park
or tediously made their way south to Owens River and then over
Walker Pass. The Sierra Nevada experienced a new period of ex-

ploration, and California took a marked step toward the climax of interest in her offerings.

This pre-Mexican War, pre-gold-rush immigration takes a prominent place in the history of the state, and the tragedy and success of its participants provide a story of engrossing interest. They had forced their slow way across the continent to find a permanent home beside the western sea, and their arrival presaged the overthrow of Mexican rule in California. The Mexican, Castro, stated before an assembly in Monterey: "These Americans are so contriving that some day they will build ladders to touch the sky, and once in the heavens they will change the whole face of the universe and even the color of the stars."

In one of the parties of settlers was a man of no signal traits, who, by a chance discovery, was to set the whole world agog. This was James W. Marshall, an employee of John A. Sutter of the Sacramento. On January 24, 1848, he found gold in a millrace belonging to Sutter. About a week later the inevitable took place. California became a part of the United States.

The news of the gold discovery spread like wildfire, and by the close of 1848 every settlement and city in America and many cities of foreign lands were affected by the California fever. Gold seekers swarmed into the newly acquired territory by land and by sea. The overland routes of the fur trader and the pioneer settler found such a use as the world had never seen. From the Missouri frontier to Fort Laramie the procession of Argonauts passed in an unbroken stream for months. Some 35,000 people traversed the Western wilderness and 230 American vessels reached California ports in 1849. The western slope of the Sierra from the San Joaquin on the south to the Trinity on the north was suddenly populous with the gold-mad horde. On May 29, the *Californian* of Yerba Buena issued a notice to the effect that its further publication, for the present, would cease because its employees and patrons were going to the mines. On July 15 its editor returned and published an account of his personal experiences as a gold seeker. He wrote: "The country from the Ajuba [Yuba] to the San Joaquin, a distance of about 120 miles, and from the base toward the summit of the mountains . . . about seventy miles, has been explored and gold found on every part."

By 1849 the Mariposa hills were occupied by the miners, and the claims to become famous as the "Southern Mines" were being located. Jamestown, Sonora, Columbia, Murphys, Chinese Camp, Big Oak Flat, Snelling, and Mariposa, all adjacent to the Yosemite region, came to life in a day. Stockton was the immediate base of supply for these camps.

The history of Mariposa is replete with fascinating episodes. May Stanislas Corcoran, a daughter of Mariposa, has supplied the Yosemite Museum with a manuscript entitled "Mariposa, the Land of Hidden Gold," which comes from her own accomplished pen. From it the following brief account is abstracted as an introduction to the beginnings of human affairs in the Mariposa hills.

In 1850, Mariposa County occupied much of the state from Tuolumne County southward. A State Senate Committee on County Subdivision, headed by P.H. de la Guerra, determined its bounds, and a Select Committee on Names, M.G. Vallejo, Chairman, gave it its name — a name which was first applied by Moraga's party in 1806 to Mariposa Creek.[1] Gradually through the years, the original expansive unit was reduced by the creation of other counties — Madera, Fresno, Tulare, Kings, and Kern, and parts of Inyo and

1. The first legislature of the state appointed a committee to report on the derivation and definition of the names of the several counties of California. The report is dated April 16, 1850, and from it is quoted the following:

"In the month of June, 1806 (in one of their yearly excursions to the valley of the rushes—Valle de los Tulares—with a view to hunt elks), a party of Californians pitched their tents on a stream at the foot of the Sierra Nevada, and whilst there, myriads of butterflies, of the most gorgeous and variegated colors, clustered on the surrounding trees, attracted their attention, from which circumstance they gave the stream the appellation of Mariposa. Hence Mariposa River, from which the county (also heavily laden with the precious metal) derives its poetical name."

Mono counties.

Agua Fria was at first the county seat, but even in the beginning the town of Mariposa was the center of the scene of activity.
Four mail routes of the Pony Express converged upon it. Prior to
the arrival of Americans, the Spanish Californians had scarcely penetrated the Sierra in the county, but these uplands were well populated with Indians. One of the strongest tribes, the
Ah-wah-nee-chees, lived in the Deep Grassy Valley (Yosemite) during the summer months and occupied villages along the Mariposa
and Chowchilla rivers in the winter.

Mariposa proved to be the southernmost of the important
southern mines. Of the people who were drawn to it during the
days of the gold rush, many were from the Southern States. They
brought "libraries . . . horses from Kentucky . . . silk hats, chivalry,
colonels, and culture from Virginia; and from most of the states that
later became Confederate, lawyers, doctors, writers, even painters —
miners all . . . Pennsylvania, Massachusetts, New York, and Europe
also sent representatives, and there were Mexican War veterans,
such as Jarvis Streeter, Commodore Stockton, Colonel Fremont,
and Capt. Wm. Howard." By Christmas, 1849, more than three
thousand inhabitants occupied the town of Mariposa, which extended from Chicken Gulch to Mormon Bar.

In February, 1851, a remarkable vein of gold was discovered in
the Mariposa diggings, first designated as the "Johnson vein of
Mariposa," and extensive works were developed from Ridley's Ferry
(Bagby) to Mount Ophir. These properties were acquired by a
company having headquarters in Paris, France, which became
known as "The French Company."

The Frémont Grant, also known as the Rancho Las Mariposas,
was a vast estate of 44,386 acres of grazing land in the Mariposa
hills, which Colonel J. C. Frémont acquired by virtue of a purchase
made in 1847 from J. B. Alvarado. It was one of several so-called

"floating grants." After gold was discovered in the Mariposa region in 1848, Frémont "floated" his rancho far from the original claim to cover mineral lands including properties already in the possession of miners. The center of Frémont's activities was Bear Valley, thirteen miles northwest of Mariposa. Lengthy litigations in the face of hostile public sentiment piled up court costs and lawyer fees. However, the United States courts confirmed Frémont's claims, and other claimants, including the French Company, lost many valuable holdings. Tremendous investments were made in stamp mills, tunnels, shafts, and the other appurtenances related to the mining towns as well as to the mines which Frémont attempted to develop.

In spite of its phenomenal but spotty productiveness, the Frémont Grant brought bankruptcy to its owner and was finally sold at sheriff sale. The town of Mariposa, which was on Frémont's Rancho, became the county seat in 1851, and the present court house was built in 1854. The seats and the bar in the courtroom continue in use today, and the documents and files of the mining days still claim their places in the ancient vault. They constitute some of the priceless reminders of a dramatic period in the early history of the Yosemite region. In these records may be traced the transfer of the ownership of the Mariposa Grant from Frémont to a group of Wall Street capitalists. These new owners employed Frederick Law Olmsted as superintendent of the estate. He arrived in the Sierra in the fall of 1863 to assume his duties at Bear Valley. The next year he was made chairman of the first board of Yosemite Valley commissioners, so actively linking the history of the Mariposa estate with the history of the Yosemite Grant. Olmsted continued his connection with the Mariposa Grant until Aug. 31, 1865, at which time he returned to New York and proceeded to distinguish himself as the "father" of the profession of landscape architecture.

His son, Frederick Law Olmsted, Jr., born July 24, 1870, has continued in the Olmsted tradition. As an authority on parks, municipal improvements, city planning and landscape architecture, and the preservation of the American scene he has exerted a leadership comparable to his father's pioneering. He has entered the Yosemite picture as National Park Service collaborator in planning and as a member of the Yosemite Advisory Board, to which organization he was appointed in 1928.

One of the few members of the small army of early miners in the Mariposa region who left a personal record of his experiences was L.H. Bunnell. His writings provide most valuable references on the history of the beginning of things in the Yosemite region. He was present in the Mariposa hills in 1849, and from his book, *Discovery of the Yosemite*, we learn that Americans were scattered throughout the lower mountains in that year. Adventurous traders had established trading posts in the wilderness in order that they might reap a harvest from the miners and Indians.

James D. Savage, the most conspicuous figure in early Yosemite history, whose life story, if told in full, would constitute a valuable contribution to Californiana, was one of these traders. In 1849 he maintained a store at the mouth of the South Fork of the Merced, only a few miles from the gates of Yosemite Valley. Now a half million people a year hurry by this spot in automobiles; a monument with sign and text indicates that the site is one of the most significant, historically, of all the localities in the Yosemite region. It was here that the first episode in the drama of Yosemite Indian troubles took place. The story of the white man's occupancy of the valley actually begins at the mouth of this canyon in the Mariposa hills.

CHAPTER III

WHITE CHIEF OF THE FOOTHILLS

*T*he entire story of very early events in the Yosemite region is pervaded by the spirit of one individual. In spite of the fact that no historian has chronicled the events of his brief but exciting career, the name of James D. Savage is legendary throughout the region of the Southern Mines. It has been the ambition of more than one writer of California history to pin down the fables of this pioneer and to establish his true life story on stable supports of authentic source. Scattered through the literature of the gold days are sketchy accounts of his exploits, and rarely narratives of firsthand experiences with his affairs may be found. Before relating Savage definitely to Yosemite itself we shall do well to consider his personal history.

During the beginning years of the gold excitement, his fame spread throughout the camps and to the ports upon which the mines depended for supplies. Savage was the subject of continual gossip, conjecture, and acclaim. His career was short, but it was crowded with thrilling happenings and terminated with violence in a just cause. Throughout it, Savage was brave — a man born to lead.

Because he played a leading role in the discovery of Yosemite Valley, national park officials have been energetic in their attempt to complete his life story and give it adequate representation in the Yosemite Museum. For several years, as historical material had been accumulating there, and details of most events in the Yosemite drama unfolded and took their proper place in the exhibits, Savage still remained a mystery.

At last there came a Yosemite visitor who was descended from the grandfather of James D. Savage. This lady, Ida Savage Bolles, after learning of the local interest in her relative, communicated

with yet another relative, who today resides in the same Middle
Western state from which "Jim" Savage came. The result was that
Mrs. Louise Savage Ireland took up the challenge and devoted
many months to the determining of the California pioneer's ancestry.
To her we acknowledge indebtedness for her persevering search,
which involved considerable travel and correspondence. Not only
did she reveal the ancestry of Jim Savage, but she located a "delightful old lady" who, as a girl, knew Jim of California fame. This
unexpected biographical material provides firsthand information
about the youth of James D. Savage such as has not been obtained
from any living Californian who knew him in his halcyon days.[b]

The following story of the life of the first white man to enter
Yosemite Valley, though incomplete, is much more comprehensive
than anything that has previously appeared in print, and is, we believe, gathered from sources[1] wholly dependable.

James D. Savage was one of six children born to Peter Savage
and Doritha Shaunce. Henry C. Pratt of Virginia, Illinois, a second
cousin, writes, "My mother, Emily Savage, born in 1817, and her
cousin, James Savage, were near the same age." This is the best ap-
proximation of his age contained in the biographical material accumulated by Mrs. Ireland. The parent, Peter Savage, went by ox cart
and raft from Cayuga County, New York, to Jacksonville, Morgan
County, Illinois, in 1822. Sixteen years later Peter's family removed
to Princeton, Bureau County, Illinois.

....

1. Foremost among the references is L. H. Bunnell's *Discovery of the Yosemite*, published in 1880.
Bunnell was closely associated with Savage during three of his most active years in the Mariposa re-
gion; his account is intimate and rich in detail and unprejudiced. We catch an interesting glimpse of
Savage, the 'fortyniner, through the pages also of George H. Tinkham's *California Men and Events*.
Something additional of his gold mining and trading is gleaned from the writings of W. E. Wilde and
S. P. Elias. Elliot's *History of Fresno County* contributes a number of authenticated incidents, and J. M.
Hutchings reveals matters regarding influences that undoubtedly figured in his tragic death. United
States Senate documents record his official dealings with the Indians; L. A. Winchell gives some infor-
mation on his enemies; contemporary newspapers describe his meeting with death; and finally
Depositions from the Papers of Geo. W. Wright, One of Two First Congressmen from California, provides papers
pertaining to the Court of Claims, 1858, in which appears sworn testimony regarding the shooting of
Savage. This last paper formed a part of the Boutwell Dunlap Collection.

Mrs. Ireland in her quest met Mrs. Sarah Seton Porter of Princeton, who at the time of the interview in 1928 was ninety-eight years old. Mrs. Porter knew James D. Savage as a youth. She recalls that

> Jim Savage was grown when his father, Peter, brought the family to Princeton from Morgan County. Jim was smart as a whip, shrewd, apt in picking up languages, such as German and French—for both tongues were spoken here, the two races having settlements in and about Princeton. He was vigorous and strong, had blue eyes and a magnificent physique, loved all kinds of sports engaged in in his day, was tactful, likable, and interesting....
>
> Sometimes Jim would come to church, but, oh, he was such a wag of a youth. More often than not, he would remain outside, and when he knew time had come for prayer, he'd flick the knees of his horse and make him kneel, too, and then wink at us inside. We couldn't laugh of course, but we always watched for this trick of Jim's. He got such a lot of fun out of doing it.

Savage took a wife, Eliza, and settled in Peru, Illinois. A daughter was born to this union. He and his brother, Morgan, were caught in the wave of California fever that affected many of the border settlements in the 'forties and they joined one of the overland parties in 1846. Lydia Savage Healy, another second cousin, expresses the opinion that the brothers joined Frémont's third expedition. However, since it is known that Savage's wife and child made the start, it is evident that they were with one of the parties of emigrants who, that year, made the journey. Mrs. Porter, then Sarah Seton, with two brothers and a sister drove from Princeton to Peru to bid them farewell.

On this journey, "suffering and discouragement went hand in hand." The wife and child did not survive the trip. Only the physically fit endured the hardships, and among these were Savage and his brother. By what route they entered California is not known, but S. P. Elias reports that Savage volunteered beneath the Bear flag and fought through the war against the Mexicans. A member of Frémont's battalion, he was with Frémont both in Oregon and in California. After peace and before the discovery of gold, and shortly after the disbanding of Frémont's battalion, he went to the south, settled among the Indians, and through José and Jésus, two of the most powerful chiefs in the valley of the San Joaquin, he established an intimacy with the principal tribes. By his indomitable energy, capability of endurance, and personal prowess he acquired a complete mastery over them to such an extent that he was elected chief of several of the tribes. He obtained great influence over the Indians of the lowlands and led them successfully against their mountain enemies, conquering a peace wherever he forayed.

In any event, when Frémont and Pico put their signatures to the Cahuenga peace treaty on January 13, 1847, the Mexican War, so far as California was concerned, was at an end. Frémont's battalion was disbanded, and we may believe, with Elias, that James D. Savage then established his intimacy with the principal Indian tribes of the San Joaquin.

His aptitude for "picking up languages" apparently came to the fore, for he mastered the Indian dialect and extended his influence until it amounted to something of a barbaric despotism. The Indians acknowledged his authority, and he, no doubt, improved their condition. In the wars with the mountain tribes Savage's tactics won them victories, and he brought about progress, generally.

Prior to the gold rush, his territory was seldom visited by whites, but early in 1848, hardly a year subsequent to his conquest of the Indians, there poured in that flood of miners which transformed the entire picture. Savage adapted himself to it forthwith, and soon his name was on the lips of everyone. When he let it be known among his Indian followers that he would like to acquire a lot of the yellow metal, the squaws set to work and turned the product of their labors into the lap of the white chief. W. E. Wilde writes that Savage was associated with the Rev. James Woods in 1848 and that he and his Indians were working the gravel deposits at what became known as Big Oak Flat. It was here that a white Texan stabbed Luturio, one of the Indian leaders, and the Texan in turn was killed by the Indians. Savage, knowing the potentialities of enraged Indians, pacified them and withdrew with them to other localities.

George H. Tinkham next throws a spotlight on Savage at Jamestown in May (?) 1849. Cornelius Sullivan related to Tinkham that

> under a brushwood tent, supported by upright poles, sat James D. Savage, measuring and pouring gold dust into the candle boxes by his side. Five hundred or more naked Indians, with belts of cloth bound around their waists or suspended from their heads brought the dust to Savage, and in return for it received a bright piece of cloth or some beads.

Just how much gold dust Savage acquired was never reported, but that it was an enormous amount is not to be questioned. For some two years his army of Indian followers busied themselves in gleaning the creeks and ravines of the foothills, and considering the facility with which gold could be gathered; it is small wonder that he was reputed to have barrels full of it.

We learn from L. H. Bunnell, one of Savage's intimate acquaintances of long standing, that in 1849-1850 Savage had established his trading post at the mouth of the South Fork of the Merced, not more than fifteen miles below Yosemite Valley, and on the line of the present Merced-Yosemite highway.

> At this point, engaged in gold mining, he had employed a party of native Indians. Early in the season of 1850 his trading-post and mining camp were attacked by a band of the Yosemite Indians. This tribe, or band, claimed the territory in that vicinity, and attempted to drive Savage off. Their real object, however, was plunder. They were considered treacherous and dangerous, and were very troublesome to the miners generally.
>
> Savage and his Indian miners repulsed the attack and drove off the marauders, but from this occurrence he no longer deemed this location desir-

able. Being fully aware of the murderous propensities of his assailants, he removed to Mariposa Creek, not far from the junction of the Agua Fria, and near to the site of the old stone fort. Soon after, he established a branch post on the Fresno, where the mining prospects became most encouraging, as the high water subsided in that stream. This branch station was placed in charge of a man by the name of Greeley.

This event on the South Fork constitutes the initial step in the hostilities that were to result in Savage's renown as the discoverer of Yosemite Valley. Since he had remained so close to the remarkable canyon for some months prior to the Indian attack, and because the threatening Indians frequently boasted of a "deep valley in which one Indian is more than ten white men," Bunnell once asked Savage whether he had ever entered the mysterious place. Savage's words were: "Last year while I was located at the mouth of the South Fork of the Merced, I was attacked by the Yosemites, but with the Indian miners I had in my employ, drove them off, and followed some of them up the Merced River into a canyon, which I supposed led to their stronghold, as the Indians then with me said it was not a safe place to go into. From the appearance of this rocky gorge I had no difficulty in believing them. Fearing an ambush, I did not follow them. It was on this account that I changed my location to Mariposa Creek. I would like to get into the den of the thieving murderers. If ever I have a chance I will smoke out the Grizzly Bears [the Yosemites] from their holes, where they are thought to be so secure."

Savage built up an exceedingly prosperous business at his trading posts on the Fresno and on Mariposa Creek. He stocked his stores with merchandise from San Francisco Bay and exchanged the goods at enormous profits for the gold brought in by the Indians. An ounce of gold bought a can of oysters, five pounds of flour, or a pound of bacon; a shirt required five ounces, and a pair of boots or a hat brought a full pound of the precious metal. His customers included white prospectors as well as his subservient Indians, for the white men would agree to his exacting terms in preference to leaving their diggings to make a trip for supplies to the growing village of Mariposa.

The Indians never questioned the rate of exchange, for to them it seemed that their white chief was working miracles in providing quantities of desirable food and prized raiment in return for something that was to be had for the taking. To guarantee a continuance of cordial relations with his Indian friends, and to cement the alliance of several tribes, Savage had taken wives from among the young squaws of different tribes. Two of these were called Eekino and Homut. It is not known which tribes were represented in his household, but the wives are reported to have totaled five. If their bridal contract was recognized by all their tribesmen, it is not difficult to understand how Savage's supporters numbered five hundred.

The Mariposa Creek store retinue of whites was thrown into a state of some agitation one fall day in 1850 when one of Savage's wives confided the information that the mountain Indians were combining to wipe the whites from the hills. Confirmation of her rumor was obtained from some of the friendly bucks who had long followed Savage. These Indians declared that they had learned that the mountain tribe, the Yosemites, were ready to descend upon Savage again for the purpose of plunder and that they were maneuvering to secure the combined forces of other tribes.

Savage did not misunderstand the threat, as did some others of the white men. Hoping to impress the Indians with the wonders, numbers, and power of the whites, he conceived the idea of taking some of them to that milling base of supply, San Francisco. It is probable, too, that he planned to put some of his great store of accumulated gold in safekeeping on the same trip. Accordingly, he announced that he was going to "the Bay" for a new stock of goods and invited José Juarez, a chief of influence with the Chowchillas and Chukchansies, to accompany him. José accepted the invitation.

With them went some of Savage's dependable Indian friends, including a wife or two.

It was the occasion of this trip that provided the crowning touch for Savage's reputation among the whites of all the gold camps. The story of the affair spread to as many localities as were represented in San Francisco's picturesque population at the time of the visit, and legends of Jim Savage's barrel of gold are handed down to this day. How large the barrel may have been it is now impossible to ascertain, but certainly a fabulous fortune traveled with the strange party.

They made their headquarters at the Revere House and became the sensation of the hour.[2] The Indians arrayed themselves in gaudy finery and gorged themselves with costly viands and considerable liquor. To the great distress of Savage, José maintained himself in a state of drunkenness throughout most of their stay. In order to prevent disturbances Savage locked him up on one occasion and when he was somewhat sobered remonstrated with him. José flew into an excited rage, became abusive with his tongue, and finally disclosed his secret of the war against the whites. Savage knocked him down.

The party remained to witness the celebration of the admission of California into the Union on October 29, 1850. Savage deposited his gold in exchange for goods to be delivered as needed, gilded his already colorful visit with enough gambling and reckless spending to stagger the residents, and gathered his retinue for the return journey.

José had maintained a silence and dignity ever after the violent quarrel with his chief.

No sooner had they reached the foothill territory from which they had traveled a fortnight before than they were greeted with news of Indian threats. As the Fresno station maintained by Savage

---

2. Bell (1927) records that the photographer, Vance, made pictures of Savage and his Indians on this occasion.

seemed to be in immediate danger, the party went there at once. Numerous Indians were about, but all seemed quiet. However, the white agents employed by Savage revealed that the Indians were no longer trading.

Savage thereupon invited all Indians present to meet with him and proceeded at once to conduct a peaceful confab before his store. Addressing them he said:

"I know that some of the Indians do not wish to be friends with the white men and that they are trying to unite the different tribes for the purpose of a war. It is better for the Indians and white men to be friends. If the Indians make war on the white men, every tribe will be exterminated; not one will be left. I have just been where the white men are more numerous than the wasps and ants; and if war is made and the Americans are aroused to anger, every Indian engaged in the war will be killed before the whites will be satisfied."

Having made himself clearly understood in the Indian language he turned to his fellow traveler, José, for confirmation of his statements regarding the power of the whites. José stepped forward and delivered himself of the following brief but energetic oration:

"Our brother has told his Indian relatives much that is truth; we have seen many people; the white men are very numerous; but the white men we saw on our visit are of many tribes; they are not like the tribe that dig gold in the mountains." He then gave an absurd description of what he had seen while below, and continued: "Those white tribes will not come to the mountains. They will not help the gold diggers if the Indians make war against them. If the gold diggers go to the white tribes in the big village, they give their gold for strong water and games; when they have no more gold, the white tribes drive the gold diggers back to the mountains with clubs. They strike them down [referring to the police], as your white relative struck me while I was with him. The white tribes will not go to war with the Indians in the mountains. They cannot bring their big ships and big guns to us; we have no cause to fear them. They will not injure us."

His climax came as a bold argument for the immediate declaration of war upon the whites.

Chief José Rey of the Chowchillas then contributed his plea for immediate hostilities, and Savage withdrew before the two hostile chiefs. Upon his return to the Mariposa Station, his appeals for immediate preparation for war were given small hearing by the whites. A few were inclined to scoff.

Close on the heels of the warnings, however, came news of an attack on the Fresno store. All the whites except the messenger who had brought the news were killed. The Mariposa Indian War was on.

Savage had gone to Horse Shoe Bend in the Merced Canyon to solicit aid. He had hoped to find a more attentive audience there than among the county officials at Agua Fria. In his absence his Mariposa store was burned, its three white attendants were killed, and his wives were carried off by the assailants.[c]

Cassady, one of the rival traders who had scoffed at Savage's first news of impending disaster, was surprised in his establishment and met quick death.[d] Three other murderous attacks took place in the immediate vicinity, and the whites finally leaped to the defense of their holdings.

James Burney, the county sheriff, took a place at the head of a body of volunteers who had banded for mutual protection. On January 6, 1851, James D. Savage accompanied this party in an attack made upon an Indian encampment of several hundred squaws and bucks under the leadership of José Rey. This was the first organized movement of the whites against the Indians of the Mariposa Hills.

By this time Governor McDougal had issued a proclamation calling for volunteers, and the Mariposa Battalion came into existence. Savage was made major in full command. Three companies, under John J. Kuykendall, John Boling, and William Dill, were organized and drilled near Savage's ruined Mariposa store.[3] The affairs of this punitive body of men are dealt with in another chapter. Let it here suffice to say that its activities were especially directed against the mountain tribe of "Grizzlies," and that on March 25, 1851, Savage and his men entered the mysterious stronghold, Yosemite Valley.[c]

In 1928 it was my privilege to interview Maria Lebrado, one of the last members of the Yosemite tribe who experienced subjection by the whites. I eagerly sought ethnological and historical data, which was forthcoming in gratifying abundance. Purposely I had avoided questioning the aged squaw about Major Savage; but presently she asked, in jumbled English and Spanish, if I knew about the "Captain" of the white soldiers. She called him "Chowwis,' and described him as a blond chief whose light hair fell upon his shoulders and whose beard hung halfway to his waist. She had been much impressed by his commanding blue eyes and declared that his shirts were always red. To this member of the mountain tribe of Yosemite the Major was recalled as something of a thorn in her flesh. That he was a beloved leader of the foothill tribes she agreed, but hastened to explain that those Indians, too, were enemies of her people. Maria is the only person I have met who had seen Savage.

For five months Savage commanded the movements of the Mariposa Battalion. Its various units were active in the Sierra Summit region above Yosemite, at the headwaters of the Chowchilla, and on the upper reaches of the San Joaquin. In every encounter the Indians were defeated and they finally sued for peace. The prowess of Savage as a mountaineer and military leader is

3. A muster roll of the Mariposa Battalion that appears in Elliott, 1881, is included as Document IV in the Appendix of this book.

borne out in a letter, published in *Alta California* on June 12, 1851, in which the battalion's sergeant major describes at length for the adjutant a foray at the headwaters of the San Joaquin:

> . . . I am aware that you have been high up and deep in the mountains and snow yourself, but I believe this trip ranks all others. The Major himself has seen cañons and snow peaks this trip which he never saw before. It is astonishing what this man can endure. Traveling on day and night, through snow and over the mountains, without food, is not considered fatigue to him, and as you are well aware the boys will follow him as long as he leaves a sign.

The same *Alta* carries a resolution, signed by men in Dill's and Boling's companies, affirming in great detail their high confidence in Savage.

In addition to his activities with the battalion in the field, Major Savage functioned conspicuously in aiding the United States Indian Commissioners in preparing a peace treaty. He maintained a friendly attitude toward the oppressed Indians and, had the government made good its promises, or had the appropriations not been absorbed elsewhere, the tribes of the Sierra would have been more adequately provided for. The treaty, signed April 29, 1851, does not carry the "signatures" of Tenaya of the Yosemites or of the leader of the Chowchillas.

On July 1, 1851, the Mariposa Battalion was mustered out. Major Savage resumed his trading operations in a store on the Fresno River near Coarse Gold. In compliance with the treaty, a reservation for the Indians was set aside on the Fresno, and another on the Kings River. In the fall of 1851 the Fresno store was the polling place for a large number of voters for county officers. That winter Savage built Fort Bishop, near the Fresno reservation, and prepared to carry on a prosperous trade. He spoke as follows on this subject to L. H. Bunnell:

If I can make good my losses by the Indians *out* of the Indians, I am going to do it. I was the best friend the Indians had, and they would have destroyed me. Now that they once more call me "Chief," they shall build me up. I will be just to them, as I have been merciful, for, after all, they are but poor ignorant beings, but my losses must be made good.

During the first months of 1852, Major Savage conducted a substantial, if not a phenomenal, business with the miners of the Fresno and surrounding territory, and with the Indians at the agency. No Indian hostilities were in evidence, but a policy of excluding them from the store proper was adhered to. The goods which they bought with their gold dust were handed out to them through small openings left in the walls. These openings were securely fastened at night.

Not infrequently the Indians were subjected to abusive treatment at the hands of certain whites. The mistreatment was enough to provoke an uprising, but with a few exceptions they remained on the reservations. An important light on subsequent events in Savage's life is brought out in this statement by L. H. Bunnell:

As far as I was able to learn at the time, a few persons envied them the possession of their Kings River reservation and determined to "squat" upon it, after they should have been driven off. This "border element" was made use of by an unprincipled schemer, who it was understood was willing to accept office, when a division of Mariposa County should have been made, or when a vacancy of any kind should occur. But population was required, and the best lands had been reserved for the savages. A few hangers-on, at the agencies, that had been discharged for want of employment and other reasons, made claims upon the Kings River reservation; the Indians came to warn them off, when they were at once fired upon, and it was reported that several were killed.

Further details of the deplorable act committed by the would-be "squatters" are provided by the following news item which appeared in the *Alta California* of July 7, 1852:

ANTICIPATED INDIAN DIFFICULTIES ON KING'S RIVER

By Mr. Stelle, who came express to Stockton on the 5th inst., we have
received the annexed correspondence from

San Joaquin, (Evening,) July 2, 1852.

EDITORS ALTA CALIFORNIA:—A few days ago, the Indians on
King's River warned Campbell, Poole & Co., ferrymen, twenty miles from
here, to leave, showing at the same time their papers from the Indian
Commissioners. The Indians then left, and threatened to kill the ferrymen
if on their reservation when they returned. Mr. Campbell has been col-
lecting volunteers, many have joined him. Major Harvey left this evening
with some eighteen or twenty men. A fine chance for the boys to have a
frolic, locate some land, and be well paid by Uncle Sam.

These agitations and murders were denounced by Major
Savage in unsparing terms. Although the citizens of Mariposa were
at the time unable to learn the details of the affair at Kings River,
which was a distant settlement, the great mass of the people were
satisfied that wrong had been done to the Indians; however, there
had been a decided opposition by citizens generally to the establishment of two agencies in the county, and the selection of the best
agricultural lands for reservations. Mariposa then included nearly
the whole San Joaquin Valley south of the Tuolumne.

The opponents to the recommendations of the commissioners
claimed that "The government of the United States has no right to
select the territory of a sovereign State to establish reservations for
the Indians, nor for any other purpose, without the consent of the
State." The state legislature of 1851-1852 instructed the senators
and representatives in congress to use their influence to have the
Indians removed beyond the limits of the state.

W. W. Elliot, in his *History of Fresno County* (1881), reveals further details: "Sometime previous to August 16, 1852, one Major
Harvey, the first county Judge of Tulare County, and Wm. J.
Campbell, either hired or incited a lot of men, who rushed into one
of the rancherias on Kings River and succeeded in killing a number
of old squaws."

Elliott's assertions are supported by the following news item
from the *San Francisco Daily Herald*, August 21, 1852:

Among other acts by white men calculated to excite the Indians, a ferry was established over the San Joaquin, within an Indian reservation, above Fort Miller, some miles above Savage's. The Indians, no doubt, considered this an encroachment; and from an idea that the ferry stopped fish from ascending the river, some straggling Indian, acting without authority from chiefs or council, spoke of this notion about the fish at the ferry, and saying that the ferry was within their lands, added that it would have to be broken up. The proprietor of the ferry, assuming this as a threatened hostility, or making a pretence of it, assembled a few willing friends, who, armed with rifles, appeared suddenly among some Indian families while most of the men were many miles off, peaceably at work at Savage's, without dreaming of danger, and without justifiable provocation the white men fired upon the families, killing two women, as it is stated, and some children, and wounding several others.

With such conditions prevailing on the Kings, it is small wonder that numerous Kings Agency Indians traveled to the Fresno in order to trade with Savage. Needless to say, this aroused the further ire of the traders on the Kings. The white malcontents continued their agitation, and the wronged Indians of the Kings wailed to Savage of their troubles. Consistently with his earlier acts, wherein the public good was involved, Major Savage attempted to pacify the Indians. He also denounced the "squatters" with all the emphasis of his personality and high standing. He asserted that they should be punished under the laws which they had violated and presented the case to the Indian Commissioners.

Harvey and the trader Campbell made common cause of denouncing Major Savage in return. Word was sent to the Major that they dared him to set foot in Kings River region. Upon its receipt, Savage mounted his horse and traveled to the Kings River Agency.

The events that occurred upon his arrival have been variously described by half a dozen writers. Elliott's description, which agrees essentially with Bunnell's, is as follows:

On the 16th day of August, 1852, Savage paid a visit to the Kings River Reservation, but previously to this Harvey declared that if Savage ever came there he would not return alive. Arriving at the reservation early in the forenoon, Savage found there Harvey and Judge Marvin, and a quarrel at once ensued between Savage and Harvey, the latter demanding of Savage a retraction of the language he had used regarding Harvey, whereupon Savage slapped Harvey across the face with his open hand, and while doing so, his pistol fell out of his shirt bosom and was picked up by Marvin. Harvey then stepped up to Marvin and said: "Marvin you have disarmed me; you have my pistol." "No," said Marvin, "this is Major Savage's pistol," whereupon Harvey, finding Savage unarmed, commenced firing his own pistol, shooting five balls into Savage, who fell, and died almost instantly. Marvin was standing by all this time, with Savage's pistol in his hands, too cowardly or scared to interfere and prevent the murder. At this time Harvey was County Judge of Tulare County, and one Joel H. Brooks, who had been in the employment of Savage for several years, and who had received at his hands nothing but kindness and favors, was appointed by Harvey, Justice of the Peace, for the sole purpose of investigating Harvey's case for the killing of Savage. Of course Harvey was acquitted by Brooks—was not even held to answer before the Grand Jury. Harvey finally left, in mortal fear of the Indians, for he imagined that every Indian was seeking his life to avenge the murder of Savage. Afterwards, Harvey died of paralysis.

In 1926 the late Boutwell Dunlap unearthed 169 pages of depositions in manuscript form, taken in a law case of 1858 in which the death of Savage was made an issue. The incidents related by the witness under oath are redolent of the old wild days. This testimony comes from the same Brooks who as magistrate had acquitted Harvey. It is quoted as follows:

Twenty-four hours after the Indians had ordered Campbell to leave, Harvey and his company had a fight with the Indians, killing some and whipping the balance. Savage was then an Indian agent appointed by Wozencroft. Savage and Wozencroft made a great fuss about the American people abusing the Indians and succeeded in getting the Commanding General of the U.S. forces on the Pacific to send up a couple of companies of troops to Tulare County, to take up Major Harvey and the men that were under his command and that had assisted him in this horrible murder of "the poor innocent savages."

The circumstances which led to Savages' death grew out of this difficulty. The troops had crossed Kings River. This was some time in August 1852 in the morning. Major Savage and Judge John G. Marvin rode up to the door of Campbell's trading-house. Savage called for Harvey. Harvey stepped to the door. Savage remarked, "I understand, Major Harvey, that you say I am no gentleman." Harvey replied, "I have frequently made that statement." Savage remarked, to Harvey, "There is a good horse, saddle, bridle, spurs and leggings which belong to me. I fetched them, for the purpose of letting you have them to leave this country with." Harvey replied, "I have got a fine mule and I will leave the country on my own animal, when I want to leave it." Savage called for breakfast. Savage and Marvin ate breakfast by themselves in a brush house outside the store. After they had got through their breakfast, Savage tied up his hair, rolled up his sleeves, took his six-shooter out of its scabbard and placed it in front of him under the waistband of his pantaloons. He then walked into Campbell's store and asked Major Harvey if he could not induce him to call him a gentleman. Harvey told him that he had made up his mind and had expressed his opinion in regard to that, and did not think he would alter it. He knocked Harvey down and stamped upon him a little. They were separated by some gentlemen in the house, and Harvey got up. Savage says, "To what conclusion have you come in regard to my gentlemancy?" Harvey replies, "I think you are a damned scoundrel." Savage knocked Harvey down again. They were again separated by gentlemen present. As Harvey straightened himself onto his feet, he presented a six-shooter and shot Major Savage through the heart. Savage fell without saying anything. It was supposed that Harvey shot him twice after he was dead, every ball taking effect in his heart. That is all I know about the fight. I gained this information by taking the testimony as magistrate of those who saw it.

What may have become of the court records of the so-called trial is unknown, but a scrap of testimony by the proprietor of the house in which the killing took place was preserved by the *San Francisco Daily Herald*, September 3, 1852, as follows:

The People of the State of California *vs.* Walter H. Harvey, for the killing of James D. Savage, on the 16th day of August, 1852, contrary to the laws of the State of California, &c.

Mr. Edmunds sworn, says—"Yesterday morning Major Savage came into my house and asked Major Harvey if he had said he was no gentleman. Major Harvey replied he had said it. Major Savage struck Major Harvey on the side of the head and knocked him down on some sacks of flour, and then proceeded to kick and beat him. Judge Marvin and some one else interfered, and Major Savage was taken off of Major Harvey. Major Savage still had hold of Major Harvey when Major Harvey kicked him. Major Savage then struck Major Harvey on the cheek, and knocked him down the second time, and used him, the same as before. By some means I cannot say, Major Savage was again taken off, and they separated. Major Savage was in the act of attacking him again, when Major Harvey drew his pistol and shot him."

Question by the Court—Did Major Harvey shoot more than once?

Answer—I think he did; I found four holes in him.

Question—Did Major Savage knock Major Harvey down before he drew his pistol?

Answer—The prisoner had been knocked down by Major Savage twice before he drew his pistol, or made any attempt to shoot him.

Mr. Gonele sworn—corroborates the evidence of Mr. Edmunds. Mr. Knider sworn, also does the same.

This is all the testimony given in as to the fight, Major Fitzgerald, U.S.A., sworn, testified to some facts which induced him to think Major Savage not a gentleman.

The Court, upon this testimony, discharged Major Harvey without requiring bail.

So passed the leading figure in early Yosemite history. In this day of greater appreciation of individual heroism, sacrifice, and pioneer accomplishment in public service, how one covets unprejudiced narratives of such lives as was that of James D. Savage! Bunnell comments feelingly on "his many noble qualities, his manly courage, his generous hospitality, his unyielding devotion to friends, and his kindness to immigrant strangers." A writer in the *Daily Herald* of September 4, 1852, contributes more details of events that followed the murder.

EFFECT OF MAJOR SAVAGE'S DEATH UPON THE INDIANS

We have received a letter dated August 31st. on the Indian Reservation, Upper San Joaquin, giving some further particulars of the murder of Major James Savage and the effect produced thereby upon the Indians. The writer has resided among them upwards of two years, understood their language and their habits, and for a long time assisted Major Savage in managing them. His opinions therefore are entitled to weight. The following extracts will show the probable effect this murder will have on the prospects of the southern section of the State:

"You have doubtless ere this heard of the death, or rather murder, of Major Savage upon King's River. It has produced considerable sensation throughout the country and is deeply regretted, for the country and the government have lost the services of a man whom it will not be easy to replace. He could do more to keep the Indians in subjection than all the forces that Uncle Sam could send here. The Indians were terribly excited at his death. Some of them reached the scene of the tragedy soon after it occurred. They threw themselves upon his body, uttering the most terrific cries, bathing their hands and faces in his blood, and even stooping and drinking it, as it gushed from his wounds. It was with difficulty his remains could be interred. The Chiefs clung to his body, and swore they would die with their father.

"The night he was buried the Indians built large fires, around which they danced, singing the while the mournful death chaunt, until the hills around rang with the sound. I have never seen such profound manifestations of grief. The young men, as they whirled wildly and distractedly around in the dance, shouted the name of their 'father' that was gone; while the squaws sat rocking their bodies to and fro, chaunting their mournful dirges, until the very blood within one curdled with horror at the scene.

"I have not the slightest doubt that there will be a general outbreak this winter. Just as soon as the rainy season sets in we shall have the beginning of one of the most protracted and expensive wars the people of California have ever been engaged in. The Indians are quiet now, but are evidently contemplating some hostile movement. They told me, a few days since, that their 'father' was gone and they would not live with the whites any longer.

"I have studied the character of these Indians, as you know, for more than two years, and have acquired my experience in managing them under Savage himself. I do not speak lightly nor unadvisedly, therefore, when I assert that no more disastrous event could have occurred to the interests of this State, than the murder of the gallant Major Savage."

It is possible that more details of Savage's biography may be brought to light, and it is with that hope, coupled with the desire to give his memory just due, that this material is presented for public perusal.

On the Fresno River, near the site of his old trading post, rest the bones of the "white chief." In 1855, Dr. Leach, who had been associated with Savage in trading with the Indians, journeyed to the Kings River, disinterred the remains, and transferred them to their present resting place. A ten-foot shaft of Connecticut granite, bearing the simple inscription, "Maj. Jas. D. Savage," marks the spot. On July 4, 1929, the little city of Madera, California, honored the memory of Savage by placing an inscribed plaque on a city gate. These memorials, presumably, are the only public reminders of the importance of James D. Savage in the history of the state.

The story of Major Savage may be concluded with a reference to his family ties. As has been related, Californians were, until 1928, wholly mystified about his origin. Through the researches of Louise Savage Ireland we are made to sense the human side of his saga and are brought to an understanding of his intimate family connections and his faithfulness to blood ties. L. H. Savage of El Paso, Texas, writes that his father, John W. Savage, first cousin of James D. Savage, made a vain attempt to join the Major in California. Returning miners in 1850 told the Illinois Savages that "Jim" invited them to come to California, where he would make them rich. John, then a boy of nineteen years, financed by older members of the family, shipped for the Golden State and sailed around the Horn. Almost a year elapsed before he reached San Francisco. There he learned that his noted relative had met death six months before.

What became of any wealth that the Major may have amassed remains a mystery. The Indians he struggled to protect and the lands he tried to save for them long ago passed out of the reckoning. By way of explanation we quote from Hutchings' *In the Heart of the Sierras*:

> The reservation on the Fresno gradually became unpopular on this account [because the Indians craved their mountain homes], but mainly from bad management; was afterwards abolished by the Government; and, finally, its lands and buildings were gobbled up by sharp-sighted, if not unprincipled men, who, like many others of that class, became rich out of the acquisition.

One cannot but wonder what counteracting influences James

D. Savage would have exercised in the Fresno Agency business had he been permitted to live.

CHAPTER IV

PIONEERS IN THE VALLEY

*B*y March of 1851 the Indian Commissioners McKee, Barbour, and Woozencraft were actively assembling representatives of the numerous Sierra Indian tribes and driving sharp bargains with them to quitclaim their lands. On March 19, 1851, the commissioners in their camp (Camp Frémont) in the Mariposa region reached an agreement with six tribes and proceeded to establish a reservation for them. Their report refers to one tribe, the "Yosemetos," who were expected at this confab but failed to appear. The friendly Indians who signed the treaty reported that this mountain tribe had no intentions of coming in. It was, therefore, decided to send Major Savage and a part of his Mariposa Battalion after them.

On the evening of March 19, the day on which the Camp Frémont treaty was signed, Major Savage set out with the companies of Captains Boling and Dill. Captain Kuykendall's company had traveled to the region of the San Joaquin and Kings rivers, in which locality the commissioners planned to negotiate another treaty. The force under the command of Major Savage followed a route very near that which is now known as the Wawona Road to Yosemite Valley.

On the South Fork of the Merced, at what is now called Wawona, a Nuchu camp was surprised and captured. Messengers sent ahead from this camp returned with the assurance that the Yosemite tribe would come in and give themselves up. Old Chief Tenaya of the Yosemites did come into camp, but, after waiting three days for the others, Major Savage became impatient and set out with the battalion to enter the much-talked-of Yosemite retreat. When they had covered about half the distance to the valley, seventy-two Indians were met plodding through the snow. Not convinced that this band constituted the entire tribe, Savage sent them to his camp on the South Fork while he pushed on to the valley. His route again was that followed by the present Wawona road.

On March 25, 1851, the party went into camp near Bridalveil Fall.ᶠ That night around the campfire a suitable name for the remarkable valley was discussed. Lafayette H. Bunnell, a young man upon whom the surroundings and events had made a deeper impression than upon any of the others, urged that it be named Yosemite, after the natives who had been driven out. This name was agreed upon. Although the whites knew the name of the tribe, they were apparently unaware that the Indians had another name, Ahwahnee, for their Deep Grassy Valley.

The next morning the camp was moved to the mouth of Indian Canyon, and the day was spent in exploring the valley. Only one Indian was found, an ancient squaw, too feeble to escape. Parties penetrated Tenaya Canyon above Mirror Lake, ascended the Merced Canyon beyond Nevada Fall, and explored both to the north and to the south of the river on the valley floor. No more Indians were discovered, and on the third day the party withdrew from the valley. The Indians who had been gathered while the party was on the way to the valley escaped from their guard while en route to the Indian Commissioner's camp on the Fresno; so this first expedition accomplished nothing in the way of subduing the Yosemites.

In May, 1851, Major Savage sent Captain John Boling and his company back to Yosemite to surprise the elusive inhabitants and to whip them well. Boling followed the same route taken previously and arrived in Yosemite on May 9. He made his first camp near the site of the present Sentinel Bridge. Chief Tenaya and a few of his followers were captured, but the majority of the Yosemites eluded their pursuers. It was during this stay in Yosemite that the first letter from the valley was dispatched. On May 15, 1851, Captain Boling wrote to Major Savage of his affairs, and the letter was published in the *Alta California*, June 12, 1851. It follows:

On reaching this valley, which we did on the 9th inst., I selected for our encampment the most secluded place that I could find, lest our arrival might be discovered by the Indians. Spies were immediately despatched in different directions, some of which crossed the river to examine for signs on the opposite side. Trails were soon found, leading up and down the river, which had been made since the last rain. On the morning of the 10th we took up the line of march for the upper end of the valley, and having traveled about five miles we discovered five Indians running up the river on the north side. All of my command, except a sufficient number to take care of the pack animals, put spurs to their animals, swam the river and caught them before they could get into the mountains. One of them proved to be the son of the old Yosemety chief. I informed them if they would come down from the mountains and go with me to the U. S. Indian Commissioners, they would not be hurt; but if they would not, I would remain in their neighborhood as long as there was a fresh track to be found; informing him at the same time that all the Indians except his father's people and the Chouchillas had treated . . . He then informed me that . . . if I would let him loose, with another Indian, he would bring in his father and all his people by twelve o'clock the next day. I then gave them plenty to eat and started him and his companion out. We watched the others close, intending to hold them as hostages until the despatch-bearers returned. They appeared well satisfied and we were not suspicious of them, in consequence of which one of them escaped. We commenced searching for him, which alarmed the other two still in custody, and they attempted to make their escape. The boys took after them and finding they could not catch them, fired and killed them both. This circumstance, connected with the fact of the two whom we had sent out not returning, satisfied me that they had no intention of coming in. My command then set out to search for the Rancheria. The party which went up the left toward Can-yarthia [?] found the rancheria at the head of a little valley, and from the signs it appeared that the Indians had left but a few minutes. The boys pursued them up the mountain on the north side of the river, and when they had got near the top, helping each other from rock to rock on account of the abruptness of the mountains; the first intimation they had of the Indians being near was a shower of huge rocks which came tumbling down the mountain, threatening instant destruction. Several of the men were knocked down, and some of them rolled and fell some distance before they could recover, wounding and bruising them generally. One man's gun was knocked out of his hand and fell seventy feet before it stopped, whilst another man's hat was knocked off his head without hurting him. The men immediately took shelter behind large rocks, from which they could get an occasional shot, which soon forced the Indians to retreat, and by pressing them close they caught the old Yo-semity chief, whom we yet hold as a prisoner. In this skirmish they killed one Indian and wounded several others.

You are aware that I know this old fellow well enough to look out well for him, lest by some stratagem he makes his escape. I shall aim to use him to the best advantage in pursuing his people. I send down a few of my command with the pack animals for provisions; and I am satisfied if you will send me ten or twelve of old Ponwatchez' best men I could catch the women and children and thereby force the men to come in. The Indians I have with me have acted in good faith and agree with me in this opinion.

On May 21, some members of the invading party discovered the fresh trail of a small party of Indians traveling in the direction of the Mono country. Immediate pursuit was made, and on May 22 the Yosemites were discovered encamped on the shores of Tenaya Lake in a spot much of which was snow-covered. They were completely surprised and surrendered without a struggle. This was the first expedition made into the Yosemite high country from the west, and it was on this occasion that the name Lake Tenaya was applied by Bunnell. The old Indian chief, on being told of how his name was to be perpetuated, sullenly remonstrated that the lake already had a name, "Py-we-ack"—Lake of the Shining Rocks.

The Indians were on this second occasion successfully escorted to the Fresno reservation. Tenaya and his band, however, refused to adapt themselves to the conditions under which they were forced to live. They begged repeatedly to be permitted to return to the mountains and to the acorn food of their ancestors. At last, on his solemn promise to behave, Tenaya was permitted to go back to Yosemite with members of his family. In a short time his old followers quietly slipped away from the reservation and joined him. No attempt was made to bring them back.

During the winter of 1851-52, no complaints against the Yosemites were registered, but in May of 1852 a party of eight prospectors made their way into the valley, where two of them were killed by the Indians. A remarkable manuscript, prepared by Stephen F. Grover, a member of this party, was obtained by Mrs. A. E. Chandler, of Santa Cruz, who in 1901 mailed it to Galen Clark. Upon Clark's death it was turned over to the pioneer Yosemite photographer, George Fiske. When Mr. Fiske died, the papers were given to National Park Service officials for safekeeping in the Yosemite Museum. Grover's reminiscences are apparently authentically presented and divulge much that was not recorded elsewhere. Those familiar with Yosemite history as it has been accepted since the appearance of Bunnell's *Discovery of Yosemite* will recognize a number of incidents that are at variance with previous records.

GROVER'S NARRATIVE—A REMINISCENCE

On the 27th of April, 1852, a party of miners, consisting of Messrs. Grover, Babcock, Peabody, Tudor, Sherburn, Rose, Aich, and an Englishman whose name I cannot now recall, left Coarse Gold Gulch in Mariposa County, on an expedition prospecting for gold in the wilds of the Sierra Nevada Mountains. We followed up Coarse Gold Gulch into the Sierras, traveling five days, and took the Indian trail through the Mariposa Big Tree Grove, and were the first white men to enter there. Then we followed the South Fork of the Merced River, traveling on Indian trails the entire time.

On reaching the hills above Yosemite Valley, our party camped for the night, and questioned the expediency of descending into the Valley at all. Our party were all opposed to the project except Sherburn, Tudor, and Rose. They over-persuaded the rest and fairly forced us against our will, and we finally followed the old Mariposa Indian trail on the morning of the 2nd of May, and entering the Valley on the East side of the Merced River, camped on a little opening, near a bend in the River free from any brush whatever, and staked out our pack mules by the river. I, being the youngest of the party, a mere boy of twenty-two years, and not feeling usually well that morning, remained in camp with Aich and the Englishman to prepare dinner, while the others went up the Valley, some prospecting, and others hunting for game. We had no fear of the Indians, as they had been peaceable, and no outbreaks having occurred, the whites traveled fearlessly wherever they wished to go. Thus, we had no apprehension of trouble. To my astonishment and horror I heard our men attacked, and amid firing, screams, and confusion, here came Peabody, who reached camp first, wounded by an arrow in his arm and another in the back of his neck, and one through his clothes, just grazing the skin of his stomach, wetting his rifle and ammunition in crossing the river as he ran to reach camp. Babcock soon followed, and as both men had plunged through the stream that flows from the Bridal Veil Falls in making their escape, they were drenched to the skin.

On reaching us, Aich immediately began picking the wet powder from Babcock's rifle, while I with my rifle stood guard and kept the savages at bay the best I could. (The other men, with the exception of Sherburn, Tudor, and Rose, came rushing into camp in wild excitement.) Rose, a Frenchman, was the first to fall, and from the opposite side of the steam where he fell, apparently with his death wound, he screamed to us, "'T is no use to try to save ourselves, we have all got to die." He was the only one of our company that could speak Indian and we depended upon him for an interpreter. Sherburn and Tudor were killed in their first encounter, Tudor being killed with an ax in the hands of a savage, which was taken along with the party for cutting wood. The Indians gathered around as near as they dared to come, whooping and yelling, and constantly firing arrows at us. We feared they would pick up the rifles dropped by our companions in their flight and turn them against us, but they did not know how to use them. As we were very hard pressed, and as the number of Indians steadily increased, we tried to escape by the old Mariposa trail, the one by which we entered the Valley, one of our number catching up a sack of a few pounds of flour and another a tin cup and some of our outer clothing and fled as best we could with the savages in hot pursuit. We had proceeded but a short distance when we were attacked in front by the savages who had cut off our retreat. Death staring at us on almost every hand, and seeing no means of escape, we fled to the bluff, I losing my pistol as I ran. We were in a shower of arrows all the while, and the Indians were closing in upon us very fast; the valley seemed alive with them—on rocks, and behind trees, bristling like Demons, shrieking their war whoops, and exulting in our apparently easy capture. We fired back at them to keep them off while we tried to make our way forward hugging the bluff as closely as possible. Our way was soon blocked by the Indians who headed us off with a shower of arrows (two going through my clothing, one through my hat which I lost), when from above the rocks began to fall on us and in our despair we clung to the face of the bluff, and scrambling up we found a little place in the turn of the wall, a shelf-like projection, where, after infinite labor, we succeeded in gathering ourselves, secure from the falling rocks, at least, which were being thrown by Indians under the orders from their Chief. The arrows still whistled among us thick and fast, and I fully believe—could I visit that spot even now after the lapse of all these years—I could still pick up some of those flint arrow points in the shelf of the rock and in the face of the bluff where we were huddled together.

We could see the old Chief Tenieya way up in the Valley in an open space with fully one hundred and fifty Indians around him, to whom he gave his orders, which were passed to another Chief just below us, and these two directed those around them and shouted orders to those on the top of the bluff who were rolling the rocks over on us. Fully believing ourselves doomed men, we never relaxed our vigilance, but with the two rifles we still kept them at bay, determined to sell our lives as dearly as possible. I recall, with wonder, how every event of my life up to that time passed through my mind, incident after incident, with lightning rapidity, and with wonderful precision.

We were crowded together beneath this little projecting rock (two rifles were fortunately retained in our little party, one in the hands of Aich and one in my own), every nerve strung to its highest tension, and being wounded myself with an arrow through my sleeve that cut my arm and another through my hat, when all of a sudden the Chief just below us, about fifty yards distant, suddenly threw up his hands and with a terrible yell fell over backwards with a bullet through his body. Immediately, the firing of arrows ceased and the savages were thrown into confusion, while notes of alarm were sounded and answered far up the Valley and from the high bluffs above us. They began to withdraw and we could hear the twigs crackle as they crept away.

It was now getting dusk and we had been since early morning without food or rest. Not knowing what to expect we remained where we were, suffering from our wounds and tortured with fear till the moon went down about midnight; then trembling in every limb, we ventured to creep forth, not daring to attempt the old trail again; we crept along and around the course of the bluff and worked our way up through the snow, from point to point, often feeling the utter impossibility of climbing farther, but with an energy born of despair, we would try again, helping the wounded more helpless than ourselves, and by daylight we reached the top of the bluff. A wonderful hope of escape animated us though surrounded as we were, and we could but realize how small our chances were for evading the savages who were sure to be sent on our trail. Having had nothing to eat since the morning before, we breakfasted by stirring some of our flour in the tip cup, with snow, and passing it around among us, in full sight of the smoke of the Indian camps and signal fires all over the Valley.

Our feelings toward the "Noble Red Man" at this time can better be imagined than described.

Starting out warily and carefully, expecting at every step to feel the stings of the whizzing arrows of our deadly foes, we kept near and in the most dense underbrush, creeping slowly and painfully along as best we could, those who were best able carrying the extra garments of the wounded and helping them along; fully realizing the probability of the arrow tips with which we were wounded having been dipped in poison before being sent on their message of death. In this manner we toiled on, a suffering and saddened band of once hopeful prospectors.

Suddenly a deer bounded in sight. Some objected to our shooting as the report of our rifle might betray us—but said I, as well die by our foes as by starvation, and dropping on one knee with never a steadier nerve or truer aim, the first crack of my rifle brought him down. Hope revived in our hearts, and quickly skinning our prize we roasted pieces of venison on long sticks thrust in the flame and smoke, and with no seasoning whatever it was the sweetest morsel I ever tasted. Hastily stripping the flesh from the hind quarters of the deer, Aich and myself, being the only ones able to carry the extra burden, shouldered the meat and we again took up our line of travel. In this manner we toiled on and crossed the Mariposa Trail, and passed down the south fork of the Merced River, constantly fearing pursuit. As night came on we prepared camp by cutting crotched stakes which we drove in the ground and putting a pole across enclosed it with brush, making a pretty secure hiding place for the night; we crept under and lay close together. Although expecting an attack we were so exhausted and tired that we soon slept.

An incident of the night occurs to me: One of the men on reaching out his foot quickly, struck one of the poles, and down came the whole structure upon us. Thinking that our foes were upon us, our frightened crowd sprang out and made for the more dense brush, but as quiet followed we realized our mistake and gathering together again we passed the remainder of the night in sleepless apprehension.

When morning came we started again, following up the river, and passed one of our camping places. We traveled as far as we could in that direction, and prepared for our next night to camp and slept in a big hollow tree, still fearing pursuit. We passed the night undisturbed and in the morning started again on our journey, keeping in the shelter of the brush, and crossed the foot of the Falls, a little above Crane Flat—so named by us, as one of our party shot a large crane there while going over, but it is now known as Wawona. We still traveled in the back ground, passing through Big Tree Grove again, but not until we gained the ridge above Chowchilla did we feel any surety of ever seeing our friends again.

Traveling on thus for five days, we at last reached Coarse Gold Gulch once more, barefooted and ragged but more glad than I can express. An excited crowd soon gathered around us and while listening to our hair-breadth escapes, our sufferings and perils, and while vowing vengeance on the treacherous savages, an Indian was seen quickly coming down the mountain trail, gaily dressed in war paint and feathers, evidently a spy on our track, and not three hours behind us. A party of miners watched him as he passed by the settlement. E. Whitney Grover, my brother, and a German cautiously followed him. The haughty Red Man was made to bite the dust before many minutes had passed.

My brother Whitney Grover quickly formed a company of twenty-five men, who were piloted by Aich, and started for the Valley to bury our unfortunate companions. They found only Sherburn and Tudor, after a five days march, and met with no hostility from the Indians. They buried them where they lay, with such land marks as were at hand at that time. I have often called to mind the fact that the two men, Sherburn and Tudor, the only ones of our party who were killed on that eventful morning, were seen reading their Bibles while in camp the morning before starting into the Valley. They were both good men and we mourned their loss sincerely.

After we had been home six days, Rose, who was a partner of Sherburn and Tudor in a mine about five miles west of Coarse Gold Gulch, where there was a small mining camp, appeared in the neighborhood and reported the attack and said the whole party was killed, and that he alone escaped.

On being questioned, he said he hid behind the Waterfall and lived by chewing the leather strap which held his rifle across his shoulders. This sounded strange to us as he had his rifle and plenty of ammunition and game was abundant. Afterward hearing of our return to Coarse Gold Gulch camp, he never came to see us as would have been natural, but shortly disappeared. We thought his actions and words very strange and we remembered how he urged us to enter the Valley, and at the time of the attack was the first one to fall, right amongst the savages, apparently with his death wound, and now he appears without a scratch, telling his version of the affair and disappearing without seeing any of us. We all believed he was not the honest man and friend we took him to be. He took possession of the gold mine in which he held a one-third interest with Sherburn and Tudor, and sold it.

Years afterward, in traveling at a distance and amongst strangers, I heard this story of our adventures repeated, as told by Aich, and he represented himself as the only man of the party who was not in the least frightened.

I told them that "I was most thoroughly frightened, and Aich looked just as I felt."

STEPHEN F. GROVER
Santa Cruz, California

The commander of the regular army garrison at Fort Miller was notified of these events, and a detachment of the 2d Infantry under Lieutenant Tredwell Moore was dispatched in June, 1852. Five Indians were captured in the Yosemite Valley, all of whom were found to possess articles of clothing belonging to the murdered men. These Indians were summarily shot.[g] Tenaya's scouts undoubtedly witnessed this prompt pronouncement of judgment, and the members of the tribe fled with all speed to their Piute allies at Mono Lake.

The soldiers pursued the fleeing Indians by way of Tenaya Lake and Bloody Canyon. They found no trace of the Yosemites and could elicit no information from the Piutes. The party explored the region north and south of Bloody Canyon and found some promising mineral deposits. In August they returned to Tuolumne Soda Springs and then made their way back to Mariposa by way of the old Mono Trail that passed south of Yosemite Valley.

Upon arrival at Mariposa they exhibited samples of their ore discoveries. This created the usual excitement, and Lee Vining with a party of companions hastened to visit the region to prospect for gold. Leevining Canyon, through which the Tioga Road now passes, was named for the leader of this party.

Tenaya and his refugee band remained with the Mono Indians until late in the summer of 1853, when they again ventured into their old haunts in the Yosemite Valley. Shortly after they had reestablished themselves in their old home, a party of young Yosemites made a raid on the camp of their former hosts and stole a band of horses which the Monos had recently driven up from southern California. The thieves brought the animals to Yosemite by a very roundabout route through a pass at the head of the San Joaquin, hoping by this means to escape detection. However, the Monos at once discovered the ruse and organized a war party to wreak vengeance upon their ungrateful guests. Surprising the

Yosemites while they were feasting gluttonously upon the stolen horses, they almost annihilated Tenaya's band with stones before a rally could be effected. Eight of the Yosemite braves escaped the slaughter and fled down the Merced Canyon. The old men and women who escaped death were given their liberty, but the young women and children were made captive and taken to Mono Lake.

The story of this last act in the elimination of the troublesome Yosemites was made known to Bunnell by surviving members of the tribe.

In 1928, when I talked with Maria, a member of the original Yosemite tribe, her version of the massacre differed widely from the story told by Bunnell. Through her daughter she stoutly assured me that no Indians died in Yosemite Valley except those killed by whites and those who were ill. I asked her how Tenaya died and where. She explained that while the Yosemites were at Mono Lake they engaged in hand games with the Monos. These games are stirring affairs among the Indians. A. L. Kroeber states, "It is impossible to have seen a California Indian warmed to his work in this game when played for stakes—provided its aim and method are understood—and any longer justly to designate him mentally sluggish and emotionally apathetic, as is the wont. It is a game in which not sticks and luck, but the tensest of wills, the keenest perceptions and the supplest of muscular responses are matched ... Seen in this light, the contortions, gesticulations, noises, and excitement of the native are not the mere uncontrolledness of an overgrown child, but the outward reflexes of a powerfully surcharged intensity."

According to Maria, it was in the heat of such a game that a quarrel developed between Tenaya and his Mono allies. In the fight that followed, Tenaya and four of his Yosemite braves were stoned to death. At least, this stoning feature agrees with former accounts of the killing. Horse stealing and a gluttonous feast in Yosemite Valley do not figure in Maria's story. She insists that Tom

"Hutchings," the Yosemite Indian befriended by J. M. Hutchings, attended to the burning of the bodies and packed the charred remains upon his own back from Mono Lake to Hites Cove. There a great "cry" was held for two weeks; the remaining Yosemite Indians and all their friends bewailed the loss of Chief Tenaya and the four tribesmen.

A number of parties of miners, emboldened by the news of the disbanding of the Yosemites, visited the valley in the fall of 1853. During 1854 no white men are known to have entered Yosemite Valley.[h]

By 1855 several accounts written by members of the three punitive expeditions that had entered Yosemite had been published in San Francisco papers. The difficulties of overcoming hostile Indians in the search for gold were far more prominent in the minds of these writers than the scenic wonders of the new-found valley. Nevertheless, the mention of a thousand-foot waterfall in one of these published letters awakened James M. Hutchings, then publishing the *California Magazine*, to the possibilities that Yosemite presented. Hutchings organized the first tourist party in June, 1855, and with two of the original Yosemites as guides proceeded from Mariposa over the old Indian trail via Wawona and Inspiration Point to the valley. Thomas Ayres, an artist, was a member of the party and during this visit he made the first sketches ever made in Yosemite. Ten of these original pencil drawings are now preserved in the Yosemite Museum.[i]

In 1853, James Alden, then a commander in the United States Navy, came to California on a commission to settle the boundary between Mexico and California. He remained until 1860. Some time between 1856 and 1860 he visited Yosemite Valley. Probably on his return to San Francisco he came upon Ayres's work, which appealed to him as the best mementos of his Yosemite experience, and he procured ten originals and one lithograph. Mrs. Ernest W. Bowditch,

Mrs. C. W. Hubbard, and Mrs. A. H. Eustis, descendants of Admiral Alden and heirs to these priceless drawings, have presented them to the Yosemite Museum, which stands near the spot where some of them were made.

In the years that have elapsed since these drawings were created, they have journeyed on pack mules, sailed the seas in old United States men-of-war, jolted about in covered wagons, and at last made a transcontinental journey to come again to the valley that gave them birth.

CHAPTER V

TOURISTS IN THE SADDLE

*H*utchings and his first sight-seers "spent five glorious days in luxurious scenic banqueting" in the newly discovered valley and then followed their Indian guides over the return trail to Mariposa. Upon their arrival in that mountain city, they were besieged with eager questioners, among whom was L. A. Holmes, the editor of the *Mariposa Gazette*, which had recently been established. Mr. Holmes begged that his paper be given opportunity to publish the first account from the pen of Mr. Hutchings. His request was complied with, and in the *Gazette* of July 12, 1855, appears the first printed description of Yosemite Valley, prepared by one uninfluenced by Indian troubles or gold fever.[j]

Journalists the country over copied the description, and so started the Hutchings Yosemite publicity, which was to continue through a period of forty-seven years. Parties from Mariposa and other mining camps, and from San Francisco, interested by Hutchings' oral and printed accounts, organized, secured the same Indian guides, and inaugurated tourist travel to the Yosemite wonder spot.

Milton and Houston Mann, who had accompanied one of these sight-seeing expeditions, were so imbued with the possibilities of serving the hordes of visitors soon to come that they set to work immediately to construct a horse toll trail from the South Fork of the Merced to the Yosemite Valley.[k] Galen Clark, who also had been a member of one of the 1855 parties, was prompted to establish a camp on the South Fork where travelers could be accommodated. This camp was situated on the Mann Brothers' Trail and later became known as Clark's Station. It is known as Wawona now. The Mann brothers finished their trail in 1856.

Old Indian trails were followed by much of the Mariposa-Yosemite Valley route. The toll was collected at White and Hatch's, approximately twelve miles from Mariposa. At Clark's Station (Wawona), the trail detached itself from the Indian route and ascended Alder Creek to its headwaters. Here it crossed to the Bridalveil Creek drainage and passed through several fine meadows, gradually ascending to the highest point on the route above Old Inspiration Point on the south rim of Yosemite Valley. From this point it dropped sharply to the floor of the valley near the foot of Bridalveil Fall. The present-day Alder Creek and Pohono trails traverse much of the old route.

Several years after the pioneer trail was built, sheep camps were established on two of the lush meadows through which it passed. They were known as Westfall's and Ostrander's. The rough shelters existing here were frequently used by tired travelers who preferred to make an overnight stop on the trail rather than exhaust themselves in completing the saddle trip to the valley in one day. Usually, however, Westfall's or Ostrander's were convenient lunch stops for the saddle parties.

In 1869, Charles Peregoy built a hotel, "The Mountain View House," at what had been known as Westfall Meadow and with the help of his wife operated a much-praised hospice every summer until 1875, when the coming of the stage road between Wawona and Yosemite Valley did away with the greater part of the travel on the trail.

The Mann Brothers' Trail, which was some fifty miles in length, was purchased by Mariposa County and made available to public use without charge before construction of the stage road from Mariposa had been completed.

In 1856, the year that witnessed the completion of the Mariposa-Yosemite Valley Trail, L. H. Bunnell, George W. Coulter, and others united in the construction of the "Coulterville Free

Trail." Very little, if any, of this route followed existing Indian trails. The Coulterville Trail started at Bull Creek, to which point a wagon road already had been constructed, and passed through Deer Flat, Hazel Green, Crane Flat, and Tamarack Flat to the point now known as Gentry, and thence to the valley. Its total length was forty-eight miles, of which seventeen miles could be traveled in a carriage[l].

A second pioneer horse trail on the north side of the Merced began at the village of Big Oak Flat, six miles north of Coulterville, and followed a route north of the Coulterville Free Trail through Garrote to Harden's Ranch on the South Fork of the Tuolumne River, thence to its junction with the Coulterville Trail between Crane Flat and Tamarack Flat.[m]

Sections of all of these early routes passed over high terrain where deep snow persisted well into the spring. Early fall snow storms in these vicinities sometimes contributed to the hazards of travel. The trails found use during a relatively short season. The Merced Canyon offered opportunity to establish a route at lower elevation, but the difficulties of construction in the narrow gorge deterred all would-be builders until a short time prior to the wagon-road era. The Hite's Cove route, which came into use in the early 'seventies, partly answered the need for a snow-free canyon trail. Hite's Cove, where the John Hite Mine was located in 1861, is on the South Fork of the Merced some distance above its confluence with the Merced River. A wagon road eighteen miles in length made it accessible from Mariposa. Tourists using this route stopped overnight in Hite's Cove and then traveled twenty miles in the saddle up the Merced Canyon to the valley.

Another means of reaching the valley on horseback via the Merced Canyon was developed soon after wagon roads had been built. Some Yosemite visitors, perhaps because of the poor condition of the roads at certain seasons, elected to leave the Coulterville stage route at Dudley's, from where they went to Jenkins Hill on the rim of the steep walls of the Merced gorge. Here a horse trail enabled them to descend to the bottom of the canyon, thence up the Merced to the valley. This thirty mile saddle trip involved an overnight stop at Hennesey's, situated a short distance below the present El Portal.

Travel in the saddle, of course, was regarded by the California pioneer with few qualms. Likewise, the conveyance of freight on the backs of mules was looked upon as commonplace, and the success attained by those early packers is, in this day and age, wonderful to contemplate. In Hutchings' *California Magazine* for December, 1859, appears a most interesting essay on the business of packing as then practiced among the mountaineers of the gold camps.

Pack animals and packers have not yet passed from the Yosemite scene, for much of the back country is, and always will be, we hope, accessible by trail only. Government trail gangs are dependent for weeks at a time upon the supplies brought to them upon the backs of mules. Likewise, those who avail themselves of High Sierra Camp facilities are served by pack trains. Present-day packing differs in no essential way from the mode of the 'fifties, except that it is often done by Indians instead of the old-time Mexican *mulatero*.

What one visitor of the pre-wagon days thought of the saddle trip into Yosemite Valley may be gathered from J. H. Beadle in his *Undeveloped West*. Beadle visited the Sierra in 1871 and approached the valley from the north.

> Thirty-seven miles from Garrote bring us to Tamarack Flat, the highest point on the road, the end of staging, and no wonder. The remaining five miles down into the valley must be made on horseback.
> While transferring baggage—very little is allowed—to pack mules, the guide and driver amuse us with accounts of former tourists, particularly of Anna Dickinson, who rode astride into the valley, and thereby demonstrat-

ed her right to vote, drink "cocktails," bear arms, and work the roads, without regard to age, sex, or previous condition of servitude. They tell us with great glee of Olive Logan, who, when told she must ride thus into the valley, tried practising on the back of the coach seats, and when laughed at for her pains, took her revenge by savagely abusing everything on the road. When Mrs. Cady Stanton was here a few weeks since, she found it impossible to fit herself to the saddle, averring she had not been in one for thirty years. Our accomplished guide, Mr. F. A. Brightman, saddled seven different mules for her (she admits the fact in her report), and still she would not risk it, and "while the guides laughed behind their horses, and even the mules winked knowingly and shook their long ears comically, still she stood a spectacle for men and donkeys." In vain the skillful Brightman assured her he had piloted five thousand persons down that fearful incline, and not an accident. She would not be persuaded, and walked the entire distance, equal to twenty miles on level ground. And shall this much-enduring woman still be denied a voice in the government of the country? Perish the thought. With all these anecdotes I began to feel nervous myself, for I am but an indifferent rider, and when I observed the careful strapping and saw that my horse was enveloped in a perfect network of girths, cruppers and circingles, I inquired diffidently, "Is there no danger that this horse will turn a somerset with me over some steep point?" "Oh, no, sir," rejoined the cheerful Brightman, "he is bitterly opposed to it."

We turn again to the left into a sort of stairway in the mountain side, and cautiously tread the stony defile downward; at places over loose boulders, at others around or over the points of shelving rock, where one false step would send horse and rider a mangled mass two thousand feet below, and more rarely over ground covered with bushes and grade moderate enough to afford a brief rest. It is impossible to repress fear. Every nerve is tense; the muscles involuntarily make ready for a spring, and even the bravest lean timorously toward the mountain side and away from the cliff, with foot loose in stirrup and eye alert, ready for a spring in case of peril. The thought is vain; should the horse go, the rider would infallibly go with him. And the poor brutes seem to fully realize their danger and ours, as with wary steps and tremulous ears, emitting almost human signs, with more than brute caution they deliberately place one foot before the other, calculating seemingly at each step the desperate chances and intensely conscious of our mutual peril. Mutual danger creates mutual sympathy—everything animal, everything that can feel pain, is naturally cowardly—and while we feel a strange animal kinship with our horses, they seem to express a half-human earnestness to assure us that their interest is our interest, and their self-preservative instinct in full accord with our intellectual dread. We learn with wonder that of all the five thousand who have made this perilous passage not one has been injured—if injured be the word, for the only injury here would be certain death. One false step and we are gone bounding over rocks, ricocheting from cliffs, till all semblance of humanity is lost upon the flat rock below. Such a route would be impossible to any but those mountain-trained mustangs, to whom a broken stone staircase seems as safe as an ordinary macadamized road.

At length we reach a point where the most hardy generally dismount and walk—two hundred feet descent in five hundred feet progress. Indeed half the route will average the descent of an ordinary staircase. Then comes a passage of only moderate descent and terror, then another and more terrible stairway—a descent of four hundred feet in a thousand. I will not walk before and lead my horse, as does our guide, but trail my long rope halter and keep him before,—always careful to keep on the upper side of him, springing from rock to rock, and hugging the cliff with all the ardor of a young lover. For now I am scared. All pretense of pride is gone, and just the last thing I intend to risk is for that horse to stumble, and in falling strike me over that fearful cliff. At last comes a gentler slope, then a crystal spring, dense grove and grass-covered plat, and we are down into the valley. Gladly we take the stage, and are whirled along in the gathering twilight.

The vehicle that whirled Beadle over the flat of the valley floor was brought to Yosemite before roads were constructed and is now exhibited at the Yosemite Museum as "the first wagon in Yosemite Valley."[n]

The arrival of visitors prompted the building of shelters. The first habitation to be constructed by white men in Yosemite was a rough shack put up in 1855 by a party of surveyors, of which Bunnell was a member. A company had been organized to bring water from the foot of the valley into the dry diggings of the Mariposa estate. It was supposed that a claim in the valley would doubly secure the water privileges.

The first permanent structure was built in 1856 by Walworth and Hite. It was constructed of pine boards that were rived out by hand, and occupied the site of the 1851 camp of Boling's party (near the foot of the present Four-Mile Trail to Glacier Point). It was known as the Lower Hotel until 1869, when it was pulled down, and Black's Hotel was constructed on the spot.

In the spring of 1857, Beardsley and Hite put up a canvas-covered house in the old village. The next year this was replaced by a wooden structure, the planks for which had been whipsawed by hand. J. M. Hutchings was again in the valley in 1859, and his *California Magazine* for December of that year tells of the first photographs to be made in Yosemite. C. L. Weed, a pioneer photographer apparently working for R. H. Vance, packed a great instrument and its bulky equipment through the mountains to the Yosemite scenes. Photography was just then taking its place in American life. Mr. Weed's first Yosemite subject was this Upper Hotel of Beardsley and Hite.° Hutchings and Weed decided on this occasion that they must visit the fall now called Illilouette, and Hutchings wrote:

> The reader would have laughed could he have seen us ready for the start. Mr. Beardsley, who had volunteered to carry the camera, had it inverted and strapped at his back, when it looked more like an Italian "hurdy gurdy" than a photographic instrument, and he like the "grinder." Another carried the stereoscopic instrument and the lunch; another, the plate-holders and gun, etcetera; and as the bushes had previously somewhat damaged our broadcloth unmentionables, we presented a very queer and picturesque appearance truly.

Hutchings published a woodcut made from the first photograph of the Yosemite hostelry in November of 1859; his book, *In the Heart of the Sierras*, again alludes to his presence in the valley when this first photograph was taken. Naturally, students of California history have been interested in learning more about the work of Weed, but in spite of serious attempts to procure more information on this photographer of 1859, nothing was brought to light. It was then something of a thrill to me to find myself in possession of an original print from the earliest Yosemite negative. That the print is genuine seems to be a fact, and the incidents relative to its discovery are worth the telling here.

Its donor, Arthur Rosenblatt, resided as a small boy within a
few blocks of the Hutchings San Francisco home on Pine Street.
Mr. Rosenblatt and his brothers played with the Hutchings children. In 1880 the Hutchings home was destroyed by fire. The
small boys of the neighborhood searched the debris for objects
worth saving, and Irving and Wallace Rosenblatt salvaged a pack of
large water-stained photographs. Arthur Rosenblatt with fore-
thought mounted these pictures in an old scrapbook. He has cher-
ished them through the years that have passed. In June, 1929, he
visited the Yosemite Museum and was interested in the historical exhibits. In his study of the displayed materials, he came upon a photographic copy of the old drawing of the "Hutchings House," which
has been taken from *In the Heart of the Sierras*. He recognized its subject as identical with one of the old photographs which he had preserved since 1880. He made his find known to the park naturalist,
and immediately phoned to his San Francisco home and requested
that the scrapbook be mailed at once to the Yosemite Museum.
Upon its receipt, the old hotel photograph was segregated from the
others, and comparisons were made with the drawing in the old
Hutchings book and with the building itself. The print is obviously
from the original Weed negative.

Hutchings' visit of 1859 apparently convinced him of the desir-
ability of residing in Yosemite Valley. During the next few years he
spared no effort in making its wonders known to the world through
his *California Magazine*. The spirited etchings of Yosemite wonders
that were reproduced in the magazine from Weed's photos and from
Ayres's drawings did much to convince travelers of the magnificence
of Yosemite scenery. The stream of tourists who entered the valley
grew apace in spite of the hardships to be endured on the long journey in the saddle. Horace Greeley was one of those who braved the
discomforts in 1859 and gave his description of the place to hundreds of thousands in the East. Greeley, foolishly, determined to

make the 57-mile saddle trip via the Mariposa route in one day. He arrived at the Upper Hotel in Yosemite Valley at 1:00 A.M., more dead than alive, yet shortly afterward he wrote, "I know no single wonder of Nature on earth which can claim a superiority over the Yosemite." His visit was made at a season when Yosemite Falls contained but little water, and he dubbed them a "humbug," but his hearty praise of the general wonders played a significant part in turning the interest of Easterners upon the new mecca of scenic beauty.

In 1864 J. M. Hutchings came to the Upper Hotel (Cedar Cottage) in the role of proprietor. The mirth and discomfiture engendered among Hutchings' guests by the cheesecloth partitions between bedrooms prompted him to build a sawmill near the foot of Yosemite Falls in order to produce sufficient lumber to "hard finish" his hostelry. It was in this mill that John Muir found employment for a time. The hotel was embellished with lean-tos and porches, and an addition was constructed at the rear in which was completely enclosed the trunk of a large growing cedar tree. Hutchings built a great fireplace in this sitting room and proceeded to make the novel gathering place famous as the "Big Tree Room."ᴾ

A winter spent in the frigid shade of the south wall of Yosemite Valley convinced the Hutchings family that their "Big Tree Room" was not a pleasant winter habitation. They built anew and moved into the warm sunshine of the north side of the valley. With their own hands members of the family constructed a snug cabin among giant black oaks near the foot of Yosemite Falls and there spent the remainder of their Yosemite days.

Papers, letters, and photographs relating to the Yosemite experiences of the Hutchings family have been preserved by J. M. Hutchings' daughter, Mrs. Gertrude Hutchings Mills, and by the family of his wife, the Walkingtons of England. Materials generously donated from these sources take important places in the collections of the Yosemite Museum and have greatly aided in the preparation of this volume.

J. M. Hutchings invested heavily in the construction of the Sentinel group of buildings and continued to be identified with the Yosemite as publicity agent, hotel proprietor, resident, official guardian, and unofficial champion until 1902. In that year, he met his death on the zigzags of the Big Oak Flat Road. In the 1902 register of the hotel, which was once the Hutchings House, is the following entry made by Mrs. Hutchings, the second wife[q] of J. M. Hutchings:

November 8, 1902

Today leaving Yo Semite and all I love best.

EMILY A. HUTCHINGS

Thinking that some who come here may wish to know a little about the sad tragedy of Mr. J. Hutchings death, I would like to write a few words.

Because I had never seen Yo Semite in the autumn, my dear husband brought me here for a short holiday, on our way to San Francisco. We started from the Calaveras Big Trees and came via Parrots Ferry, and its beautiful gorge — the wonderful old mining center of Columbia, and its hitherto only surface-skimmed Gold Fields — Sonora and its good approaches, in its oiled and well graded roads — and thence to Chaffee and Chamberlains and to Crockers and their hearty hospitality. It has been a very pleasant experience, to see many friends on the way — most of them honored "Old Timers," who have been the thews and sinews of the State, and who still hold their own in the rugged strength, which has brought them through to 1902.

From Crockers, we started on the last day of our journey [Oct. 31, 1902], continuing through the glorious Forests of the Sierras, the autumnal tints of which this year, have been of unusual grandeur — these beauties all being intensified in Yo Semite.

Coming down the Grade we were impressed beyond expression, and, when we reached the point where El Capitan first presents itself, my Husband said, "It is like Heaven."

There was no apparent danger near but one of the horses took fright (probably a wild animal was at hand) and dashed away. When the Angel of Death reached Mr. Hutchings a few moments later—under the massive towering heights of that sun-illumined Cliff—"He" found him in the full vigour of life and high energetic purpose—but his grief-stricken wife prayed in vain that the ebbing tide would stay.

From the moment the sad accident was known, the greatest sympathy and kindness were shown, loving hands gave reverent aid—and on Sunday, Nov. 2, 1902, my dear husband was borne from the Big Tree Room and its time honored memories. The residents of the Valley and many of the Indians, who had long known him, followed. We laid him to rest, surrounded by nature in Her most glorious garb, and under the peaks and domes he had loved so well and had explored so fearlessly.

EMILY A. HUTCHINGS
Nov. 8, 1902

In 1941 and for several years thereafter, Yosemite Valley was visited by Cosie Hutchings Mills, daughter of J. M. Hutchings, born October 5, 1867, the second white child born in the valley. Elizabeth H. Godfrey, of the Yosemite Museum, obtained from Mrs. Mills both written and oral statements regarding the pioneer experiences of the Hutchings family in Yosemite. The interviews with Mrs. Mills were recorded by Mrs. Godfrey. Her manuscript, "Chronicles of Cosie Hutchings Mills," and Mrs. Mills' written reminiscences are preserved in the Yosemite Museum.

"Cosie" passed away in June of 1956 at the age of 88 years. She spent her last years with one of her sons, William E. Mills, Jr. at Stamford, Connecticut.

CHAPTER VI

STAGECOACH DAYS

*F*or twenty-three years after the coming of the first sight-seers, Yosemite Valley was accessible only by horse trail. The twelve thousand tourists, who frantically clung to their Yosemite-bound steeds during this period, included many Easterners and Europeans not accustomed to mountain trails. They had departed surcharged with enthusiasm but sometimes were caustic in their expressions regarding their mode of conveyance and the crudity of the facilities found at their disposal both en route and in the valley. Not a few of the comments made by visitors found their way into print. Yosemite bibliography is not limited to items printed in English. The entire world sent representatives to the valley during that first period of travel, and foreign literature carried the story of Yosemite wonders quite as did American publications.

The merchants of the towns along the routes of approach, as well as the businessmen within the valley itself, felt the need of providing more adequately for the greater numbers that might be brought to their attractions. Foremost among the provisions, naturally, was the construction of wagon roads.

To Dr. John T. McLean, the president of the Coulterville and Yosemite Turnpike Company, belongs the honor of first making the Yosemite Valley accessible to wheeled vehicles. The Coulterville Company was formed in 1859. It had extended its road to Crane Flat, and, at the insistence of Dr. McLean, arranged with the Yosemite commissioners to build and maintain a toll road to the floor of Yosemite Valley. The commissioners had agreed that this company should have exclusive rights on the north side of Yosemite Valley; that is, no other company was to build a road into the valley from the north for a period of ten years. Under this agreement, the

Coulterville Road was projected in 1870 and completed to the Merced River in 1874.[r] The following paragraph from a letter sent by Dr. McLean to the president of the Yosemite National Park Commission, 1899, gives interesting information on the discovery[1] of the Merced Grove of Big Trees, as well as a statement regarding the opening of the Coulterville Road:

> While making a survey for this road a grove of big trees was discovered, its existence not having been previously known except to Indians before these explorations for the building of this road were prosecuted. It was determined to carry the road directly through this grove, which was named the Merced Grove by me because of its nearness to the Merced River. In order to carry the proposed road through this new-found grove of *Sequoia gigantea* it was necessary, in order to secure the best grades and shortest distances to Yosemite, to leave the road already built at Hazel Green instead of at Crane Flat six miles farther east. It was thought the greater length of road required to start from Hazel Green and build through the Merced Grove would be compensated by the advantage the road would have of passing through this grove of over 50 *Sequoias* on the way to Yosemite. The additional cost in construction of the road by reason of this new departure from Hazel Green instead of from Crane Flat was about $10,000. The work of construction was vigorously prosecuted, and on June 17, 1874, the Yosemite was first opened to travel by wheeled vehicles over this road, on that day a number of stage coaches and passenger and freight teams passing over it to the level of the valley.[2]

The Big Oak Flat and Yosemite Turnpike Company applied to extend their road to Yosemite Valley after the commissioners had conveyed exclusive rights to the Coulterville Road. The commissioners refused to violate their agreement with McLean's company, but the Big Oak Flat Company secured the passage of an act by the state legislature, which granted the privilege asked. In July, 1874, the Big Oak Flat Road was completed to the floor of Yosemite. Needless to say, this second road functioned to the everlasting detriment of the Coulterville route.

1. The Walker party, 1833, may have been the first to see the Merced Grove. See p. 8. See also Wegner, J. H., *Yosemite Nature Notes* (1930), p. 67.

In the fall of 1874, Washburn, Chapman, Coffman and Company of Mariposa sought the right to extend their Mariposa Road to Yosemite Valley. The commissioners granted their request on the same terms as given to the Coulterville Company. On July 22, 1875, amid much celebrating, the Mariposa Road was completed to the valley floor.[t]

The easier mode of travel introduced by this road construction, coupled with the increased publicity from the pen and brush of enthusiasts, made for a substantial increase in the number of Yosemite visitors.[u] In keeping with this wagon-road building was the steady extension of the Central Pacific Railroad. Stockton, Modesto, Copperopolis, Berenda, Merced, and Madera were, in turn, the terminals. Seven routes to Yosemite made bids for the tourist travel. The Milton and Calaveras route permitted of railroad conveyance to Milton. Those who were induced to take the Berenda-Grants Springs route took the train to Raymond. The Madera-Fresno Flats route afforded railroad-coach transportation to Madera. The Modesto-Coulterville route meant leaving the rails at Modesto. The Merced-Coulterville route involved staging from Merced. The Mariposa route also required detraining at Merced, but the stage route that followed took travelers through Hornitos and Mariposa. Those tourists who chose the Milton-Big Oak Flat route left the train at Copperopolis and traveled in the stage to Chinese Camp, Priests, and into the valley on the Big Oak Flat Road.[v] Dodgers, pamphlets, and guidebooks furnished by the competing towns and stage companies produced a confusion to say the least.

The conveyances were of two types. At the height of the season, when travel was heavy and roads dry, the Standard Concord Coach was employed. At other times, a vehicle commonly termed a "mud wagon" was put to use. During this era of horse-drawn vehicles, the trains of pack mules were, of course, replaced by great freight wagons. Today, in driving over the old wagon roads, one is led to wonder how passenger vehicles succeeded in passing the great freight outfits.

Some years ago, in searching through the objects left in a deserted house in the ghost town, Bodie, I came upon a manuscript describing staging as it was practiced in that famous mining camp. What the unknown author has to say about the business there applies to neighboring mountain regions, and is a reminder of a phase of life of the 'eighties.

> The stage coach is to California what the modern express train is to Indiana, and people unaccustomed to mountain life can form but little conception of the vast amount of transportation carried on by means of coaches and freight wagons.
>
> Even though California may truly be termed the "Eden" of America, yet there is not a county in the state but has more or less traffic for the stage coach, and in the northern and eastern part of the state, especially, there is an entire network of well-graded roads, resembling Eastern pikes. These roads are mostly owned by corporations and, consequently, are toll roads.
>
> Over these are run the fast stages drawn by from two to ten large horses, and the great freight wagons drawn by from fourteen to twenty mules.
>
> The stage lines have divisions, as do railroads, and at the end of each division there is a change of horses, thus giving the greatest possible means for quick conveyance. Over each line there are generally two stages per day, one each way. These carry passengers, mail, and all express traffic. At each town is a Wells Fargo office, and business is carried on in a similar manner to that of railroad express offices. Telegraph lines are in use along the most important roads.
>
> The stage lines have time cards similar to railroads, and in case a stage is a few minutes late, it causes as much anxiety as does the delay of an O. & M. express. A crowd is always waiting at the express office; some are there for business, others through some curiosity and to size up the passengers.
>
> A stage from a mining town usually contains a bar of gold bullion worth $25,000, which is being shipped to the mint. Bullion is shipped from each mine once a month, but people always know when this precious metal is aboard by the appearance of a fat, burly officer perched beside the stage-driver, with two or three double-barreled shotguns. He, of course, is serving as a kind of scarecrow to the would-be stage robbers.
>
> The average fare for riding on a stage is 15 cents per mile.

The manner in which freight is transported is quite odd, especially to a "Hoosier." Wagons of the largest size are used. Some of these measure twelve feet from the ground to the top of the wagon bed; then bows and canvas are placed over this, making a total height of fifteen feet, at least. Usually three or four of these wagons are coupled together, like so many cars, and then drawn by from fourteen to twenty large mules. All these are handled by a single driver. A team of this kind travels, when heavily loaded, about fifteen miles per day, the same being spoken of always as the slow freight. In some mining districts, however, where business is flush, extra stages are put on for freight alone. These are termed the fast freights. This business involves a large capital, and persons engaged in it are known as forwarding companies. Even the freight or express on goods from New York is sometimes collected a hundred miles from any railroad, and so even to those living in the remote mountain regions, this is about as convenient, and they seem to enjoy life as well as if living in a railroad town.

The city of Bodie has its entire freight and passenger traffic carried as mentioned above. A short time ago its population was 10,000; there were three daily papers and free mail delivery, and all the improvements necessary to any modern town or city.

The prospect of a holdup always added to the thrill of staging. Yosemite literature is not replete with road agent episodes, but highwaymen did occasionally appear along the routes to the valley. "Black Bart," whose fame as a gentleman stage robber was worldwide during the early 'eighties, met his downfall in the Yosemite region on his twenty-eighth robbery.

Black Bart was a very unusual bandit. He took no human lives. In fact, he never fired a weapon in any of his exploits. He carried an unloaded shotgun and bluffed, successfully, twenty-seven times. His forays began in 1877, and his returns were such that he was enabled to reside in San Francisco as a respected and rather dapper citizen. His absence from the city on the occasions of his robberies was accounted for through his story of visiting mines in which he held interests. His desire to be well dressed and his penchant for clean linen proved his undoing. It was a laundry mark on a handkerchief which brought about his capture after his twenty-eighth robbery.

Not all the holdups along Yosemite roads took place in the distant past.ᵂ D. J. Foley's *Yosemite Tourist* for July 10, 1906, carries the following account of a robbery that brings the melodramatic influence of highwaymen into the very end of the period of stage coach days. It was entitled "Five Stages Held Up by the Lone Highwayman of the Chowchilla, An Event Full of Excitement and Interest," and reads:

> This is the story of a plain, ordinary "hold-up" of the Raymond-Wawona-Yosemite stages; and the time was Saturday afternoon at ten minutes of four. The place was about six miles this side of Ahwahnee, upon the side of the Chowchilla Mountain, about a mile and a half this side of where a similar, but less important, event took place last August.
>
> The point, carefully selected by the bold robber was an ideal one. The road here is in the form of the letter S, flattened out, and he selected the upper part of the letter, about all of the other parts being visible.
>
> The first stage was in charge of Will Palmer, one of the new drivers. Puffing and sweating, the team of four were rounding the turn in the road, when Walter Brode, who, with Mrs. F. J. House, occupied the front seat, yelled: "Hold up!" For up the road a hundred or more feet away he saw the fellow jump out from behind some brush and, with his old 44 Winchester up to his shoulder, he was advancing toward them. And in tones, musical and soft but determined, he said:
>
> "Throw out that box!"
>
> The driver was not aware of the presence of the express box, but it was there and Mr. Seth Hart threw it out like a gentleman.
>
> "Get out of that stage," came the cool, determined command, supplemented with that ugly-looking 44.
>
> And out they got.
>
> Then he requested one of the ladies, Miss Bowen, to "pass the hat around," which she did under protest.
>
> The other stage was then about due and so he moved down the road a bit to a point where he could keep them well "covered," and yet not be seen by the approaching stage. In the meantime all their hands were up, for that big "44" was pointed their way.
>
> Around the turn came the second stage with "Josh" Wrenn as driver. No especial importance was attributed to the unusual sight, believing it to be a joke. But the illusion was quickly dispelled when out rang that soft and musical command: "Get out of the stage," and out they got, the vi-

cious-looking "44" being much in evidence. He lined them up with the others and then ordered a boy of about fifteen to "pass the hat around." The boy was badly scared, and justly, too, and was about to comply with the request, when up spoke C. E. McStay, a well-known business man of Los Angeles, who very kindly offered to take the boy's place. To this the robber consented, not suspecting the "job" that was so quickly put up on him. For "job" it was, and one, too, that saved the passengers many dollars and valuables. "I quickly thought of and settled this proposition," said Mr. McStay. "If that boy passes the hat and searches us, for this is what he was ordered to do, he will not use any discretion, and we will all be heavy losers; whereas, if I can do that honor I shall take but little, unless I have to." All this and more, too, was thought out by Mr. McStay in less time than it takes to write this, and so he acted at once, and to him is due the credit of the "buncoing" that followed; for this mild-mannered, soft-voiced Lone Highwayman of the Chowchilla was most thoroughly "buncoed" in this change of "hat passers," and he suspected it even before the first stage was ordered to "move on." But that's another story.

And so in the fullness of his nerve—it's the real California-Los Angeles kind, too, Mr. McStay became the apparent Chief Assistant of the Lone Highwayman of the Chowchilla.

The third stage drove up in due time with the experience of the second stage duplicated. The fourth wagon had a load of ladies, and he did not order them to get out. Tho thus honored it was from this wagon that he secured most of his coin. The passengers of the fifth wagon "lined up" with the others. On this stage, in charge of the driver, Ed Gordon, was a sack, for the Sugar Pine Mills, with over $500 in it. From the zig-zag below they saw the crowd "lined up" and they, suspecting the cause, helped the driver to hide the sack under the cushion of the seat.

During the forty-year period which rightly may be considered as the stagecoach era, a combination of influences were at work. Politics sadly affected the management of the state grant (brought into existence in 1864), and sheep threatened the upper country not under the jurisdiction of the Yosemite commissioners. A national park came into existence which physically encompassed the state park and figuratively engulfed the state management.

Improvements grew apace. New hotels and public camp grounds were created; trails were built; the road system was improved and enlarged; electricity developed; and a climax reached with the construction of a railroad almost to the very gates of the valley. In 1907 the Yosemite Valley Railroad changed the entire aspect of stagecoach days by bringing its coaches to El Portal.

With the advent of this new transportation, the long stage ride was no longer necessary, but great fleets of horsedrawn vehicles were still employed to convey visitors from the railhead to Yosemite Valley. The various stage companies continued to operate, but except for the Big Tree routes, their traffic was greatly reduced. The Yosemite Valley Railroad menaced the business of staging, but a far more ominous threat had already appeared on the scene. Motor-driven vehicles were proving to be a success. The automobile was introduced to Yosemite more than a decade prior to the time when its official entry was permitted by park regulations. The first car to climb the Yosemite grades was a Stanley Steamer, and its driver was A. E. Holmes of San Jose.[x] In a letter to J. V. Lloyd, Mr. Holmes testifies as follows:

> This trip was made in the month of July [1900] by way of Madera and Raymond in a Stanley Steamer car that was manufactured just outside of the city of Boston. I was accompanied on this trip by my brother, F. H. Holmes.
>
> At that time Boysen took our photographs in the Valley; one at the foot of Yosemite Falls, and another near Mirror Lake.
>
> The body that is shown in the photograph is not the original body that came with the car, but one that was made just for the trip into the Yosemite.

To what extent noisy automobiles were regarded as a menace may be sensed upon considering the following "Instruction" posted about the park and published with *Rules and Regulations* during the later years of the stagecoach era:

(4) *Bicycles*.—The greatest care must be exercised by persons using bicycles. On meeting a team the rider must stop and stand at side of road between the bicycle and the team—the outer side of the road if on a grade or curve. In passing a team from the rear, the rider should learn from the driver if his horses are liable to frighten,

in which case the driver should halt, and the rider dismount and walk past, keeping between the bicycle and the team....

(9) *Miscellaneous.* — Automobiles and motor cycles are not permitted in the park.

What the railroad did to the stagecoach, the automobile, aided by storm, did to the railroad. On December 11, 1937, as a result of prolonged and heavy warm rains which melted the early snow cover at elevations as high as 10,000 feet, a flood developed in the basins of Yosemite and Tenaya creeks, and to a lesser degree in the other Yosemite watersheds. The notch at the top of Yosemite Falls was filled almost to the brim with muddy water that was estimated to leap 150 feet away from the cliff at the top. In the valley itself Yosemite Creek was half a mile wide, and the Merced River overflowed its banks on a similar rampage. Flood scars were clearly visible in the chutes of the valley walls nine years later. In the Merced Canyon far below the valley several miles of both the All-Year Highway and the Yosemite Valley Railway were destroyed.

The expense of replacing miles of twisted rails and missing roadbed, the loss of passenger traffic to automobile travel, and finally the loss of freight revenue when the Yosemite Sugar Pine Lumber Company sold its major holdings, combined to put the railway out of business. In 1945, wrecking crews took up the track, and another pioneer railroad disappeared.

CHAPTER VII

EXPLORERS

*T*he influx of travelers even in the days of horse trails and the stagecoach brought a demand to know more of the valley and the region as a whole. Maps were needed, and the desires of travelers for dependable information brought survey parties into the park. The first of these, the Geological Survey of California, was in Yosemite in the years 1863-1867. Josiah Dwight Whitney was director of the survey, and William H. Brewer, his principal assistant. A guidebook based upon their investigations was published in 1868. Most of the mapping was done by Clarence King, Charles F. Hoffmann, and James T. Gardiner. King was later to become the first director of the United States Geological Survey and to write a dramatized account of his adventures in Yosemite and the Sierra as one of the important contributions to the literature of the range, *Mountaineering in the Sierra Nevada*. Later mountaineers have not always been able to find terrain hazards he described but they have enjoyed his story, admittedly written for an armchair audience, and have made due allowance for an aspect of greater severity that existed in the Sierra of his day.

A party of the Wheeler Survey, under George Montague Wheeler, in general charge of the Geographical Surveys west of the 100th Meridian, was in Yosemite in the late 'seventies and early 'eighties and in 1883 produced a large-scale topographic map of Yosemite Valley and vicinity. Lieut. M. M. Macomb was responsible for the Yosemite work.

During July and August, of 1890, Professor George Davidson of the United States Coast and Geodetic Survey, together with his assistants, occupied the summit of Mount Conness for the purpose of closing a link in the main triangulation which connected with the transcontinental surveys.

Large instruments and much equipment had to be transported to the summit of the mountain by pack animals and upon the shoulders of men.

Astronomical observations were made at night, and during the daylight hours horizontal angles were measured on distant peaks in the Coast Ranges from which heliotropes were constantly showing toward Mount Conness. A small square wooden observatory, 8 by 8 feet, housed the 20-inch theodolite mounted upon a concrete pier. Sixteen twisted-wire cables fastened the observatory to the granite mountain top and kept it from being blown away.

The officers of the Coast and Geodetic Survey party under Professor Davidson were J. J. Gilbert, Isaac Winston, Fremont Morse, and Frank W. Edmonds.

As a result of his own travels and surveys in the region, J. N. LeConte prepared a map of the Sierra adjacent to Yosemite and Hetch Hetchy valleys, which was published by the Sierra Club in 1893, and army officers in charge of park administration did much important map making in the 1890's. The United States Geological Survey began its mapping of the region embraced within the present park in 1891 and completed the surveys in 1909. R. B. Marshall and H. E. L. Feusier surveyed the Yosemite, Dardanelles, and Mount Lyell sheets; A. H. Sylvester and George R. Davis, the Bridgeport Quadrangle. Operating as they did with limited funds, their efforts spread over a vast territory, and confronted with a short season, they inevitably made some errors on their maps. In correct editions of these maps some ridges, lakes, and canyons have been moved, but today's travelers may still find lakes and glaciers which are not on the map, and may find a few of these features on the map but not on the ground. It is not the errors of Sierra mapmakers, however, but the measure of success they achieved, which is remarkable. In the higher reaches of the Sierra today it is extremely difficult to discover, after a particularly heavy winter, which snow field conceals a lake and which covers merely a meadow or an expanse of ice. Nor is the Sierra itself utterly static. At least two small lakes which formed behind dams of glacial moraine have disappeared recently when the dams were undermined.

Perhaps the ultimate in Yosemite mapping, from the geomorphologist's point of view, is the Yosemite Valley Sheet, prepared by the United States Geological Survey in cooperation with the State of California. The map is of large scale, and the topography, the work of François E. Matthes, is extremely accurate, giving it something of the quality of a relief map on a plane surface. Even the overhangs of the cliffs are depicted. The 1946 edition of this sheet falls short in that detail has been lost through the overprinting of topographical shading.

Considered for their practical guidance to the user of Yosemite trails, the U. S. Geological Survey maps of the back country are most important. The 700-odd miles of maintained trails which make much of the park accessible to the hiker and rider appear upon these topographical maps in true relationship to the physical features through which they pass. A useful guidebook covering the routes in and around Yosemite Valley, as well as many of the park trails south of the Tuolumne River, is the *Illustrated Guide to Yosemite Valley*, by Virginia and Ansel Adams. In this volume road and trail diagrams are stylized to impart, simply and directly, information on distances, altitudes, and relative positions. Walter A. Starr, Jr.'s *Guide to the John Muir Trail and the High Sierra Region* includes a section (Part I) on the trails of the Yosemite National Park region, and the map which accompanies it relates the high country trails to the road systems of both the east and west slopes. This guide, published by the Sierra Club, is kept up-to-date through the production of frequent editions.[y]

EARLY INDIAN ROUTES

Before the story of trail building within the national park is presented, it is worthwhile to review briefly the history of the approach routes outside the present limits of the park — the trails followed by the Indian fighters and miners.

Most of the early routes of the white man across the Yosemite Sierra and out of the valley itself followed Indian trails. The discovery of arrow points and knife blades on the slopes of some of the higher Yosemite peaks indicates that the Miwok Indians entered the high, rough country in pursuit of game. Their regularly established trade with the Monos also is a matter of record. Indian Canyon and the Vernal and Nevada falls gorge of the Merced provided two much used routes out of the valley to the east, and the Old Inspiration Point-Wawona-Fresno Flats-Coarse Gold route gave access to the foothill country to the west. There were other ancient routes on the valley walls accessible to an able-bodied Indian; however, except in emergency they probably found little use.

Walker, west-bound in 1833, followed the Miwok-Mono trail on the divide between the Merced and Tuolumne watersheds, having reached this divide, in all likelihood, via the maze of canyons formed by the tributaries of the East Walker River and the feeder streams of the Tuolumne River. White men in pursuit of eastward-fleeing Indians in 1851 penetrated to the Tenaya Lake basin, and one party in 1852 crossed to the east side via Bloody Canyon, as already described. This party returned to the San Joaquin on a branch of the Mono Trail which crossed Cathedral Pass, thence into Little Yosemite Valley, Mono Meadows, Peregoy Meadows, and Wawona. In all these travels definite trails of the aborigines could be followed even though many parts of the routes were buried in snow.

In the foothill region west of the park ancient Indian paths enabled gold seekers to reach much of the terrain in which they were interested. Barrett and Gifford (1933, p. 128) report that a Mr. Woods discovered gold on Woods Creek near the present Jamestown, Tuolumne County, in June, 1848, several months before the general rush of miners into the territory of the Southern Miwok.[z] In this locality Indian trails connected the several rancherias near the present town, Sonora, with similar Indian villages on the Merced. In the Tuolumne country, also, a primitive transmountain route gave access via Sonora Pass to the favored locality now known as Bridgeport Valley. The wagon road which was opened here very early in the gold-rush period followed closely the route of the Indians. That there were prehistoric lanes of travel in the high mountains which connected the Sonora Pass and Mono (Bloody Canyon) routes seems likely but no record of such north-south trails of the Indians has been handed down, other than the statements made by Walker and Leonard regarding their route from the Walker River country to the Tuolumne-Merced divide.

The country south of the Merced drainage system was popular, both with the Miwok and the Chukchansi, a group of the Yokuts Indians. Kroeber (1925, pp. 446, 481-482, 526) has recorded the distribution of ancient Miwok villages on the South Fork of the Merced, on Mariposa Creek, and on the Chowchilla and Fresno rivers. The primitive trails which connected these villages provided a network of lanes through the hills well known to J. D. Savage and his contemporary forty-niners who frequented the hills and stream courses north of the San Joaquin River. These Indian trails became the first routes followed by the miner and his pack outfits. A few were "improved" by their first white users to become fairly good horse trails and later some of them were transformed into wagon roads. Today the old routes are not easily distinguished from the more recent logging roads which lace back and forth everywhere through the pine country south of the park, but the investigative motorist who will check against the maps made prior to the period of logging at the turn of the century may identify the old routes and follow them in exploring the country surrounding Wawona, Mariposa, Miami, Nipinnawasee, Hites Cove, Fish Camp, Bear Valley, Hornitos, and several other historic and prehistoric sites in the Mariposa region.

The Chukchansi, northernmost of the Yokuts, occupied the country south of the Fresno River and at times crossed that stream and overlapped upon the lands of the Miwok. Prior to the Yosemite Indian War with the whites, 1850-1852, they seem to have been on friendly terms with the Miwok. Chukchansi villages close to the border of Miwok territory existed at Fresno Flats (near the present Oakhurst, Madera County), Coarse Gold, Magnet, and on the San Joaquin near Hutchins. As was true of the Miwok villages, primitive trails connected these rancherias and extended into the country of the Chukaimina on the south and into the Mono territory to the east. In this part of the Sierra, the Monos claimed a goodly part of the west slope, including the present Bass Lake region and the higher country drained by the San Joaquin and Kings rivers. At the time of the Yosemite Indian War, these west-slope Piutes (Monos) were allied with the Chowchillas and Chukchansi. The intricate trail system of the densely populated belts, characterized by the Digger pine (Upper Sonoran Zone) and the oaks and ponderosa pine (Transition Zone), fed westward into major routes to the great San Joaquin Valley and eastward to high passes on the crest of the Sierra. Of these last-mentioned routes, those across Sonora Pass, Bond Pass, Buckeye Pass, Bloody Canyon, Agnew Pass, Mammoth Pass, Mono Pass (headwaters of the South Fork of the San Joaquin River), Pine Creek Pass, and Piute Pass were especially important to the Indians of the Yosemite region. At least some of these passes were traversed by horses before the advent of the white man.

More than a few of the Indians of the Yosemite region had, prior to the gold rush, lived in the Spanish mission towns along the coast. Adam Johnston, Indian agent at the time of the Yosemite Indian War, stated of the Chowchilla and Chukchansi, "The most of them are wild, though they have among them many who have been educated at the missions, and who have fled from their real or supposed oppressors to the mountains. These speak the Spanish language as well as their native tongue." (Russell, 1931, p. 172.) As might be expected, the mountain tribes maintained their long-established contact with the Indian population of the lower valleys, and numerous routes led from the rancherias of the hill tribes out upon the San Joaquin Valley and to the coast.

As we have seen, the first penetration of the Yosemite Valley by white men was the result of miners' activities in the Mariposa hills. In reaching the hills and in entering the valley, the white prospectors of the gold-rush period followed well-defined trails long used by Indians. Within a few years after the close of hostilities with the Sierra tribes, the events described in the chapter on early mining excitements east of Yosemite took place. Here, also, the primitive paths of the Indian opened the way. The sheepherder, contemporary with the miner of the high country, also followed the trails of the Indian, and his flocks, together with the cattleman's herds, did their part in "grading" the routes and making them conspicuous.

TRAIL BUILDERS

When Yosemite National Park was created in 1890, the U. S. Army took over the administration of the federal area which almost surrounded the state reservation. To aid patrolling in the park, a full program of exploration and mapping was launched. Capt. Alexander Rodgers, Col. Harry C. Benson, Major W. W. Forsyth, and Lts. N. F. McClure and Milton F. Davis made particularly important contribution to the work.

The existing fine system of trails so important to protection and enjoyment of Yosemite National Park had its inception in the plan of the U. S. Army. Almost at once after assuming responsibility for the care of the park, commanding officers initiated construction of trails, and at this juncture the location of primitive Indian trails was no longer a prime consideration in defining routes. The story of trail building by the U. S. Army will be told in a later part of this chapter.

It was inevitable that in the exploration for trails and passes, certain peaks should be climbed. The first recorded ascents of Yosemite's peaks are attributed to members of the various survey parties. Perhaps the first was the ascent of Mount Hoffmann in 1863 by Whitney, Brewer, and Hoffmann. King climbed it in 1864 and with Gardiner climbed Mount Conness that same year, following with an ascent of Mount Clark, not without adventure, in 1866. Muir climbed Mounts Dana and Hoffmann, and far more difficult Cathedral Peak, three years later. Probably the first Yosemite ascent for the challenge of it by a casual tourist was that of Mount Lyell, highest peak in the park, in 1871. According to Hutchings:

> Members of the State Geological Survey Corps having considered it impossible to reach the summit of this lofty peak, the writer was astonished to learn from Mr. A. T. Tileston [John Boies Tileston] of Boston, after his return to the Valley from a jaunt of health and pleasure in the High Sierra, that he had personally proven it to be possible by making the ascent. Incredible as it seemed at the time, three of us found Mr. Tileston's card upon it some ten days afterward.

Mr. Tileston, writing to his wife from Clark and Moore's after the climb on Mount Lyell, explained that he ascended nearly to the snow line on August 28, 1871, and next morning "climbed the mountain and reached the top of the highest pinnacle ('inaccessible, according to the State Geological Survey') before eight." (Tileston, 1922, pp. 89-90.)

John Muir reached the summit of Mount Lyell later that year. Muir undoubtedly climbed in part as a response to the challenge of summits but could hardly be considered a casual tourist.

Four years later another summit, of which Whitney had said, it "never has been, and never will be trodden by human foot," was ascended by a man climbing merely for the fun of it. In 1875, George G. Anderson, continuing where John Conway, a valley resident, had been stopped by difficulty and danger, tackled the climb of Half Dome with ideas of his own. According to Muir:

> Anderson began with Conway's old rope, which had been left in place, and resolutely drilled his way to the top, inserting eye-bolts five or six feet apart, and making his rope fast to each in succession, resting his feet on the last bolt while he drilled a hole for the next above. Occasionally some irregularity in the curve, or slight foothold, would enable him to climb a few feet without the rope, which he would pass and begin drilling again, and thus the whole work was accomplished in less than a week.

Anderson's climb was the beginning of a search for routes to prominent heights in Yosemite that continues today. The fame of Yosemite's wonders was spreading through the world, and the advent of stage roads brought a multitude of visitors who preferred to see the region without having to drill to do so. It was imperative that officials in charge of the state reservation improve and multiply the faint Indian trails in order that eager visitors might reach the valley rim and the High Sierra beyond.

Because appropriations made by the state legislature for the use of the Yosemite Valley Commission were too small to enable that executive body to undertake a program of trail building, toll privileges were granted to certain responsible individuals in return for the construction of some of the much-needed trails. Albert Snow, John Conway, James McCauley, Washburn and McCready, and James Hutchings were prominent in this contractual arrangement with the Yosemite commissioners.

Two trails antedate the regime of the Yosemite Valley Commissioners—the trail to Mirror Lake and the Vernal Fall Trail.

No record exists identifying the builders of these pioneer trails. Albert Snow, 1870, built a horse trail from "Register Rock" on the Vernal Fall Trail, via Clark Point, to his "La Casa Nevada" on the flat between Vernal and Nevada falls. In 1871, John Conway, working for McCauley, started construction of the Four Mile Trail from the base of Sentinel Rock to Glacier Point. The project was completed in 1872. The old Mono Trail of the Indians between Little Yosemite and Glacier Point was followed by Washburn and McCready when they constructed their toll route here in 1872. In 1874, James Hutchings met the cost of a horse trail up Indian Canyon, which by 1877 already had fallen into such disrepair as to make it accessible only to hikers. The disintegration progressed rapidly, and the "improved" aboriginal route to the north rim found use during a comparatively few years of Yosemite tourist travel. Geographically and topographically it has much to commend it; in the current master plan of Yosemite National Park it is carried as the trail proposal calculated "to provide the best all-year access to the upper country on the north side of the valley." Early action is expected which will place it on the map again. The Yosemite Falls Trail, started by John Conway in 1873 and completed to the north rim in 1877, was carried by its builder and owner still higher to the summit of Eagle Peak, highest of the Three Brothers. John Conway's homemade surveying instruments used in trail building are preserved in the Yosemite Museum.

By 1882 the State Legislature initiated a program of purchasing and maintaining the Yosemite trails which had been privately built and operated on a toll basis. The Four Mile Trail to Glacier Point was first on the docket. A number of the other toll trails reverted to the state at this time through the expiration of leases. In 1886 rights to all remaining trails and to those portions of the Coulterville and Big Oak Flat roads within the boundary of the Yosemite Grant were purchased by the state and made free to the public.[a]

At the time Yosemite National Park was established a great part of the northern section of the reservation was quite unknown except to cattlemen, sheepmen, and a few prospectors and trappers. As previously mentioned, the U. S. Army officers responsible for the administration of the national park at this time opened a new era in High Sierra trail development. From 1891 to 1914 a succession of officers, with a number of troops of cavalry, worked with diligence and with great ingenuity in locating trails, in contracting for their construction, and in counteracting the forces of exploiters who looked upon this great mountain domain as their own. At that time the back country trails were limited to the Tioga Road, which had deteriorated to the status of a horse trail; a trail along the southern boundary from Wawona to Crescent and Johnson lakes and Chiquito Pass, thence to Devils Postpile; the old Indian route from Wawona to Tuolumne Meadows via Cathedral Pass; two trails to Hetch Hetchy and Lake Eleanor from Hog Ranch, near the present Mather Ranger Station; and a trail from Tuolumne Meadows to Mount Conness. This dearth of marked routes was corrected quickly. Regular patrol routes for protective purposes were established, and the soldiers located, marked, and supervised the construction of the trails needed in policing the area. The large "T" blazed on the trees along the routes of the cavalrymen remain as evidences of the Army's activities and are still familiar signs in much of the Yosemite back country.

By the time of the return of the Yosemite Grant and the Mariposa Grove of Big Trees to Federal administration in 1906, the Army had worked wonders in providing a system of trails. C. Frank Brockman (1943, p. 96) summarizes the story as follows:

> The original trail system of 1891 had been extended to include a trail up Little Yosemite Valley to Merced Lake, Vogelsang Pass and thence down Rafferty Creek to Tuolumne Meadows, a route that is familiar to all High Sierra hikers of the present day. The Isberg Pass trail to the east boundary of the park had been marked and Fernandez Pass, farther to the south,

had also been rendered accessible by a trail that branched from the original trail along the southern boundary. The present trail from Tuolumne Meadows up the Lyell Fork of the Tuolumne to Donohue Pass also dates from this period. From Tuolumne Meadows a trail also reached out into the remote northern portion of the park to the vicinity of Glen Aulin, thence up Alkali Creek to Cold, Virginia, and Matterhorn canyons. From the latter point this route continued westward to Smedberg Lake, down Rogers Canyon, eventually passing through Pleasant Valley and over Rancheria Mountain to Hetch Hetchy Valley. The Ten Lakes area was accessible by means of a trail originating on the Tioga Road near White Wolf, and from Hetch Hetchy Valley trails radiated to Tiltill Mountain, Miguel Meadow, Lake Eleanor, Vernon Lake, and up Moraine Ridge to a point near what is today known as the "Golden Stairs," overlooking the lower portion of Jack Main Canyon. A route approximating the present Forsythe trail from Little Yosemite around the southern shoulder of Clouds Rest to Tenaya Lake had been established, and from Tenaya Lake the point now known as Glen Aulin could be reached by the McGee Lake trail. The routes taken by these early trails were essentially the same as those of the present day and points mentioned will be familiar to all who enjoy roaming about the Yosemite back country.

When the National Park Service came into existence in 1916, the broad design of the trail system was essentially as it is at present. The more important trails constructed during the last years of Army administration and in the first years of the National Park Service regime include the Tenaya zigzags built in 1911; the Glen Aulin-Pate Valley route, 1917-1925; the Babcock Lake Trail; the Yosemite Creek-Ten Lakes Trail; the Ledge Trail to Glacier Point, 1918; the Harden Lake-Pate Valley Trail, 1919; Pate Valley-Pleasant Valley Trail, 1920; and the Ottoway Lakes-Washburn Lake Trail in 1941.

Gabriel Sovulewski, who for more than thirty years supervised the construction of Yosemite trails, once outlined for me the amazing story of the evolution of the trail system from Indian routes and sheep trails (Sovulewski, 1928, pp. 25-28). Mr. Sovulewski stated, "Most of these improvements were made on my suggestion, and sometimes at my insistence, yet it is necessary to bear in mind that the credit is not all due to me, even though I did work hard. I share the credit with all superintendents under whom I have served. They gave me freedom to do the work which I have enjoyed immensely."

Col. H. C. Benson, one of the superintendents referred to by Mr. Sovulewski, wrote in 1924:

> The successful working out of the trails and the continuation of developing them is due largely to the loyalty and hard work of Mr. Gabriel Sovulewski. Too much credit can not be given to this man for the development of Yosemite National Park. (Brockman, 1943, p. 102.)

THE JOHN MUIR TRAIL

A fitting climax to the High Sierra trails in Yosemite National Park is found in that portion of the trail system which has been designated the John Muir Trail. Beginning at the LeConte Lodge in Yosemite Valley, this route follows the Merced River Trail to Little Yosemite, thence along the ancient Indian route over Cathedral Pass to Tuolumne Meadows, up the Lyell Fork of the Tuolumne to Donohue Pass (where the trail leaves the national park), along the east slope to Island Pass, then back to the headwaters of westward-flowing streams to Devils Postpile and Reds Meadow on the San Joaquin, south to Mono Creek and other tributaries of the South Fork of the San Joaquin, into Kings Canyon National Park at Evolution Valley, over Muir Pass to the headwaters of the Middle Fork of the Kings, over Mather Pass in the South Fork of the Kings, over Pinchot Pass, Glen Pass, and into Sequoia National Park at Foresters Pass, thence south to Mount Whitney. At Whitney Pass the route descends the east slope until it connects with a spur of the El Camino Sierra at Whitney Portal above the town of Lone Pine. Along the route are 148 peaks more than 13,000 feet in height. The Sierra crest, itself, is more than 13,000 feet above the sea for eight and one-half miles adjacent to Mount Whitney. The trail traverses one of the most extensive areas yet remaining practically free from automobile roads.

In Sequoia National Park, the High Sierra Trail from Giant Forest to Mount Whitney enters the John Muir Trail on Wallace Creek, a tributary of the Kern. Thus does the John Muir Trail connect the national parks of the Sierra, traversing in some 260 miles most of the grandest regions of the High Sierra.

The National Park Service, the Forest Service, and the State of California have cooperated in making the John Muir Trail a reality. The phenomenal route had its inception during the 1914 Sierra Club Outing, when it was suggested to officers of the club that the State of California might well appropriate funds with which to develop trails in the High Sierra. Upon the death of John Muir, president of the club, appropriation bills were introduced for the purpose of creating a memorial trail. The first appropriation of $10,000 enabled the state engineer, Wilbur F. McClure, to explore a practical route along the crest of the Sierra from Yosemite to Mount Whitney. McClure made two trips into the Sierra and then conferred with the Sierra Club and officers of the U. S. Forest Service before designating the route. During the next twenty years several state appropriations were forthcoming, and the federal agencies most concerned, the Forest Service and the National Park Service, entered into the program of locating and building the trail. The earlier explorations of Muir, Solomons, LeConte, and numerous state and federal survey parties contributed to the success of the undertaking. The maps of the Geological Survey greatly facilitated the work.

While Stephen T. Mather was still Assistant Secretary of the Interior and before the National Park Service was created, the "Mather Mountain Party of 1916" assembled in Yosemite Valley preparatory to an inspection of the John Muir Trail. This expedition received the support of the Geological Survey. Frank B. Ewing, at that time an employee of the Geological Survey, was chief guide and general manager. As an employee of the National Park

Service, he has remained in Yosemite National Park ever since that early march along the John Muir Trail and has been a principal party to the National Park Service trail developments previously described. The section of the John Muir Trail in Yosemite National Park was born and has matured under Ewing's personal supervision. Mr. Mather's expedition of 1916 helped to crystallize ideas regarding the Muir Trail and established it in the official minds and master plans of the new National Park Service and the U. S. Forest Service. Robert Sterling Yard, a member of the Mather party and later editor for the new bureau, wrote a sparkling account of the expedition (Yard, 1918). The route at that time was the same within Yosemite National Park as it is today, but the physical condition of the trail has improved mightily. The Mather party traveled the John Muir Trail to Evolution Valley, beyond which the trail was described as impassable to horses. From there the party moved westward to the North Fork of the Kings, then south to the Tehipite Valley, Kanawyers on the South Fork, and yet further southward to the Giant Forest. Today the Giant Forest is more accessible from the John Muir Trail via the High Sierra Trail.

In promoting the development of the John Muir Trail and in fostering the use of High Sierra trails, generally, the Sierra Club has ever been preeminent among the advocates of mountaineering. Among its members are many individuals who have contributed to the shaping of National Park Service policies. This club, which was organized about the same time that Yosemite National Park was created, defined its purposes: "To explore, enjoy, and render accessible the mountain regions of the Pacific Coast; to publish authentic information concerning them; to enlist the support and cooperation of the people and the Government in preserving the forests and other natural features of the Sierra Nevada." For nearly half a century the Sierra Club has centered its attention upon the security and well-being of the natural attributes of Yosemite and has worked to make those attributes known and appreciated. The national parks, national forests, and state parks, generally, have benefited greatly by the continuous interest of the club, and the trail and road systems of Yosemite National Park, especially, have received its study.

A NEW EMPHASIS ON THE HIGH COUNTRY

With the completion of an all-year highway into Yosemite Valley and the realignment of portions of the Big Oak Flat and Tioga roads, the accessibility of Yosemite National Park to the motorist reached its peak, and since that time serious thought has been given to modification of the road system. The Commonwealth Club, in a comprehensive report entitled, "Should We Stop Building New Roads into California's High Mountains?" concluded that accessibility had already reached, if it had not passed, a desirable maximum, on the basis of a stand for the preservation of mountain wilderness values made by many sportsmen's organizations and the Sierra Club. The National Park Service gave consideration, in its Yosemite Master Plan, to the abandonment and obliteration of certain roads which were either superseded by highways or which could be relocated to reduce any detrimental effects upon the mountain landscape. Col. C. G. Thomson led in establishing this trend.

Studies were made by the park administration, the concessionaire, and various organizations outside of the park of means by which present-day visitors, who were now arriving by automobile in hurried throngs numbering as many as 30,000 persons on a single holiday week end, might enjoy the park to some degree at least in the manner that the pioneers had enjoyed it. Improvement of the trails, of outlying facilities, education in the means of trail travel, and the development of an all-season program that would help to spread the peak of travel into a plateau, were steps taken and which are being taken in the attempt to halt the tendency of the public to make of Yosemite Valley an urban "resort."

High Sierra camps were developed, as described elsewhere in this book. They were visited by travelers afoot or in the saddle, and "foot-burners" and pack outfits visited the remote regions of the park, where no improvements upon nature are permitted other than those which a man can carry in—and carry back out again when he leaves. The numbers of people who are attracted to the back country have increased mightily, but the congestion of crowds in Yosemite Valley is still great. This fact in itself constitutes a reason for increasing the effort to introduce visitors to the wonders of the wild high country.

David R. Brower, an officer of the Sierra Club and an ardent proponent of rock-climbing as a sport, and an accomplished skier, has reviewed the development of these forms of recreation in Yosemite. He has kindly agreed to my use of the following portion of an enlightening account, most of which has not previously appeared in print:

"To a few people—fortunately, perhaps, a very few—even a trail detracts a little from the feeling of 'roughing it.' Too clearly, the foot of man, or of mule, has trod there before them. Consequently, those who would get especially close to nature have become skilled in woodcraft so as to take care of themselves and have then struck off not only from the highways and roads, but also from the horse trails and footpaths. Muir and Anderson were pioneers in this form of recreation. A few have carried on where they left off. Routes were found through trailless Tenaya Canyon to the high country above; Muir Gorge, in the Grand Canyon of the Tuolumne, presented an obstacle where the waters of that river were confined in a narrow, vertical-walled box canyon, but it has proved not to be an obstacle to good swimmers in periods of low water. Muir discovered Fern Ledge and crossed it along the tremendous face of the Yosemite Falls cliff, until he was under the upper fall itself. Charles Michael, years later, and William Kat, to this day, followed Muir's footsteps and made new ones of their own on other Yosemite byways, such as the Gunsight to the top of Bridalveil Fall, Mount Starr King, the Lower Brother. For the most part these men, and others of similar bent, climbed alone. Michael was almost to regret it when, on an ascent of Piute Point, he fell a few feet, broke his leg, and was just able to drag himself back to the valley — to climb again when the break had knitted.

"These pioneers of the byways were limited, not by lack of enterprise, but by lack of modern equipment and the technique for its use; both of these required assets came to Yosemite in 1933. A year before that a Rock-Climbing Section was formed in the Sierra Club, and its members brought Alpine technique, which they had practiced and improved in local metropolitan rock parks, to Yosemite. Skillfully using rope and piton technique, and developing their balance climbing to a point where they are able to ascend Half Dome without recourse to any artificial aids, much less cableways, members of this and similar sections, men and women alike, have pioneered many new routes on the valley walls, some extremely difficult. The present total of routes to the rim, exclusive of the trails, is forty-five. Spires and pinnacles not accessible by other means were especially challenging. The higher and lower Cathedral Spires were climbed in 1934 by the party of Jules M. Eichorn, Richard M. Leonard, and Bestor Robinson. The routes for this and other climbs are described in the Yosemite Valley section of a comprehensive 'Climber's Guide to the High Sierra' being published serially by the Sierra Club.

"Construed at present as the ultimate in technical rockclimbing was the ascent, September 2, 1946, of the Lost Arrow by the party of Jack Arnold, Robin Hansen, Fritz Lippmann, and Anton Nelson. The party used more than a thousand feet of rope and many pounds of mountaineer's hardware. They first managed to throw a light line over the summit. Two men remained in support at the rim. The other two went down a rope to the notch separating the pinnacle from the valley wall, and with expert technique were able to climb 100 feet of the rock's outer face, nearly 3,000 sheer feet above the valley floor, until they could reach the lower end of the line. With this they pulled rope over the summit. Another 100 feet of climbing on that rope, with help from the men on the rim, brought them to the top on the evening of the third day. On the crowded, rounded summit they drilled small holes for two expansion bolts, anchored ropes to them, and in the moonlight worked across the gap to the rim on the airy, swinging ropes.

"Needless to say, such climbs as this should not be undertaken without the necessary background of experience. Foolhardy attempts by the overoptimistic to take short cuts or cross-country routes into unknown hazards all too often result in arduous and dangerous rescue operations by park rangers. The National Park Service requires, in Yosemite and in other 'mountaineering' parks, that persons desiring to climb off the trail register first at park headquarters, where, as a matter of the visitor's own protection, he can be advised whether he has the adequate equipment or skill for his proposed undertaking, and where he announces his destination so that rangers will know where to look for him in case of trouble.

"If trails or cross-country routes have afforded the summer visitor a fuller knowledge of Yosemite National Park and its hidden wild places, certainly the improvement of access to various park areas in winter has also increased the enjoyment of the superlative scenery for which Yosemite was set aside as a national park in the first place.

"In the first days of winter sports in Yosemite, snowballing, tobogganing, skating, and sliding down small hills on toestrapped skis was enough for the winter visitor. Snow, to Californians at least, was novelty enough in itself. But the surge of interest in skiing as a sport of skill that arrived after World War I, the resulting vast improvement in ski equipment and apparel, and the winter accessibility brought about by use of snow-removal equipment, inevitably stimulated skiers to demand greatly improved facilities for skiing. The National Park Service, required by law to be custodians of outstanding scenic resources for all the people, in all seasons, for present and future enjoyment, very properly 'made haste slowly.' Other areas, administered by agencies whose obligations were less exacting, developed facilities far more rapidly, and the pressure on the National Park Service, in Yosemite and elsewhere, was greatly increased.

"Ski development in Yosemite involved serious scenic, economic, and geographic considerations. The development should not damage the scenic values for which the park was created. It should, nevertheless, be so situated that the skier could enjoy that scenery without going far beyond the areas in which utilities were available; otherwise, the facilities would be used primarily by persons who wanted only to ski and not to enjoy the Yosemite scene. Such persons could be better accommodated elsewhere. The area developed for skiing should not be so close to the valley rim as to be dangerous. From the concessionaire's standpoint, the development should make use of, and not duplicate, hotel facilities already available; otherwise, it would not be worth the financial risk. Where the Park Service is concerned, economically it should be close enough to the valley not to require excessive road maintenance and snow removal and should not be too difficult to administer, for the Park Service, after all, could only spend what Congress appropriated in the annual budget. As for the man who skied in Yosemite for the sake of skiing, his wants were simple. In the aggregate, he wanted high and low cost accommodations built at an elevation where the best snow lay the longest and the slopes were most open; he wanted satisfactory uphill transportation to enable him to spend most of his time and energy sliding down; he wanted cleared runs and marked trails, outlying huts for touring, and excellent ski instruction patterned after the best European ski schools. He wanted ski competition scheduled, and long courses on which to race. He, moreover, wanted all this in a quantity that would take care of four thousand or more skiers on a week end, without overcrowding the facilities or overburdening his purse.

"What could the National Park Service do? The development at Badger Pass was the result. The ski house, upski, rope tows, Constam lift, the runs of various types, the ski school, the cleared roads and parking area, the ranger ski patrol, the marked touring trails, and the touring hut at Ostrander Lake are all part of a development that is compatible with the national park concept. Improvements will inevitably follow. In the development so far, full enjoyment has been provided for the tens of thousands of skiers who, although they like improvements, would still prefer that the administrators of the national parks continue to make haste slowly in any attempt to improve upon the natural scene."

CHAPTER VIII

HOTELS AND THEIR KEEPERS

The early public interest manifested in the scenic beauties of Yosemite prompted a few far-sighted local men of the mountains to prepare for the influx of travelers that they felt was bound to occur. J. M. Hutchings had no more than related his experiences of his first visit in 1855 before Milton and Houston Mann undertook the improvement of the old Mariposa Indian trail leading to the valley. The next year Bunnell developed a trail from the north side of the gorge. The first visitors were from the camps of the Southern Mines, chiefly, but there were a few from San Francisco and interior towns, as well. During those first years of travel the few visitors expected to "rough it"; they were men and women accustomed to the wilds, and comforts were hardly required. Yet those pioneer hotelkeepers who had provided crude shelters found that their establishments were patronized. Hotelkeeping takes a place very near the beginning of the Yosemite story.

The valley was then public domain. Although unsurveyed, it was generally conceded that homesteads within it might be claimed by whosoever persevered in establishing rights. The prospect of great activity in developing Frémont's "Mariposa Estate" caused certain citizens of Mariposa to turn their attention to Yosemite Valley as the source of a much-needed water supply. Bunnell reveals that commercial interests had designs upon the valley as early as 1855. A survey of the valley and the canyon below was made in that year by L. H. Bunnell and George K. Peterson with the idea of making a reservoir.

The first house to be constructed there was built in 1856 by the company interested in this water project.[b] Bunnell states: "It was of white cedar 'puncheons,' plank split out of logs. The builders of it supposed that a claim in the valley would doubly secure the water privileges. We made this building our headquarters, covering the roof with our tents."

The first permanent hotel structure was also started that year. It became known as the "Lower Hotel." During the next decade it and the Upper Hotel found no competitors. At the close of the 'sixties, however, the hotel business of Yosemite Valley flashed rather prominently in the commerce of the state.

A volume might be written on the efforts of honest proprietors to serve the early tourist; on the scheming of less scrupulous claimants to capitalize on their Yosemite holdings; on the humorous reaction of unsuspecting visitors within the early hostelries; and, finally, on the story of later-day developments which now care for the throng that, annually, partakes of Yosemite offerings. The full history of Yosemite hotels is eminently worth the telling, but the present work will be content in pointing to interesting recorded incidents in the story.

THE LOWER HOTEL

Messrs. Walworth and Hite were the first to venture in serving the Yosemite public. Hite was a member of that family whose fortune was made from the golden treasure of a mine at Hite's Cove. Walworth seems to have left no record of his affairs or connections. The partners selected a site opposite Yosemite Falls, very near the area that had been occupied by Captain Boling's camp in 1851, and set up their hotel of planks split from pine logs. The building, started in 1856, was not completed until the next year, and in the meantime a second establishment was started near the present Sentinel Bridge, so the first became, quite naturally, the "Lower Hotel." Cunningham and Beardsley, the same Beardsley who packed Weed's camera in 1859, elected to finish construction of the Lower Hotel, and they employed Mr. and Mrs. John H. Neal to run it for them.

J. C. Holbrook, the first to preach a sermon in Yosemite, writes of his stop with Mrs. Neal in 1859: "I secured a bed, such as it was, for my wife, in a rough board shanty occupied by a family that had arrived a few days before to keep a sort of tavern, the woman being the only one within fifty or sixty miles of the place. For myself, a bed of shavings and a blanket under the branches of some trees formed my resting place."

A London parson in his *To San Francisco and Back*, of the late 'sixties, offers the following description of his visit to this earliest of Yosemite hotels:

> There are in it [the valley] two hotels, as they call themselves, but the accommodation is very rough. When G_____ and I were shown to our bedroom the first night we found that it consisted of a quarter of a shed screened off by split planks, which rose about eight or ten feet from the ground, and enabled us to hear everything that went on in the other "rooms," which were simply stalls in the same shed. Ours had no window, but we could see the stars through the roof. The door, opening out into the forest, was fastened with cow-hinges of skin with the hair on, and a little leather strap which hooked on to a nail. We boasted a rough, gaping floor, but several of the other bedrooms were only strewed with branches of arbor vitae. As a grizzly bear had lately been seen wandering about a few hundred yards from our "hotel," we took the precaution of putting our revolvers under our pillows. I dare say this was needless as the bears have mostly retired to the upper part of the valley, a few miles off, but it gave a finish to our toilet which had the charm of novelty. Next morning, however, seeing the keeper of the ranch with his six-shooter in his hand, and noticing that it was heavily loaded, I asked him why he used so much powder. "Oh," said he, "I've loaded it for bears."
>
> At first G_____ and I were the only visitors at this house, but several were at the other one about half a mile off, and more were soon expected.

Cunningham, A. G. Black, P. Longhurst, and G. F. Leidig all took their turn at operating the crude establishment. It was under the management of Black when Clarence King arrived on his pioneer trip with the Geological Survey of California, and one Longhurst apparently even then anticipated future proprietorship by engaging in guiding its guests about the valley. King describes Longhurst as "a weather-beaten round-the-worlder, whose function in the party was to tell yarns, sing songs, and feed the inner man." His account, in *Mountaineering in the Sierra Nevada*, continues:

> We had chosen, as the head-quarters of the survey, two little cabins under the pine-trees near Black's Hotel. [Black was then owner of the Lower Hotel.] They were central; they offered us a shelter; and from their doors, which opened almost upon the Merced itself, we obtained a most delightful sunrise view of the Yosemite.
>
> Next morning, in spite of early outcries from Longhurst, and a warning solo of his performed with spoon and fry-pan, we lay in our comfortable blankets pretending to enjoy the effect of sunrise light upon the Yosemite cliff and fall, all of us unwilling to own that we were tired out and needed rest. Breakfast had waited an hour or more when we got a little weary of beds and yielded to the temptation of appetite.
>
> A family of Indians, consisting of two huge girls and their parents, sat silently waiting for us to commence, and, after we had begun, watched every mouthful from the moment we got it successfully impaled upon the camp forks, a cloud darkening their faces as it disappeared forever down our throats.
>
> But we quite lost our spectators when Longhurst came upon the boards as a flapjack-frier, a role to which he bent his whole intelligence, and with entire success. Scorning such vulgar accomplishment as turning the cake over in mid-air, he slung it boldly up, turning it three times, ostentatiously greasing the pan with a fine centrifugal movement, and catching the flapjack as it fluttered down, and spanked it upon the hot coals with a touch at once graceful and masterly.
>
> I failed to enjoy these products, feeling as if I were breakfasting in sacrilege upon works of art. Not so our Indian friends, who wrestled affectionately for frequent unfortunate cakes which would dodge Longhurst and fall into the ashes.

In 1869 A. G. Black tore down the Lower Hotel and on its site constructed the rambling building which became known as "Black's."

UPPER HOTEL

Prior to their interest in the Lower Hotel, S. M. Cunningham and Buck Beardsley had essayed to start a store and tent shelter on the later site of the Cedar Cottage. Cunningham, of later Big Tree fame, dropped this venture; so Beardsley united with G. Hite and in the fall of 1857 began the preparation of the timbers which made the frame of the Cedar Cottage. Mechanical sawmills had not yet been brought so far into the wilderness, and the partners whipsawed and hewed every plank, rafter, and joist in the building. It was ready for occupancy in May, 1859.

The proprietors of the Upper Hotel fared none too well in the returns forthcoming from guests. Ownership changed hands a number of times, and business dwindled to a point of absolute suspension. In 1864 it was possible for J. M. Hutchings to purchase the building and the land claim adjoining for a very nominal price. At this time the proposed state park was being widely talked of, and, as a matter of fact, Hutchings stepped into the ownership of the Upper Hotel property but a few months before the Yosemite Valley was removed from the public domain and granted to the state to be "inalienable for all time." Mr. Hutchings was, and is to this day, sharply criticized by some citizens for his presumption in purchasing public lands that had not been officially surveyed. Whatever may have been his legal claim, it must be admitted that his was the moral right to expect compensation for the expenditure of thousands of dollars for physical improvements made upon his Yosemite property.

Hutchings brought his family to the Upper Hotel in 1864 and assumed a proprietorship that awakened lengthy comments from many of his journalistic guests. Being well educated, a great lover of nature, a journalist himself, and blessed with a generous share of sentiment, it can be understood why some of his guests felt that "there are better things which he could do better." Testimonies agree that if he was not a huge success as a resort manager, his rich fund of information and hospitable enthusiasm more than compensated for his defects.

Charles Loring Brace visited Yosemite a few years after Hutchings became a local character there. He stopped at the Hutchings House and later wrote about his experience:

> One of the jokes current in the Valley is to carefully warn the traveler, before coming to this hotel, "not to leave his bed-room door unlocked, as there are thieves about!" On retiring to his room for the night, he discovers to his amazement, that his door is a sheet, and his partition from the adjoining sleeping-chamber also a cotton cloth. The curtain-lectures and bed-room conversations conducted under these circumstances, it may be judged, are discreet. The house, however, is clean, and the table excellent; and Hutchings himself, enough of a character alone to make up for innumerable deficiencies. He is one of the original pioneers of the Valley, and at the same time is a man of considerable literary abilities, and a poet. He has written a very creditable guidebook on the Canyon. No one could have a finer appreciation of the points of beauty, and the most characteristic scenes of the Valley. He is a "Guide" in the highest sense, and loves the wonderful region which he shows yearly to strangers from every quarter of the world. But, unfortunately, he is also hotel-keeper, waiter, and cook — employments requiring a good deal of close, practical attention, as earthly life is arranged. Thus we come down, very hungry, to a delicious breakfast of fresh trout, venison, and great pans of garden strawberries; but, unfortunately, there are no knives and forks. A romantic young lady asks, in an unlucky moment, about the best point of view for the Yosemite Fall. "Madam, there is but one; you must get close to the Upper Fall, just above the mist of the lower, and there you will see a horizontal rainbow beneath your feet, and the most exquisite —"
>
> Here a strong-minded lady, whose politeness is at an end, "But here, Hutchings, we have no knives and forks!" "Oh, beg a thousand pardons, madam!" and he rushes off; but meeting his wife on the way, she gives him coffee for the English party, and he forgets us entirely, and we get up good-naturedly and search out the implements ourselves. Again, from an amiable lady, "Please, Mr. Hutchings, another cup of coffee!" "Certainly, Madam!" When the English lady from Calcutta asks him about some wild flowers, he goes off in a botanical and poetical disquisition, and in his abstraction brings the other lady, with great eagerness, a glass of water. Sometimes sugar is handed you instead of salt for the trout, or cold water is poured into your coffee; but none of the ladies mind, for our landlord is as handsome as he is obliging, and really full of information.

Maria Teresa Longworth, known as Therese Yelverton, Viscountess Avonmore, visited Yosemite in 1870, where she wrote *Zanita: A Tale of the Yosemite*, published in 1872. She made the Hutchings' entourage a part of her melodrama, and Florence, eldest daughter of the Hutchingses, was the heroine, "Zanita." John Muir, of whom in real life the Viscountess was enamored, was the hero, "Kenmuir." A good analysis of Yelverton's relationships, actual and fictional, with the Hutchings family and the other pioneer residents of the valley is contained in Linnie Marsh Wolfe's great book, *Son of the Wilderness*.

Not all of the Hutchings House features were within its walls. J. D. Caton, who availed himself of the Hutchings hospitality in 1870, "walked over to the foot of the Yosemite Falls and lingered by the way to pick a market basket full of enormous strawberries in Hutchings' garden." One of the first acts of the homesteaders was to plant an orchard and cultivate the above-mentioned strawberry patch. The strawberries long ago disappeared, but many of the one hundred and fifty apple trees still thrive and provide fruit for permanent Yosemite residents.

During his regime of ownership, Hutchings added Rock Cottage, Oak Cottage, and River Cottage to his caravansary.ᶜ In 1874 the state legislature appropriated $60,000 to extinguish all private claims in Yosemite Valley, and the Hutchings interests were adjudged to be entitled to $24,000.

Coulter and Murphy then became the proprietors of the old Hutchings group and in 1876 they built the Sentinel Hotel. Their period of management was brief, and the entire property passed to J. K. Barnard in 1877, who for seventeen years maintained it as the Yosemite Falls Hotel.[1] This unit among the pioneer hostelries was torn down in 1938-1940.

---

1. See Fannie Crippen Jones, "The Barnards in Yosemite," MS in Yosemite Museum.

CLARK'S RANCH, NOW WAWONA

Galen Clark accompanied one of the 1855 Yosemite-bound parties that had been inspired by Hutchings, when that pioneer related his experiences in Mariposa. Upon his first trip to the valley over the old Indian trail from Mariposa, he recognized in the meadows on the South Fork of the Merced a most promising place of abode. His health had been impaired in the gold camps; he had, in fact, been told by a physician that he could live but a short time. The lovely vale of the Nuchu Indians offered solace, and in April of 1857 he settled there on the site of the camp occupied by the Mariposa Battalion in 1851. Nowhere in his writings does Clark intimate that he expected to be overtaken by early death at the time of his homesteading. Rather we may believe that it was with foresight and careful plan that he erected his cabin beside the new trail of the sight-seer and prepared to accommodate those saddle-weary pilgrims who mounted horses at Mariposa and made their first stop with him en route to the new mecca.

His first cabin was crude. A rough pine table surrounded by three-legged stools facilitated his homely service. As the number of visitors increased, Clark enlarged his ranch house. When ten years of his pioneer hotel keeping had passed, Charles Loring Brace was among his visitors. Brace writes:

> After fourteen miles—an easy ride—we all reached Clark's Ranch at a late hour, ready for supper and bed.
> This ranch is a long, rambling, low house, built under enormous sugar-pines, where travelers find excellent quarters and rest in their journey to the Valley. Clark himself is evidently a character; one of those men one frequently meets in California—the modern anchorite—a hater of civilization and a lover of the forest—handsome, thoughtful, interesting, and slovenly. In his cabin were some of the choicest modern books and scientific surveys; the walls were lined with beautiful photographs of the Yosemite; he knew more than any of his guests of the fauna, flora, and geology of the State; he conversed well on any subject, and was at once philosopher, savant, chambermaid, cook, and landlord.

From the scores of books written by early Yosemite visitors, one might extract a great compendium of remarks on Clark and his ranch. The proprietor, like the Grizzly Giant, was impressive. He was invariably remembered by his guests. They wrote of his generous hospitality, his simplicity, kindness, honesty, wit, wisdom, and unselfish devotion to the mountains he loved. Had they known, they might have written that he gave too freely of all his mental and physical assets and that as a businessman he was not a success. The season of 1870 found the ownership of his ranch divided with Edwin Moore.

Moore assumed general management, and Clark's became known as "Clark and Moore's." The ladies of Moore's family introduced a new element in the hospitality of the place, and for a few years it assumed an aspect of new ambition. Extensive improvements, however, resulted in foreclosure of mortgages, and the firm of Washburn, Coffman, and Chapman secured ownership in 1875 and changed the name to "Wawona."[d]

A. P. Vivian stopped at Wawona in January, 1878, and wrote:

> Although still called a "ranche," this establishment has long ceased to be mainly concerned with agriculture. Clark himself exists no longer, at any rate in this locality; that individual sold his interests some years ago to Messrs. Washburn, who "run the stage," and are now the "bosses of the route" between this and Merced. The ranche is now a small but comfortable and roomy inn, and during the tourists' season is filled to overflowing.
>
> Besides having constructed the twenty-five miles of capital road hence into the Yosemite Valley, Messrs. Washburn are again showing their enterprise by making a road direct to Merced, the object of which is to save thirty miles over the present Mariposa route.

The Yosemite Park and Curry Company now owns and operates Wawona.[e] It has become one of the largest and most favorably known family resorts in the Sierra Nevada and retains some of the flavor of its earlier years.

BLACK'S HOTEL

A. G. Black was a pioneer of the Coulterville region. In the late 'fifties, he resided at Bull Creek on the Coulterville trail. Visitors who entered the valley from the north during the first years of tourist travel have left a few records of stops made at the "Black's" of that place. The "Black's" of Yosemite Valley did not come into existence until the advent of the 'sixties, when Mrs. Black is reported to have purchased the old Lower Hotel. In 1869 this first structure was torn down, and an elongated shedlike structure built on its site, near the foot of the present Four-Mile Trail to Glacier Point. This was the "Black's" that for nineteen years served a goodly number of Yosemite tourists. In 1888, after the opening of the Stoneman House, there was among the commissioners "a unanimity of feeling that the old shanties and other architectural bric-a-brac, that had long done service for hotels and stables, and the like, should be torn down." Black's Hotel was accordingly removed in the fall of 1888, and the lumber from its sagging walls went into the construction of the "Kenneyville" property, which stood on the present site of the Ahwahnee Hotel.

LEIDIG'S

The family of George F. Leidig arrived in Yosemite Valley in 1866. For a time the old Lower Hotel was in their charge, but, when its owner, A. G. Black, assumed its management personally, the Leidigs secured rights to build for themselves. They selected a site just west of the old establishment and constructed a two-story building to become known as Leidig's. This was in 1869. Charles T. Leidig, the first white boy to be born in the valley, was born in the spring of that year.

Mrs. Leidig's ability as a cook was quickly noted by visitors, and, no doubt, the popularity of her table did much to draw patrons. Many are the printed comments in the contemporary publications of her guests. Here is an example:

> Leidig's is the best place in the line of hotels. Mrs. L_____ attends to
> the cooking in person; the results are that the food is well cooked and in-
> telligently served. There is not the variety to be obtained here as in places
> more accessible to market. After traveling a few months in California, a
> person is liable to think less of variety and more of quality. At this place
> the beds are cleanly and wholesome, although consisting of pulu mattress-
> es placed upon slat bedsteads. This house stands in the shadow of Sentinel
> Rock, and faces the great Yosemite Fall; is surrounded with porches, mak-
> ing a pleasant place to sit and contemplate the magnificence of the com-
> manding scenery. (From Caroline M. Churchill, 1876.)

When A. P. Vivian continued on to Yosemite in January of
1878, he found the Leidig family in the valley and commented as follows on his winter reception:

> Our host was glad enough to see us, for tourists are very scarce com-
> modities at this time of the year, and he determined to celebrate our arrival
> by exploding a dynamite cartridge, that we might at the same time enjoy
> the grand echoes. These were doubtless extraordinary, but I am free to
> confess I would rather have gone away without hearing them than have
> experienced the anxiety of mind, and real risk to body, which preceded the
> pleasure.

Leidig's, with Black's, was torn down after the Stoneman
House provided more fitting accommodations. The little chapel
which had been built near these old hotels in 1879 was moved to its
present site in the Old Village. In 1928 the picturesque old well
platform and crane, which had marked the Leidig site, was destroyed. Only a group of locust trees now indicates where this center of pioneer activity existed.

THE COSMOPOLITAN, 1870-1932

But the wonder—among the buildings of Yosemite—is the
"Cosmopolitan," containing saloon, billiard hall, bathing rooms, and bar-
ber-shop, established and kept by Mr. J. C. Smith. Everything in it was
transported twenty miles on mules; mirrors full-length, pyramids of elabo-

rate glassware, costly service, the finest of cues and tables, reading-room handsomely furnished and supplied with the latest from Eastern cities, and baths with unexceptionable surroundings, attest the nerve and energy of the projector. It is a perfect gem. The end of the wagon-road was twenty miles away when the enterprise began, and yet such skill was used in mule-packing that not an article was broken. I have not seen a finer place of resort, for its size. The arrangements for living are such that one could spend the summer there delightfully, and we found several tourists who remained for weeks.

The foregoing from J. H. Beadle is but one of scores of enthusiastic outbursts from amazed tourists who wrote of their Yosemite experiences. To say that J. C. Smith figured in early Yosemite affairs is hardly expressive. His baths, his drinks, and the various unexpected comforts provided by his Cosmopolitan left lasting impressions that vied with El Capitan when it came to securing space in books written by visitors. The ladies exclaimed over the cleanliness of the bathtubs; a profusion of towels, fine and coarse; delicate toilet soaps, bay rum, Florida water, arnica, court plaster; needles, thread, and buttons; and late copies of the *Alta* and the *Bulletin* for fresh "bustles." The men found joy in "a running accompaniment of 'brandy-cocktails,' 'gin-slings,' 'barber's poles,' 'eye-openers,' 'mint-julep,' 'Samson with the hair on,' 'corpse-revivers,' 'rattlesnakes,' and other potent combinations."

The Cosmopolitan boasted of a certain Grand Register, a foot in thickness, morocco-bound, and mounted with silver. Within it were the autographs and comments of thousands of visitors both great and lowly. The relic is now a part of the Yosemite Museum collection.[2]

Tommy Hall, the pioneer barber of Yosemite, found sumptuous quarters in the Cosmopolitan. The old building continued to house a barber shop until it was destroyed by fire on December 8, 1932.

---

2. See Harwell, C. A., *Yosemite Nature Notes*, 1933, Vol. XII, No. 1.

LA CASA NEVADA, 1870-1897

For fifteen years after the coming of visitors, the wonders of the Merced Canyon above Happy Isles were accessible only to those hardy mountaineers who could scramble through the boulder-strewn gorge without the advantage of a true trail. In 1869-70 one Albert Snow completed a horse trail from Yosemite Valley to the flat between Vernal and Nevada falls, and there opened a mountain chalet, which was to be known as "La Casa Nevada." The popularity of the saddle trip to the two great falls of the Merced was immediate, and the pioneer trail builder, John Conway, extended the trail from Snow's to Little Yosemite Valley the next year. It then was usual for all tourists to ascend the Merced Canyon to La Casa Nevada and Little Yosemite. Some hikers undertook the trip from Little Yosemite to Glacier Point, but another fifteen years were to elapse before Glacier Point was made accessible by a truly good horse trail from Nevada Fall.

Snow's was opened on April 28, 1870. One of the prized possessions of the Yosemite Museum is a register from this hostelry, which dates from the opening to 1875. Upon its foxed pages appear thousands of registrations and numerous comments of more than passing interest. Among these is a very interesting two-page manuscript by John Muir, describing an 1874 trip to Snow's via Glacier Point and the Illilouette. P. A. H. Laurence, once editor of the *Mariposa Gazette*, contributed to its value by inscribing within it an account of his visit to Yosemite Valley in 1855, years before the chalet was built.

A party with N. H. Davis, United States Inspector General, commented upon their destination and added: "This party defers further remarks until some further examinations are made." Under the date of the original entry is a significant second autograph by a member of the General's party: "A preliminary examination develops an abundance of mountain dew."

A great pile of broken containers, which had once held the "mountain dew," is about the only remnant of La Casa Nevada which may be viewed by present-day visitors, for the chalet was destroyed by fire in the early 'nineties.

PEREGOY'S, 1869-1878

Another pioneer hotel is represented in the Yosemite Museum collections by a register.[3] It was known as the Mountain View House and occupied a strategic spot on the old horse trail from Clark's to Yosemite Valley. Its site is known to present-day visitors as Peregoy Meadows, and the remains of the log building now repose quite as they fell many years ago. The hospitality of its keepers, Mr. and Mrs. Charles E. Peregoy, was utilized by those travelers who, coming from Clark's, took lunch there, or by those who departed from the valley via Glacier Point and made it an overnight stopping place.

The Mountain View House register indicates that guests were entertained as early as the fall of 1869. It was not, however, until the spring of 1870 that the little resort made a bid for patronage. Its capacity for overnight accommodation was sixteen; so it is not surprising that a number of writers of the 'seventies were forced to record, in their published Yosemite memoirs, that they arrived late and sat around the kitchen stove all night. In June of 1872, fifty-six tourists were overtaken by a snowstorm in the neighborhood of Peregoy's. It is to be surmised that on that night even the little kitchen did not accommodate the overflow.

The construction of the Wawona road in 1875 revised the route of all Yosemite travel south of the Merced. Peregoy's was left far from the line of travel and no longer functioned in the scheme of resorts. It had guests, however, as late as 1878.

....

3. See Taylor, Mrs. H. J., *Yosemite Nature Notes* (1929).

THE HARRIS CAMP GROUNDS

By 1878, the demand for recognition of private camping parties introduced the idea of public camp grounds in Yosemite. Large numbers of visitors were bringing their own conveyances and camping equipment so as to be independent of the hostelries. The commissioners set aside a part of the old Lamon property in the vicinity of the present Ahwahnee Hotel as the grounds upon which to accommodate the new class of visitors. Mr. A. Harris was granted the right to administer to the wants of the campers. He grew fodder for their animals, offered stable facilities, sold provisions, and rented equipment. The Harris Camp Ground was the forerunner of the present-day housekeeping camps and public auto camps, which accommodate, by far, the greater number of Yosemite visitors.

An exceedingly interesting register, kept for the comments of campers of that day, was recently presented to the Yosemite Museum by the descendants of Harris. For ten years Yosemite campers recorded their ideas of Yosemite, its management, and particularly the kindness of Harris, upon its pages. The following is representative:

Yosemite Valley,
Tuesday, July 20th, 1880

We have tented in the Valley and been contented too.
So would like to add a chapter to this *bible* for review
Of campers who come hither for study or for fun
In this Valley—of God's building the grandest 'neath the sun.
When you come into the Valley—for information go
To the owner of this Record, and directly he will show
You where to go, and how to go, and what to see when there
And will sell you all things needful, at prices that are fair.
Like Moses in the wilderness, he'll furnish food and drink
For all the tribes that come to him—cheaper than you'd think.
His bread is not from Heaven—but San Francisco Bay
And that is next thing to it—so San Franciscans say.
The water that he gives you—running through granite rock
Is the same as that which Moses gave his wonder-stricken flock.

If you ask him where to angle — he'll tell you — on the sly
Down in the Indian Camp — with silver hook and fly.
In a word this Mr. Harris is a proper kind of man,
And as a friend to campers in the Valley — leads the van.

WM. B. LAKE} San Francisco   E.D. LAKE} Sacramento
FRED W. LAKE}   NAT WEBB}

If the reader thinks this poetry — don't judge me by the style,
For 't is the kind that rhymsters make to peddle by the mile.
WBL

It may be said that from the Harris service grew the idea of camp rental, which was first practiced by the commissioners in 1898 and is now a recognized business of the housekeeping camps department of the present operators in the park.

GLACIER POINT MOUNTAIN HOUSE

After the construction of Snow's trail to Little Yosemite in 1871, some good mountaineers made the Glacier Point trip via Little Yosemite and the Illilouette basin. Prior to this time, J. M. Hutchings had been guiding parties of hikers to the famous Point over a most hazardous trail, which he had blazed up the Ledge and through the Chimney. Occasional references to a shack at Glacier Point indicate that Peregoy had made some attempt to locate there about the same time that his Mountain View House of Peregoy Meadows was opened for business. However, the real claim for Glacier Point patronage came from one James McCauley who in 1870-1871 met the expense of building a horse trail from Black's and Leidig's over a four-mile route up the 3,200-foot cliff to the famous vantage point. This new route was at first a toll trail. For sixty years it has been climbed and descended by countless thousands of riders and hikers. It has been known as the Four-Mile Trail for more than half a century, and it was not until 1929 that its grades, surveyed and built by John Conway, were changed by more skilled engineers.

It is likely that McCauley, owner of the Four-Mile Trail, made use of the insufficient little building on Glacier Point while his trail was in the making. Few records regarding the "shack" or his later Mountain House are to be found, but Lady C. F. Gordon-Cumming wrote on the tenth of May, 1878: "The snow on the upper trail [Four-Mile] had been cleared by men who are building a rest-house on the summit." After arriving at Glacier Point, she records: "The cold breeze was so biting that we were thankful to take refuge, with our luncheon-basket, in the newly built wooden house." Later, "On our way down through the snow-cuttings, we had rather an awkward meeting with a long file of mules heavily laden with furniture — or rather, portions of furniture — for the new house."[f]

It is believed that the first firefall from Glacier Point was the work of James McCauley in 1871 or 1872. He sold his trail to the state. His Mountain House was operated on a lease basis from the commissioners. One of his visitors of the early 'eighties was Derrick Dodd, who concocted something of a classic in the way of Glacier Point stories. It is too good to pass into oblivion.

DERRICK DODD'S TOUGH STORY

As a part of the usual programme, we experimented as to the time taken by different objects in reaching the bottom of the cliff. An ordinary stone tossed over remained in sight an incredibly long time, but finally vanished somewhere about the middle distance. A handkerchief with a stone tied in the corner, was visible perhaps a thousand feet deeper; but even an empty box, watched by a field-glass, could not be traced to its concussion with the Valley floor. Finally, the landlord appeared on the scene, carrying an antique hen under his arm. This, in spite of the terrified ejaculations and entreaties of the ladies, he deliberately threw over the cliff's edge. A rooster might have gone thus to his doom in stoic silence, but the sex of this unfortunate bird asserted itself the moment it started on its awful journey into space. With an ear-piercing cackle that gradually grew fainter as it fell, the poor creature shot downward; now beating the air with ineffectual wings, and now frantically clawing at the very wind, that slanted her first this way and then that; thus the hapless fowl shot down, down, until it became a mere fluff of feathers no larger than a quail. Then it dwindled to a wren's size, disappeared, then again dotted the sight a moment as a pin's point, and then—it was gone!

After drawing a long breath all round, the women folks pitched into the hen's owner with redoubled zest. But the genial McCauley shook his head knowingly, and replied:

"Don't be alarmed about that chicken, ladies. She's used to it. She goes over that cliff every day during the season."

And, sure enough, on our road back we met the old hen about half up the trail, calmly picking her way home!

In 1882, the Glacier Point road was built. Traffic to the Mountain House was, of course, doubled by the coming of those who would not walk or ride a horse up steep trails. Glacier Point trails did not fall into disuse, however. On the contrary, attempts were made to make them more attractive. Anderson's Trail from Happy Isles to Vernal Fall was constructed at great loss to its builder in 1882. The present Eleven-Mile Trail from Nevada Fall to Glacier Point was built in 1885. In spite of the variety of routes offered, it was planned as early as 1887 to provide a passenger lift to the famous vantage-point. The plan progressed as far as the making of a preliminary survey. Accommodations at the point remained unchanged until 1917, when the Glacier Point Hotel was built by the Desmond Park Service Company adjacent to the Mountain House. The two structures function as a unit of the Yosemite Park and Curry Company operation.

THE JOHN DEGNAN BAKERY AND STORE

The Degnan concession in the "Old Village" is not and never was a hotel or lodge. However, it has catered to Yosemite tourists since 1884 and is the oldest business in the park. John Degnan, an Irishman, built his first Yosemite cabin on the site of the present Degnan store. Soon thereafter, on the occasion of a spring meeting of the Yosemite Valley Commissioners, of which the governor of the state was a member, Mr. Degnan appeared before the managing body to obtain the privilege of building a suitable home. The board listened to his plea, and the Governor observed, "He seems to be the kind of man we want as an all-year resident — one who will take care of the place when it needs care." Mr. Degnan, in an interview with a National Park Service official in 1941, stated, "After that meeting the Commissioners came over to my cabin, and the Governor then assigned to me the land which I now occupy, extending from the road to the cliff."

Mrs. Degnan, who was a party to all of Mr. Degnan's pioneering in Yosemite Valley, met the tourists' demand for bread. Gradually, her bakery expanded until her ovens could turn out one hundred loaves at a baking. The business and the home grew as did the Degnan family. Mary Ellen Degnan, one of the several children born to Mr. and Mrs. Degnan, now manages the modern store and restaurant which evolved from the pioneer venture.

The record of John Degnan's activities in Yosemite National Park stands as ample testimony to the accuracy of the governor's appraisal, "He seems to be the kind of man we want." He was a respected party to much of the early physical improvement in and about the valley and to the general growth and development of facilities and services.

Mrs. Degnan died Dec. 17, 1940, and Mr. Degnan's death occurred on Feb. 27, 1943.

THE STONEMAN HOUSE

The demand for more pretentious accommodations than those afforded by the pioneer hotels of Yosemite was met in 1887, when the state built a four-story structure that would accommodate about 150 guests. The legislature in 1885 appropriated $40,000 to be expended on this building. Another $5,000 was secured for water supply and furniture. A site near the present Camp Curry garage was selected, and the building contract let to Carle, Croly, and Abernethy. Upon its completion J. J. Cook, who had been managing Black's Hotel, was placed in charge.

The bulky structure was not beautiful architecturally, and the first few years of its existence demonstrated that its design was faulty. In 1896 the Stoneman House burned to the ground.

CAMP CURRY

Mr. and Mrs. D. A. Curry originated an idea in tourist service which rather revolutionized the scheme of hostelry operation in Yosemite and other national parks. The Currys came to Yosemite in 1899. They were teachers who had turned their summer vacations into profitable management of Western camping tours in such localities as Yellowstone National Park. Their first venture in Yosemite involved use of seven tents and employment of one paid woman cook. The services of several college students were secured in return for summer expenses. The site chosen for that first camp is the area occupied by Camp Curry.

Success of the hotel-camp plan was immediately apparent. The first year 292 people registered at the resort. However, success was not attained without striving. The camp was dependent upon freight-wagon service requiring two weeks to make the round trip to Merced. Sometimes even this service failed.

Informal hospitality has always characterized Camp Curry. Popular campfire entertainments have been a feature from the beginning. In one of the first summers in Yosemite, D. A. Curry revived the firefall,[4] which it is presumed originated with James McCauley, of the Mountain House.

The coming of the Yosemite Valley Railroad in 1907 gave a powerful new impetus to the growth of Camp Curry. Automobile travel, of course, provided the climax. In 1915 the camp provided accommodations for one thousand visitors. Today, it maintains nearly 500 tents and 200 bungalow and cabin rooms.

....

4. Beatty, M. E. "History of the Firefall," *Yosemite Nature Notes* (1934), pp. 41-43; and Yosemite Park and Curry Co., 1940, *The Firefall, Explanation and History*, Yosemite National Park, pp. 1-5.

The successful operations of the Curry business induced would-be competition. Camp Yosemite, later known as Camp Lost Arrow, was started in 1901 near the foot of Yosemite Falls. It continued to function until 1915. Camp Ahwahnee, at the foot of the Four-Mile Trail, was established in 1908 and continued for seven years. The Desmond Park Service Company secured a twenty-year concession to operate camps, stores, and transportation service in 1915. This company purchased the assets of the Sentinel Hotel, Camp Lost Arrow, and Camp Ahwahnee. The two camps were discontinued, and a new venture made in the former Yosemite Lodge. The Desmond Company prevailed until 1920, when reorganization took place, and it became the Yosemite National Park Company.

The old Yosemite Lodge, which served thousands of visitors, went up in a blaze of glory in October 1956 when a welder's torch set it ablaze as it was being dismantled—after construction of the new lodge nearby. These new lodge buildings have been designed with a feeling of spaciousness yet they recapture some of the mood of pioneer architecture.

The Curry Camping Company maintained its substantial position through all of the years of varying fortunes of its less substantial contemporaries. In 1925, the Yosemite Park and Curry Company was formed by the consolidation of the Curry Company and the Yosemite National Park Company. The new organization has contracted with the government to perform all services demanded by the public in the park. Some 1,250 people are employed during the summer months, and the investment in tourist facilities totals $5,500,000.

David A. Curry did not live to witness the realization of all his plans. However, prior to his death in 1917, the march of progress had so advanced as to make evident the place of leadership the Curry operation was to maintain.

Even in her declining years Mother Curry devoted personal attention to the business of the pioneer hotel-camp almost continuously to the time of her death, which occurred in Yosemite Valley on October 10, 1948. She and her daughter, Mary Curry Tresidder, had trained a staff of workers to assume details of management. Her son-in-law, Dr. Donald B. Tresidder, presided over the operations of the Yosemite Park and Curry Company from its beginning in 1925 until his untimely death in January 1948. The Company's directors in March 1948 elected Dr. Tresidder's widow, Mary Curry Tresidder, President, and Hilmer Oehlmann, Executive Vice-President. Under the leadership of these two capable officers, the Yosemite Park and Curry Company conducts a program of public service which is appreciated by the visitor and lauded by the National Park Service. In truth, the concessioner extends a hand in partnership with the Government in conducting the Yosemite program.

HIGH SIERRA CAMPS

In 1923, Superintendent Lewis advocated the creation of a service that would enable the hiker to enjoy the wonders of the Yosemite high country and yet be free from the irksome load of blankets and food necessary to the success of a trip away from the established centers of the park. T. E. Farrow, of the Yosemite Park Company, projected tentative plans for a series of "hikers' camps," and in the fall of 1923 I was dispatched on a journey of reconnaissance for the purpose of locating camp sites in the rugged country drained by the headwaters of the Merced and Tuolumne. The sites advocated were Little Yosemite, Merced Lake,* Boothe Lake, the Lyell Fork (Mount Lyell), Tuolumne Meadows,* Glen Aulin, and Tenaya Lake.* In 1924, these sites, with the exception of Lyell Fork and Glen Aulin, were occupied by simple camps, consisting of a

---

* Camps at these spots first were established in the days of the Desmond Park Service Company, 1916-1918.

mess and cook tent, a dormitory tent for women, and a dormitory tent for men. Attendants and cooks were employed for each establishment. With two exceptions, the camps were removed from roads, and equipment and supplies were of necessity packed in on mules. Yet it was possible to offer the facilities of these high mountain resorts at a very low price, and it became apparent that saddle parties, as well as hikers, would take advantage of them. Consequently they have become known as High Sierra Camps.

The Camp beside the White Cascade at Glen Aulin was established in 1927 and has been very popular. In 1938, the Tenaya Lake Camp was moved to a beautiful location in a grove of hemlocks on May Lake, just east of Mount Hoffmann. New trails were built to make this spot more readily accessible from the Snow Creek Trail and from Glen Aulin. The Boothe Lake Camp, after a few years of operation, was abandoned in favor of a new camp near the junction of the Vogelsang, Rafferty Creek, and Lyell Fork trails. In 1940, this camp was rebuilt on the banks of Fletcher Creek. The Tuolumne Meadows Lodge is now the only one of these camps situated on a road. Each camp has a setting of a distinctive mountain character on lake or stream. All the camps represent a joint effort on the part of the National Park Service and the concessionaire to encourage and assist travel beyond the roads, where the visitor may appreciate the wild values of the park which he can hardly observe from the highways.

THE AHWAHNEE HOTEL, 1927 TO DATE

The Yosemite Park and Curry Company opened the Ahwahnee in 1927. Its interior has received quite as much study as has its exterior architectural values.

California Indian patterns have been used throughout the hotel in many ways. In the lobby, six great figures, set in multiple borders, rendered in mosaic, give color and interest to the floor. In the downstairs corridor and the dining room, other borders and simpler Indian motifs are rendered in acid-etched cement. Painted Indian ornaments play a number of different roles in the building.

In the main lounge the great beams have been related to the contents of the room with borders, spots, and panels of Indian motifs in the colors that appear in the rugs and furniture coverings, while the entire mantel end of the room serves as a bond between the ceiling and the floor with a composite of Indian figures built into one great architectural structure. At the top of each of the ten high windows is a panel of stained glass, each one different, the series forming a rhythmical frieze that bands the room. They are all composed of Indian patterns.

The arts of the whole world have been called together to give the Ahwahnee character and color. There are Colonial furniture, pottery, and textiles; furniture, cottons and linen, lights, and a clock from England; cottons from Norway; andirons from Flanders; more iron and furniture and fabrics from France; embroideries from Italy; rugs from Spain; designs from Greece and designs from Turkey; rugs, jars, and tiles, silks and cottons from Persia; more rugs from the Caucasus and tent strips from Turkestan; porcelains and paintings from China; the sturdy Temmoku ware from Japan; fabrics from Guatemala; terra cotta from Mexico, and so back to California, whence comes the basic motif of the whole, the Indian design.

On June 23, 1943, the Ahwahnee Hotel was taken over by the United States Navy and operated as a hospital. It functioned as the Naval Special Hospital until its formal decommissioning on December 15, 1945, and 6,752 patients were treated, the greatest number at one time being 853. A large and varied naval staff was assigned to duty at the Ahwahnee, including officers, nurses, Waves, and enlisted men. Representatives of the American Red Cross, Veterans' Administration, and the United States Employment Service also participated in the hospital program. The Ahwahnee as a hospital became an adequately equipped and functioning rehabilitation center, capable of handling full programs of physical training, occupational therapy, and educational work. The department of occupational therapy, especially, was recognized as outstanding among service hospitals. The program of rehabilitation extended to the out-of-doors, both summer and winter.

CHAPTER IX

EAST-SIDE MINING EXCITEMENT

*F*requently each summer, those who climb to the Sierra crest within the Yosemite National Park come upon the remains of little "cities" near the mountaintops. Because the story of these deserted towns, now within the boundaries of the park is so interwoven with the story of Mono mining affairs in general, this chapter will of necessity take some account of the events of the Mono Basin, immediately east of Yosemite.

The first white men to visit the Mono country were undoubtedly the American trappers, followed shortly afterward by the explorers and immigrants. The first records of mineral finds in this region, however, are those that pertain to Lieutenant Tredwell Moore's Indian-fighting expedition to the Yosemite in June, 1852 (see Chapter IV), which crossed the Sierra at the northern Mono Pass and brought back samples of gold ore. The miners who soon followed and, with a few others, continued to work in the Mono region, were apparently unthought-of by their former associates west of the Sierra.

John B. Trask, in his report on mines and mining in California, made to the legislature of California in 1855, says: "In my report of last year, it was stated that the placer ranges were at that time known to extend nearly to the summit ridge of the mountains; but this year it has been ascertained that they pass beyond the ridge and are now found on the eastern declivity, having nearly the same altitude as those occurring on the opposite side. Within the past season, many of these deposits have been examined, and thus far are found to be equally productive with those of similar ranges to the west, and, with a favorable season ensuing, they will be largely occupied." It is probable that Trask's statements were based on reports of the work done by Lee Vining's party.

At any rate, in 1857 it became known among the miners of the Mother Lode that rich deposits had been found at "Dogtown" and Monoville, and a rush from the Tuolumne mines resulted. The Mono Trail from Big Oak Flat, through Tamarack Flat, Tenaya Lake, Tuolumne Meadows, and Bloody Canyon, following in general an old Indian route, was blazed at this time and came into great use. The Sonora Pass route was used also, and it was over this trail that the discoverer of the famous Bodie district, later to become the center of all Mono mining, made his way.

It is not my purpose, however, to write the history of Mono County, or even to make this a lengthy story of Mono mining camps. Rather would I present a concise account of the origin of the relics found by Sierra enthusiasts, and, incidentally, tell something about the astonishing town of Bodie.

The name Tioga and the beautiful region which its mention suggests are now familiar to thousands who annually drive over the route that bisects Yosemite National Park. The original location of the mineral deposit now known as the Tioga Mine was made in 1860. Consequently, it is here that our present chronicle of Yosemite summit events should begin. In 1874, William Brusky, a sheepherder, came upon a prospect hole, shovel, pick, and an obliterated notice at this place. The notice indicated that the mine had been located as "The Sheepherder" in 1860. It was presumed by Brusky that the original locators were returning to Mariposa or Tuolumne from Mono Diggings, Bodie, or Aurora when they made the find. He flattered the claim by supposing that "the original locators probably perished, as it is not likely that they would abandon so promising a claim;" he relocated it as the "Sheepherder."

In 1878, E. B. Burdick, Samuel Baker, and W. J. Bevan organized the Tioga District. Most of the mines were owned by men of Sonora, although some Eastern capital was interested. The district extended from King's Ranch, at the foot of Bloody Canyon, over the summit of the Sierra and down the Tuolumne River to Lembert's Soda Springs. It was eight miles in extent from north to south. At one time there were 350 locations in the district. Bennettville (now called Tioga) was headquarters for the Great Sierra Consolidated Silver Company, driving a tunnel in an effort to cut, at depth, the Sheepherder Vein.

The company apparently suffered from no lack of funds, and operations were launched on a grand scale. Great quantities of supplies and equipment were packed into the camp at enormous expenditure of labor and money. At first the place was accessible only via the Bloody Canyon trail, and Mexican packers contracted to keep their pack animals active on this spectacular mountain highway. A trail was then built from the busy camp of Lundy, and that new route to Tioga proved most valuable. The *Homer Mining Index* of March 4, 1882, describes the packing of heavy machinery up 4,000 feet of mountainside to Tioga in winter:

> The transportation of 16,000 pounds of machinery across one of the highest and most rugged branches of the Sierra Nevada mountains in midwinter, where no roads exist, over vast fields and huge embankments of yielding snow and in the face of furious wind-storms laden with drifting snow, and the mercury dancing attendance on zero, is a task calculated to appall the sturdiest mountaineer; and yet J. C. Kemp, manager of the Great Sierra Consolidated Silver Company of Tioga, is now engaged in such an undertaking, and with every prospect of perfect success at an early day — so complete has been the arrangement of details and so intelligently directed is every movement. The first ascent, from Mill Creek to the mouth of Lake Canyon, is 990 feet, almost perpendicular. From that point to the south end of Lake Oneida, a distance of about two miles, is a rise of 845 feet, most of it in two hills aggregating half a mile in distance. The machinery will probably be hoisted straight up to the summit of Mount Warren ridge from the southwest shore of Lake Oneida, an almost vertical rise of 2,160 feet. From the summit the descent will be made to Saddlebags Lake, thence down to and along Lee Vining Creek to the gap or pass in the dividing ridge between Lee Vining and Slate creeks, and from that point to Tunnel, a distance of about one mile, is a rise of about

800 feet—most of it in the first quarter of a mile. The machinery consists of an engine, boiler, air-compressor, Ingersoll drills, iron pipe, etc., for use in driving the Great Sierra tunnel. It is being transported on six heavy sleds admirably constructed of hardwood. Another, or rather, a pair of bobsleds, accompanies the expedition, the latter being laden with bedding, provisions, cooking utensils, etc. The heaviest load is 4,500 pounds. Ten or twelve men, two mules, 4,500 feet of one-inch Manila rope, heavy double block and tackle, and all the available trees along the route are employed in "snaking" the machinery up the mountain—the whole being under the immediate supervision of Mr. Kemp, who remains at the front and personally directs every movement. It is expected that all the sleds will be got up into Lake Canyon today, and then the work will be pushed day and night, with two shifts of men. Meantime, the tunnel is being driven day and night, with three shifts of men under Jeff McClelland.[1]

Such difficulties prompted the Great Sierra Silver Company to construct the Tioga Road, that they might bring their machinery in from the west side of the Sierra. The road was completed in 1883 at a cost of $64,000.

In 1884, one of those "financial disasters" which always seem to play a part in mining-camp history overtook the Great Sierra Silver Company, and all work was dropped. Records show that $300,000 was expended at Tioga, and there is no evidence that their ore was ever milled.

Persons who have climbed into that interesting summit region above Gaylor Lakes have no doubt pondered over the origin of the picturesque village of long-deserted rock cabins clustered about a deep mine shaft.[2] This is the Mount Dana Summit Mine, one of the important locations of the Tioga District. Its owners were determined to operate in winter, as well as in summer. In the *Homer Mining Index*, Lundy, of October 30, 1880, we are told that the superintendent of this mine visited Lundy and employed skilled miners

1. This historic machinery is now in Yosemite. Inquire about it at the Yosemite Museum.
2. See *Ghost Mines of Yosemite* by Park Naturalist Douglass Hubbard, the Awani Press, 1957. Encouraging progress has been made in stabilizing several of the historic mining cabins in Yosemite by members of the park naturalist staff and volunteer helpers. They will be preserved as exhibits-in-place.

to spend the winter there. In December of the same year one of them descended to Bodie to obtain money with which to pay those miners. "He got tripped up on Bodie whisky and was drunk for weeks. Some of the miners returned to Lundy from the Summit Mine. The distance is but seven miles, but they were two days making the trip and suffered many hardships." Later F. W. Pike took charge of the Summit Mine, but no record appears to have been handed down of the final demise of the camp.

Another camp of the main range of the Sierra that received much notice and actually produced great wealth was Lundy, situated but a few miles north of Tioga. Prior to 1879, W. J. Lundy was operating a sawmill at the head of Lundy Lake. His product helped to supply Bodie's enormous demand for timber. In the spring of 1879, William D. Wasson took his family to Mill Canyon, near Lundy Lake, and engaged in prospecting. He was followed by C. H. Nye and L. L. Homer, who located rich veins of ore. J. G. McClinton, of Bodie, investigated and was persuaded by what he found to bring capital to the new camp at once. Homer District was organized at Wasson's residence at Emigrant Flat, in Mill Creek Canyon, September 15, 1879. Prior to this time the region was included in the Tioga District, but because the books of the Tioga recorder were kept at an inconvenient point, a new district was formed. L. L. Homer, for whom the district was named, bowed down by "financial troubles," committed suicide in San Francisco a few months later.

It is worthy of mention that in 1882 the Sierra Telegraph Company extended its line from Lundy to Yosemite Valley, where it made connection with Street's line to Sonora.

A trail was built from Tioga over the divide from Leevining Canyon into Lake Canyon, thence down Mill Creek Canyon to Lundy. In 1881 Archie Leonard, renowned as a Yosemite guide and ranger, put on a ten-horse saddle train between Lundy and

Yosemite. The trip was made in a day and a half, and the fare was $8.00 one way.

Reports of the State Mining Bureau indicate that something like $3,000,000 was taken from the May Lundy Mine. The town of Lundy proved to be substantial for many years, and the *Homer Mining Index*, printed there, is the best of all the newspapers that were produced in the ephemeral camps of Mono. Something of the spirit of mining-camp journalism may be gathered from the following note taken from a December, 1880, number of the *Index*:

> The *Index* wears a cadaverous aspect this week. It is the unavoidable result of a concatenation of congruous circumstances. The boss has gone to Bodie on special business. The devil has been taking medicine, so that his work at the case has been spasmodic and jerky. The printing office is open on all sides, and the snow flies in wherever it pleases. In the morning everything is frozen solid. Then we thaw things out, and the whole concern is deluged with drippings. It is hard to set type under such conditions. When the office is dry, it is too cold to work. When it is warm, the printer needs gum boots and oilskins. In fact, it has been a hell of a job to get this paper out.

Like the other camps, Lundy is now defunct. The May Lundy Mine has not operated for some years, and the building of a dam has raised Lundy Lake so that a part of the townsite is submerged.

Another old camp that many Yosemite fishermen and hikers come upon is the aggregation of dwellings about the "Golden Crown." At the very head of Bloody Canyon, within Mono Pass, are to be found sturdily built log cabins in various stages of decay. From the *Homer Mining Index* it has been possible to glean occasional bits of information regarding this old camp. It is stated in an 1880 number of the *Index* that Fuller and Hayt (or Hoyt) discovered large ledges of antimonial silver there in 1879. The *Mammoth City Herald* of September 3, 1879, contains a glowing account of the wealth to be obtained from the "Golden Crown," as the mine was christened, and predicts that thousands of men will be working at the head of

Bloody Canyon within one year. The *Mammoth City Herald* of August 27, 1879, under the heading, "Something Besides Pleasure in Store for Yosemite Tourists," contains an enthusiastic letter regarding these prospects.

When one observes the great number of mining claims staked out throughout the summit region about White Mountain, Mount Dana, Mount Gibbs, and Kuna Peak, it is not surprising to learn that some Yosemite Valley businessmen ventured to engage in the gamble. Albert Snow, proprietor of the famous La Casa Nevada between Vernal and Nevada falls, owned a mine in Parker Canyon; and A. G. Black, of Black's Hotel, owned the Mary Bee Mine on Mount Dana.

Some twenty miles south of the Tioga District, in a high situation quite as spectacular in scenic grandeur as any of the camps of the main range of the Sierra, was Lake District, in which Mammoth and Pine City flourished for a time — a very brief time.

In June of 1877, J. A. Parker, B. N. Lowe, B. S. Martin, and N. D. Smith located mineral deposits on Mineral Hill at an altitude of 11,000 feet. Lake District was organized here that same summer. Activity was not great until 1879, when great riches seemed inevitable, and a rush of miners swelled the population of Mammoth and Pine City. A mill was built for the reduction of ores that were not in sight, and two printing establishments cut each other's throats, the *Mammoth City Herald*, first on the ground, and the *Mammoth City Times*.

For a time hope was high. J. S. French built a toll trail from Fresno to Mammoth City. French's saddle trains met the Yosemite stages at Fresno Flats, and traveled to Basaw (or Beasore) Meadows, Little Jackass Meadows, Sheep Crossing, Cargyle Meadow, Reds Meadow, through Mammoth Pass, and then to Mammoth City, a distance of fifty-four miles. Livestock to supply the Mammoth markets was driven from Fresno Flats over this trail, also.

The first winter after propaganda had inveigled capital to take a chance on Mammoth, all activities persisted through the winter. Like those hardy men who suffered the hardships of winter on Mount Dana, the inhabitants of Mammoth contended with great difficulties.

After the winter of 1879-80, it became apparent that the Mammoth enterprise was unwarranted. The mill, constructed with such optimism, was poorly built. Had it been mechanically perfect, the fate of the camp would have been no better, for the expected ore was not forthcoming. Mammoth was another of those camps which engulfed capital and produced little or nothing. In the winter of 1880-81 the place closed.

Benton, Bodie, and Aurora are quite removed from the area likely to be reached by Sierra travelers, yet to close this account without some mention of their birth, growth, and death would be to omit some of the most important affairs of Mono mining. The first settlement in the region immediately south of Mono was made by George W. Parker, who located the Adobe Meadows in 1860. In 1861 E. C. Kelty sent "Black" Taylor, a partner of the discoverer of Bodie District, to winter some cattle in Hot Springs Valley, where he was killed by Indians. William McBride entered the region in 1853 and engaged in ranching. Float rock was found in October, 1863, by Robinson and Stuart in the foothills of the White Mountains, east of Benton. In February, 1864, these men organized the Montgomery District and succeeded in attracting some attention to their find. The region flourished for a season, but soon declined and became deserted. A few very rich deposits existed, but there seem to have been no continuous veins.

"Cherokee Joe" found lead ore in a long, low granite hill, which rises abruptly out of the valley west of the White Range, and it was here that Benton started in 1865. James Larne built the first house, and soon the camp became quite populous. Like the others, it attracted a printer, and for a time the *Mono Weekly Messenger* flaunted taunts at neighboring camps and exploited the virtues and possibilities of Benton. Like the others, too, the camp failed, and the printer moved, this time to Mammoth, where he founded the short-lived *Mammoth City Herald*.

When, in the late 'seventies, the turbulent town of Bodie was attaining its reputation as a tough place, a newspaper of Truckee, California, quoted the small daughter in a Bodie-bound family as having offered the following prayer: "Good-by, God! I'm going to Bodie." An editor of one of the several Bodie papers rejoined that the little girl had been misquoted. What she really said was, "Good, by God! I'm going to Bodie."

According to accounts printed when excitement at Bodie was high, the discoverer of the Bodie wealth, W. S. Body, came to California on the sloop *Matthew Vassar* in 1848. He had lived in Poughkeepsie, New York, and there left a wife and six children. In November, 1859, Body, Garraty, Doyle, Taylor, and Brodigan crossed Sonora Pass to test the Mono possibilities. On their way back to the west side of the mountains, they dug into placer ground in a gulch on the east side of Silver Hill, one of those now pock-marked hills just above Bodie.

The partners apparently remained on the ground and equipped themselves to work their claims. In March, 1860, Body and "Black" Taylor went to Monoville for supplies, and en route were overtaken by a severe snow-storm. Body became exhausted, and Taylor attempted to carry him but was forced to wrap a blanket around him and leave him. Taylor returned to their cabin, obtained food, and then wandered about all night in a vain search for his companion. It was not until May that Body's body was found, when it was buried on the west side of the black ridge southwest of the present town. Taylor's fate has already been mentioned.

Other miners came into the vicinity, and at a meeting, with E. Green presiding, "Body Mining District" was organized. Subsequent usage changed "Body" to "Bodie." In the summer of 1860, prospectors located lodes a few miles north of Bodie that were destined to put the Bodie find "in the shade" for some years to come. This was the Aurora discovery, upon which the Esmeralda District, organized in 1860, centered. Aurora forged ahead and became a wildly excited camp, but its bloody career was little more than a drunken orgy. The rich ores which had induced extravagance and wild speculation disappeared when shafts had been sunk about one hundred feet, and the "excitement" came to a sudden end.

It is worthy of note that the first board of county supervisors of the county of Mono met in Aurora, June 13, 1861. By 1864 it was discovered that the camp was some miles within the state of Nevada; so Bridgeport was named the county seat. Just before the move was made, a substantial courthouse had been built in Aurora, since prey to the wrecker's hammer. E. A. Sherman, first editor of the *Esmeralda Star* of Aurora, journeyed to the Eastern States prior to 1863-64, and took with him a fifty-pound specimen of rich Aurora ore. This chunk of rock had been sold and resold at mining-camp auctions to swell the Sanitary Fund, the Civil War "Red Cross." Thousands of dollars were added to the fund by this one specimen, just as had been done through repeated sale of the celebrated Austin (Nevada) sack of flour.

Mr. Sherman met Mr. Davis of the Pilgrim Society in Plymouth, Massachusetts, and exchanged the Aurora ore for a piece of Plymouth Rock. This fragment of Plymouth Rock was brought back to Aurora, and when the Mono County courthouse was built there, the Plymouth Rock fragment was placed in the cornerstone. The fifty-pound chunk of Aurora ore still may be seen in the Plymouth Society's venerable museum.

Mark Twain at one time resided in Aurora and engaged in his

humorous exaggerations. His cabin there, which even in 1878, when Wasson wrote his *Bodie and Esmeralda*, had become somewhat mythical, was recently located and moved to Reno, Nevada, where it is now exhibited. At any rate, an Aurora cabin was found which might have been occupied by Mark Twain. One part of the original Mark Twain cabin certainly did not reach Reno, according to the *Mammoth Times* of December 6, 1879. Bob Howland, who had lived with Mark Twain in Aurora, returned to their old domicile in 1879 and took down the flagpole. He had it made into canes, which he distributed among his friends.

The truly important activity in the Esmeralda region prompted the building of the Sonora Pass wagon road. The Mono County supervisors ordered that road bonds on the "Sonora and Mono road" be issued on November 5, 1863. The road was projected in 1864 and opened to travel in 1868.[3]

Bodie, in the meantime, had not given up the ghost, although only a comparatively few miners occupied the camp. From its discovery until 1877 an average of twenty votes were polled each year. In 1878, however, the Bodie Mining Company made a phenomenally rich strike of gold and silver ore, and the entire milling world was startled. Stock jumped from fifty cents to fifty-four dollars a share. The news swept all Western camps like wildfire, and by 1879 Bodie's crowd and reputation were such that the little girl's prayer of "Good-by, God! I'm going to Bodie" was representative of the opinion held by contemporaries.

Even W. S. Body, whose body had moldered in a rocky grave for nearly twenty years, was not undisturbed by the activity. In 1871 J. G. McClinton had discovered the forgotten Body grave while searching for a horse. He made no move to change the burial site, however, until some one of Bodie's several newspapers

....

3. A road of sorts crossed Sonora Pass prior to this construction work. Hittell (1911, p. 218) tells of Grizzly Adams's trip through the pass with a wagon in the spring of 1854.

launched erroneous reports of the whereabouts of Body's remains. In the fall of 1879 McClinton and Joseph Wasson exhumed the skeleton, exhibited it to Bodie's motley populace, and then gave it an elaborate burial, not excluding an eloquent address by Hon. R. D. Ferguson. Now these honored bones occupy a grave that is quite as neglected as the sage-grown niche in which they originally rested, but at least they share a place with the other several hundred dead disposed of in Bodie's forgotten cemetery.

To make Bodie's story short, let it suffice to say that for four years the camp maintained the same high-pressure activity. Men mined, milled, played, fought, and hundreds died. Some fifty companies tunneled into Bodie Bluff and all but turned it inside out. Probably twenty-five millions in bullion were conveyed in Bodie stage coaches to the railroad at Carson City, Nevada. Perhaps an amount almost as great was sunk into the hills by the numerous companies that carried on frenzied activity but produced no wealth. Only the Standard and the Bodie had proved to be immensely profitable, and in 1881 the stock market went to pieces. Bodie's mines, one after another, closed down. In 1887 the Standard and the Bodie consolidated and operated sanely and profitably for some twenty years longer. But the camp's mad days of wild speculation and excessive living were done. Gradually activities ceased, and a few years ago the picturesque blocks of frame buildings were consumed by flames.[4] To meet the opportunities of 1941 some several hundred people occupied Bodie to salvage minerals from her old mine dumps. But there was little progress in rebuilding the town. It is interesting to note, however, that the Bodie Miners' Union Hall of the 'seventies still stands. Within it Mr. and Mrs. D. V. Cain have exhibited the relics of Bodie's boom days.

---

4. Enough remains in the old town to make a visit worthwhile. Bodie is now a California State historical park.

CHAPTER X

THE INTERPRETERS

*T*he superlative qualities of the scenic features and such out-standing biological characteristics as the forests of the Yosemite region compelled the interest of scientists as soon as the area received wide mention in the press. The miners' concern with mineral values directed the attention of mining engineers upon the sections both east and west of Yosemite Valley. As early as 1853 Professor John B. Trask attempted to explain the geology of the Tuolumne-Merced watersheds.

The California State Geological Survey was established in 1860. Josiah Dwight Whitney, of Harvard University, was made State Geologist. He enlisted the services of several young men who were destined to become leaders in American geological and topographical work. William H. Brewer, William Ashburner, Chester Averill, Charles F. Hoffmann, William M. Gabb, James T. Gardiner, and Clarence King were among the members of the Whitney Survey. Over a period of ten years they penetrated the remote and unknown canyons and climbed the peaks of the Sierra Nevada, recording their findings and mapping the wild terrain. They made the first contribution to accurate and detailed knowledge of the region embraced in the present Yosemite National Park.

In 1863, Whitney himself began studies in the Yosemite region.[1] He concluded that the Yosemite Valley resulted from a sinking of a local block of the earth's crust. His assistant, King, recognized evidences of a glacier's having passed through the valley, but Whitney, although he published this fact in his official report, later stoutly denied it. Whitney at first believed the domes to have risen up as great bubbles of fluid granite.

1. See Farquhar, 1926, pp. 15-23.

Galen Clark, while not a trained geologist, was a careful observer and commanded considerable respect from the public. He believed that Yosemite Valley originated through the explosion of close-set domes of molten rock and that water action then cleared the gorge of debris and left it in its present form.

King, although he was the first to observe glacier polish and moraines in the Yosemite Valley, did not attribute any great part of the excavation of the valley to the glacier. He regarded the Yosemite as a simple crack or rent in the crust of the earth.

John Muir, who followed these early students, maintained that ice had accomplished nearly all the Yosemite sculpturing.

H. W. Turner, on the other hand, found no reason to believe that anything other than stream action, influenced by the peculiar rock structure, had had an important role in the origin of the valley, although he recognized that it had been the pathway of a glacier.

Joseph LeConte,[2] W. H. Brewer, M. M. Macomb,[3] George Davidson,[4] I. C. Russell,[5] George F. Becker, Willard D. Johnson, E. C. Andrews, Douglas W. Johnson, F. L. Ransome, J. N. LeConte, A. C. Lawson, Eliot Blackwelder, Ernst Cloos, John P. Buwalda, M.

----

2. Joseph LeConte became a faculty member at the University of California in 1869 and made his first trip to Yosemite in 1870. Of that experience, he wrote, "This trip was almost an era in my life." For the rest of his life, he devoted much time to Sierra studies. He died suddenly in the valley, July 6, 1901. The LeConte Memorial Lodge in Yosemite Valley, built by the Sierra Club in 1903, commemorates his work (see *Sierra Club Bulletin*, 1904, 1905; Farquhar, 1926, pp. 30-32).

3. Lt. Montgomery Meigs Macomb, assisted by J. C. Spiller and F. 0. Maxson, explored the Yosemite region in 1878 and 1879. Their work was a part of the program of the U. S. Geographical Surveys West of the 100th Meridian, Capt. George M. Wheeler in charge. This program received the general direction of the Chief of Engineers, U. S. Army. Macomb's field work yielded the data for a map which was standard in the Yosemite region for many years (see U. S. War Dept., 1879).

4. In 1879, the United States Coast and Geodetic Survey sent a reconnaissance party into the Yosemite high country under the leadership of George Davidson. Mount Conness was occupied on that occasion and again in 1887 and 1890 (see Chapter VII; also Davidson, 1892).

5. The United States Geological Survey was organized in 1879 under the direction of Clarence King. In 1882 and 1883, a thorough study was made of the Yosemite high country west of Mono Lake. Israel C. Russell was in charge of this field work. Willard D. Johnson and Grove Karl Gilbert assisted him. These men confirmed some of the original work done by Muir and Joseph LeConte (See U. S. Geological Survey, 1883-84, pp. 31-32, 303-328; 1886-87, I: 261-394; I. C. Russell, 1897, pp. 37-54; Farquhar, 1926, p. 42).

E. Beatty, and George D. Louderback have all studied the geology of the Yosemite Valley or the Yosemite region and have published the results of their work. The influences of the topography of the Sierra Nevada upon meteorological conditions were studied and reported upon by W. A. Glassford in the early 'nineties.

Prior to 1913, however, no one had made a comprehensive study of the geology of the entire Yosemite region. Ideas regarding the origin of the valley and related features were still hazy. In 1913, at the instance of the Sierra Club, the U. S. Geological Survey sent out a party of scientists to begin a systematic and detailed investigation. These men were François E. Matthes and Frank C. Calkins. The former was to study especially the history of the development of the Yosemite Valley; the latter to study the different types of rocks. In the years that elapsed, Matthes carried his investigations over the entire Yosemite region and into the areas to the north and south. Thus he worked out quite definitely, back to its beginning, the story of the origin of the Yosemite and of the other valleys of the same type in the Sierra Nevada. His conclusions, published by the government, have stood the test of criticism by other members of his profession. The great geologist died on June 21, 1948.

An extensive bibliography of the geology of Yosemite appears in *A Bibliography of National Parks and Monuments West of the Mississippi River*, Vol. I, 1941, pp. 95-106. The list of Matthes' contributions to Yosemite literature is long. Probably the most significant and generally useful item is *Geologic History of the Yosemite Valley*. This is a thorough report on the author's study and also contains a paper by Frank C. Calkins on the granitic rocks of the Yosemite region.[6]

Indians provided the motive for the first penetration of the whites into Yosemite Valley, but the ethnology of the region received scant attention during the first years of contacts with the aborigines. Lafayette H. Bunnell, a member of the "discovery"

6. See also Matthes' *Incomparable Valley*, University of California Press, 1956.

party of 1851, has provided satisfying accounts of the primitive Ah-wah-nee-chees in the valley, and Galen Clark, who was intimately acquainted with members of the original band, recorded their history, customs, and traditions many years after his early contacts with them. In the early 'seventies, Stephen Powers gave to them the attention of a professional ethnologist, and Constance F. Gordon-Cumming studied them in the 'eighties.

In 1898, the Bureau of American Ethnology investigated the Indians of the Tuolumne country, and William H. Holmes published the findings. Samuel A. Barrett first published on the geography and dialects of the Miwok (of which the Yosemite Indians were a part) in 1908. Barrett's work with the Miwok continued for many years, and he is credited with several important papers. Alfred L. Kroeber, a leading authority on California Indians, first published on the Miwok in 1907 and since has published extensively on the Ah-wah-nee-chees and all their neighbors. E. W. Gifford, who has been associated with both Barrett and Kroeber in the ethnological work of the University of California, has made important contributions to the published history and culture of the Miwok. His first paper on his work in the Yosemite region appeared in 1916. C. Hart Merriam devoted careful study to the myths, folk tales, and village sites of the Yosemite Indians early in the 1900's, and his published accounts appeared in 1910 and 1917. Mrs. H. J. Taylor, working in Yosemite Valley, obtained much important data from one of the last members of the Yosemite band, Maria Lebrado, and since 1932 has published several significant items. In 1941, Elizabeth H. Godfrey, of the Yosemite Museum staff, compiled a popular summary of the work done on the Yosemites entitled, "Yosemite Indians Yesterday and Today," *Yosemite Nature Notes*, 1941. The Yosemite Museum collections of objects and documents include valuable local Indian materials, which provide a most interesting and convincing story of the Ah-wah-nee-chees.

In the field of biology, the Yosemite forests attracted the first attention of scientists. Botanists generally agree that in the Big Tree, the sugar pine, the yellow pine (ponderosa and Jeffrey), the red and white firs, and the incense cedar of the Sierra is the finest and most remarkable group of conifers in the world. The Big Tree (*Sequoia gigantea*), of course, is the most phenomenal and claims first place, chronologically, in the scientific literature. In the number of workers concerned with it and in the quantity of their writings, the Big Tree also holds a respected place.

Among the early writers who dealt with the Big Tree groves of the present Yosemite National Park were Hutchings, Whitney, Asa Gray, Isaac N. Bromley, J. Otis Williams, Muir, Bunnell, and Clark. The latter was among the first to study the Sequoia groves of the Yosemite but he did not publish for nearly half a century after he made his first observations. Following the early announcements of the existence of the Tuolumne, Merced, and Mariposa groves, another group of botanists and semiprofessional workers concentrated upon the study of the Big Tree. Walter G. Marshall, Charles Palache, Paul Shoup, Julius Starke, George Dollar, and W. R. Dudley made their contributions at this time, and Muir redoubled his initial efforts. After the turn of the century, botanists and foresters in numbers concentrated upon the Big Tree. Their publications are too numerous to list, but special mention must be made of the work of Willis L. Jepson, George B. Sudworth, Ellsworth Huntington, James C. Shirley, L. F. Cook, and the continued inspired writing of Muir. The sequoia, oldest living thing, is now and always will be a fascinating subject for scientific and philosophic study. The investigations by Dr. Richard J. Hartesveldt of the effects of human impact upon the sequoias of the Mariposa Grove begun in 1954 lead toward better understanding of the ecology of the Big Trees.

Botanic studies other than investigations of the Big Tree were limited in the pioneer days to the work of John Muir. In the early 1900's, Harvey M. and Carlotta C. Hall did important work in the present national park, and their published works continue to be dependable guides for present-day botanists. Enid Michael, long a resident in Yosemite Valley, was untiring in her field studies, and her many published articles about the flora of the park are of importance to all investigators. Carl W. Sharsmith has studied intensively in the high mountain "gardens" of the park. Mary C. Tresidder published a very useful guide to the trees of the park in 1932. Emil F. Ernst has studied the forests and forest enemies in the park for many years. Willis L. Jepson's work constitutes a substantial basis for all botanical studies in Yosemite as it is for other parts of the state, and the investigations of LeRoy Abrams, 1911, have been important to subsequent workers. The studies of George M. Wright, during his residence in the park in the 1920's, resulted in significant papers on life zones in Yosemite and were the groundwork for the later important studies by him and his associates in founding and conducting broad biological surveys in the entire national park system—an undertaking briefly described later in this chapter.

The Yosemite fauna elicited no particular attention from pioneers other than James Capen Adams, who in 1854 captured grizzly bears for exhibit purposes, and John Muir, who applied himself to certain bird and mammal studies quite as enthusiastically as he did to botany and geology. In the opening years of the twentieth century, a few bird students, among them W. Otto Emerson, W. K. Fisher, Virginia Garland, C. A. Keeler, M. S. Ray, and O. Widman, published on their observations in the present park, but not until Joseph Grinnell initiated his publication program in 1911 did Yosemite zoology find reasonable representation in scientific journals. Grinnell and his staff from the Museum of Vertebrate Zoology of the University of California began formal field work in Yosemite in the fall of 1914 and continued through 1920 in making a complete survey of the vertebrate natural history of the region. Grinnell, Tracy I. Storer, Walter P. Taylor, Joseph Dixon, Charles L. Camp, Gordon F. Ferris, Charles D. Holliger, and Donald D. McLean participated in the work. The results of this survey, Grinnell and Storer's *Animal Life in the Yosemite*, published by the University of California Press in 1924, constitutes an exhaustive and most useful reference on the subject. David Starr Jordan considered it the best original work on life histories published in the West. This study, like the geological work by Matthes, was endorsed and facilitated by the Sierra Club.

After the Museum of Vertebrate Zoology paved the way, wildlife studies in the park increased, and Yosemite found better representation in the biological literature. Most of the workers who had participated in Grinnell's survey published extensively. Others who made notable contributions are Charles W. and Enid Michael, Barton W. Evermann, A. B. Howell, Vernon Bailey, J. M. Miller, John A. Comstock, E. O. Essig, and Edwin C. Van Dyke.

After 1920, when the National Park Service instituted a park-naturalist program in Yosemite, the regular and seasonal employees of the Naturalist Department made many contributions to the scientific knowledge of the park. Among the permanent park naturalists who conducted biological investigations are Ansel F. Hall, Carl P. Russell, George M. Wright, C. A. Harwell, C. C. Presnall, A. E. Borell, M. E. Beatty, James Cole, C. Frank Brockman, M. V. Walker, Harry Parker, and Russell Grater. D. D. McLean, who participated in the Grinnell Survey, also made further contributions as a regular employee of the Naturalist Department. Dr. H. C. Bryant, first as a seasonal employee and later as a regular member of the Director's staff, published extensively on his studies in the park and was influential in starting many other workers on investigations of biological nature.

One important development in biological research in Yosemite had an influence on the wildlife program of the entire National Park Service. George M. Wright, ranger and Assistant Park Naturalist, during the late 1920's sensed the dangers of the uncoordinated wildlife policy of the National Park Service and determined that there should be better administrative understanding of the normal biotic complex of Yosemite and all other national parks. In 1929, Wright was placed on a field status in order that he might organize a central unit of wildlife investigators to survey the wildlife problems of the National Park Service and recommend a broad Service-wide policy of wildlife management. Joseph S. Dixon and Ben W. Thompson were employed by Wright to assist him in this undertaking. Their work during the next several years was conducted from headquarters in Berkeley, California, and from Washington, D. C. It demonstrated that a Wildlife Division was an important administrative adjunct in the Director's organization. In 1936, Wright lost his life while in the course of his significant work. Such progress had been made in establishing policy and procedure that the program persisted. It holds a strategic place in the regular administrative set-up of the Director's office and reaches all field areas with its guidance.

The bibliography of scientific work done in Yosemite National Park since World War I is too extensive to be included here. A goodly part of it is contained in *A Bibliography of National Parks and Monuments West of the Mississippi River*. References to research projects published since the appearance of that bibliography appear in the publications of the Yosemite Natural History Association, particularly the monthly journal, *Yosemite Nature Notes*. Especially significant items dealing with wildlife policy and trends in park management are included in the references appended to the present volume. In brief, it may be said that the wildlife problems of Yosemite National Park are now fairly well defined and that administrative and technical practices are so aligned as to assure preservation of the faunal and floral characteristics of the reservation within the concept of "public enjoyment and use" of today and tomorrow. As former National Park Service Director Newton B. Drury has said, "It is national park policy to display wildlife in a natural manner. The normal habits of animals are interfered with as little as possible, and artificial management is refrained from except for protective purposes and then only as a last resort. The pauperizing or domestication of the native animals is avoided, as is also the herding or feeding of these animals to provide 'shows.' Under this policy the park is a wildlife refuge but it is neither a circus or a zoo."

The wildlife of Yosemite, like its forests and wildflower displays, its renowned cliffs and waterfalls, its glacial pavements, its meadows and valleys, and its spectacular mountaintops, has enthralled its lay visitors quite as it has galvanized the scientist and technician. When Stephen T. Mather assumed the directorship of the national parks in 1916, he determined at the outset to provide park visitors with the information on the natural and historic features which they wanted. Educational endeavors were made a part of his projected program even before a staff had been organized. Surveys of outdoor educational methods and nature teaching as practiced in several European countries had been made in 1915 by C. M. Goethe, and Mrs. Goethe, whose interest, enthusiasm, and generosity has lasted to today. Dr. Goethe's success had inspired a few Americans to establish similar educational work in the United States. The California Fish and Game Commission in 1918 sent its educational director, Dr. Harold C. Bryant, into the Sierra to reach vacationists with the message of the conservationist. Yosemite National Park and the playground areas about Lake Tahoe witnessed the introduction of "nature guiding" several years prior to the inclusion of the work in the broad field program of the National Park Service.

In 1920, Mr. Mather and some of his friends joined in supporting this nature teaching in Yosemite, and Dr. Bryant and Dr. Loye Holmes Miller were employed to lay the foundation of what has continued to be an important part of the program of the Branch of Natural History.

A personal letter from Dr. Miller, University of California, Los Angeles, provides a firsthand account of his pioneering in interpretive work in Yosemite:

> I think John Muir was the first Yosemite guide (see *A Son of the Wilderness*, by L. M. Wolfe). We smaller folk could only strive to emulate. My first experience in the valley involved a six-week period during the summer of 1917 under private auspices. Professor M. L. Maclellan (geology) and I (biology) held a summer school for public school teachers who were largely from Long Beach, California. The work consisted of lectures and field trips about the valley floor and the trails to the rim and to Merced Lake.
>
> During the summer of 1919 I was doing similar work at Tahoe when Mr. Stephen T. Mather came through on a flying trip. He asked me to confer with him on the subject of Nature Guide work in Yosemite and urged me to come at once to the valley and begin the work there. It was late in the season and I had spent most of my free time for the year. Furthermore, it seemed to me that there should be some preparation made for the work, including a measure of publicity in the park guidebooks. I therefore urged Mr. Mather to wait until 1920 for the inauguration of an official Nature Guide service. He agreed and we parted with a definite plan for 1920.
>
> In the meantime Mr. C. M. Goethe of Sacramento had become interested in the movement and had engaged Dr. H. C. Bryant in a tour of certain summer camps. I also urged the appointment of Dr. Bryant for the Yosemite work in 1920. My University schedule was such that Dr. Bryant was able to report earlier than I. He therefore gave the first official work in the valley. We cooperated in it after my arrival. I knew that I could not devote many summers to the service because of other duties as an officer of the University. Furthermore, it seemed to me that Dr. Bryant was just the man to carry on to a larger field of development. I therefore urged repeatedly that he make a full-time activity of the movement. This end was ultimately realized. Bryant made all the official reports of our work (with my endorsement). Those reports are in the files of the Superintendent's office in the park.

During the month of January, 1921, Dr. Bryant and I gave our services to the cause in an extended lecture tour through the eastern and middle western states. This effort was underwritten personally by Mr. Mather. The purpose and theme in this series was to publicize and stimulate interest in the natural history values of the park and the appreciation of nature through an increased knowledge and understanding.

I returned to Yosemite in the summer of 1921 — again in cooperation with Dr. Bryant. The movement seemed to be well on its feet so I withdrew at the end of that summer. We were appointed as temporary rangers with duties informally defined. Each morning a field trip was conducted by one or the other of us alternately, the alternate holding office hours for questions by visitors. (Questions averaged 45 to the hour). In the afternoon a children's field class was held. In the evening we alternated with talks at Camp Curry and the "Old Village" near Sentinel Bridge. They were busy days but interest was good. Week ends were devoted to overnight trips by one or the other of us.

At the urgent request of Mr. Ansel Hall I initiated the same type of work at Crater Lake Park, Oregon, in 1926 and continued it in 1927. My son, Alden Miller, was associated with me and two students, Miss Leigh Marian Larson and Miss Ruth Randall, acted as volunteers in charge of wildflower display. Reports of this work should be in the Crater Lake files. During the summer we were visited by Mr. Mather, by Dr. John C. Merriam, and by Mr. John D. Rockefeller and family. The interest of these men was immediate and finally bore material fruit in improvement of Crater Lake Park and the whole Nature Guide movement in America. Just as had been the case at Yosemite, we were appointed as rangers. My duties at Crater Lake included nature guiding, directing traffic, comforting crying babies, rounding up stray dogs, and a wild drive down the mountain to Medford Hospital with a writhing appendicitis patient and his distracted wife in the rear seat.

I have not been officially connected with the work since but have sent many graduate students to the Yosemite Field School with what I hope was the right point of view. My own retirement at 70 years leaves me out of the picture except in an advisory capacity. Just last week in conference with my associates here, I urged Park Naturalist activity as one of the public services for which our department should train young men. So you see that my interests are still with the movement. It is a field of infinite horizon.

Sincerely yours,

March 18, 1946.   LOYE MILLER

Dr. H. C. Bryant, the coworker referred to by Dr. Miller, became Assistant Director of the National Park Service in charge of interpretive work for all national parks. To Dr. Miller's statement may be added Bryant's words about interpretive work:

> In the spring of 1921, through a cooperative arrangement with the California Fish and Game Commission, the National Park Service instituted a free nature-guide service in Yosemite. The aim of this service was to furnish useful information regarding trees, wildflowers, birds, and mammals, and their conservation, and to stimulate interest in the scientific interpretation of natural phenomena. The means used to attain this aim were: trips afield; formal lectures, illustrated with lantern slides or motion pictures; ten-minute campfire talks, given alternately at the main resorts of the park; a stated office hour when questions regarding the natural history of the park could be answered; a library of dependable reference works, and a flower show where the commoner wildflowers, properly labeled, were displayed. Occasionally, visiting scientists helped by giving lectures.

About this same time, a Yosemite ranger, Ansel F. Hall, conceived the idea of establishing a Yosemite museum to serve as a public contact center and general headquarters for the interpretive program. Superintendent W. B. Lewis endorsed the plan, and the old Chris Jorgensen artists' studio was made into a temporary museum; Hall was placed in charge as permanent educational officer. The same year found a museum program under way in Yellowstone National Park, where Milton P. Skinner was made park naturalist, and in Mesa Verde National Park, where Superintendent Jesse Nusbaum organized a museum to care for the archeological treasures brought to light among the ruins of prehistoric man's abode. Glacier, Grand Canyon, Mount Rainier, Rocky Mountain, Sequoia, and Zion quickly organized educational programs similar to those established by Yosemite and Yellowstone, and in 1923 Hall, with headquarters in Berkeley, was designated to coordinate and direct the interpretive work in all parks. Working with Dr. Frank R. Oastler, Hall in 1924 organized a comprehensive plan of educational activities and defined the objectives of the naturalist group.

In 1924, C. J. Hamlin was president of the American

Association of Museums. The opportunities opened by national park museums were called to his attention by Hall, and the American Association of Museums immediately investigated the possibilities of launching adequate museum programs in the parks. In response to recommendations made by the Association and the National Park Service, the Laura Spelman Rockefeller Memorial made funds available with which to construct a fireproof museum in Yosemite National Park. This, one of the first permanent national park museums, became the natural center around which revolves the educational program in Yosemite. Even before the Yosemite museum installations had been opened to the public, demonstration of the effectiveness of the institution as headquarters for the educational staff and visiting scientists convinced leaders in the American Association of Museums that further effort should be made to establish a general program of museum work in national parks. Additional funds were obtained from the Laura Spelman Rockefeller Memorial, and new museums were built in Grand Canyon and Yellowstone national parks. Dr. Herman C. Bumpus, who had guided the museum planning and construction in Yosemite, continued as the administrator representing the association and Rockefeller interests, and Herbert Maier was architect and field superintendent on the construction projects. It was Dr. Bumpus who originated the "focal-point museum" idea.

When the museums of Yosemite, Grand Canyon, and Yellowstone had demonstrated their value to visitors and staff alike, they were accepted somewhat as models for future work, and upon the strength of their success, the Service found it possible to obtain regular government appropriations with which to build several additional museums in national parks and monuments. When P.W.A. funds became available, further impetus was given to the museum program, and a Museum Division of the Service was established in 1935, embracing historic areas of the East as well as the scenic national parks. It was my privilege to serve as the first head of this unit. The work of the Museum Division has expanded until there are more than one hundred small national park and monument museums and historic-house museums; more are planned for the future.

In order to stimulate balanced development of interpretive programs, Ray Lyman Wilbur, Secretary of the Interior, appointed a committee of educators under the chairmanship of Dr. John C. Merriam to study the broad educational possibilities in national parks (see Wilbur, 1929). In 1929, this committee recommended that an educational branch, with headquarters in Washington, be established in the Service. It was further recommended that the committee continue to function on a permanent basis as an advisory body, "whose duty it shall be to advise the Director of National Parks on matters pertinent to educational policy and developments."

Dr. Bryant, who since 1920 had served as a summer employee on the Yosemite educational staff and who had been a member of the Committee on Study of Educational Problems in National Parks, was made head of the new branch on July 1, 1930. Antedating the establishment of the branch by one year was the previously mentioned wildlife survey instituted in national parks by George M. Wright, who began his career in the National Park Service as a park ranger in Yosemite in 1927.

Thus it is evident that the pioneer interpretive work done in Yosemite projected its influence and its personnel into the wider fields of "nature guiding" and museum programs throughout the National Park Service. It may be shown, also, that the educational work done by the Yosemite staff has been instrumental in advancing the naturalist programs in state parks and elsewhere where out-of-door nature teaching is offered to the public. Some three hundred public areas and agencies in the United States provide naturalist services modeled on the Yosemite plan. Only ten per cent of these are in the National Park System.

One of the far-reaching influences of the Yosemite naturalist department is the Yosemite School of Field Natural History, a summer school for the training of naturalists,[7] where emphasis is placed on the study of living things in their natural environment. The School was founded in 1925 by Dr. H. C. Bryant in answer to a demand for better trained naturalists for the Yosemite staff. There was need for a training not furnished by the universities. The California Fish and Game Commission cooperated with the National Park Service in starting this school program. The staff is composed of park naturalists and the regular Yosemite ranger-naturalist force, aided by specialists from universities and other government bureaus. The last week of the field period is spent in making studies at timberline.

As the name implies, emphasis is placed on field work. The work is of university grade, although no university credit is offered. Graduates of this school are filling positions as nature guides in parks and summer camps throughout the country. Many of the naturalist and ranger-naturalist positions in the National Park Service are held by graduates of this field school.

The Park Naturalist position in Yosemite National Park has been held by Ansel F. Hall, 1922-1923; Carl P. Russell, 1923-1929; C. A. Harwell, 1929-1940; C. Frank Brockman, 1941-1946; Donald E. McHenry, 1947-1956; and now Douglass H. Hubbard. These men and their assistants have supervised programs including the Yosemite Museum program, directed the Yosemite School of Field Natural History, and the activities of the Yosemite Natural History Association, including the editing and publishing of *Yosemite Nature Notes*. This last-named organization has existed since 1924 as a society cooperating with the National Park Service in advancing the work of the Yosemite Naturalist Department. It is the successor of the Yosemite Museum Association formed by Ansel F. Hall in 1920.

----

7. Suspended at present.

On April 24, 1925, members of its advisory council and board of trustees defined these purposes:

1. To gather and disseminate information regarding birds, mammals, flowers, trees, Indians, history, geology, trails, scenic features, and other subjects so well exemplified by Nature in Yosemite National Park and elsewhere in the Sierra Nevada.

2. To develop and enlarge the Yosemite Museum (in cooperation with the National Park Service) and to establish subsidiary units, such as the Glacier Point Lookout and branches of similar nature.

3. To contribute in every way possible to the development of the educational activities of the Yosemite Nature Guide Service.

4. To publish (in cooperation with the National Park Service) *Yosemite Nature Notes*, a periodical containing articles of scientific interest concerning the matters referred to in this statement of purposes.

5. To promote scientific investigation along the lines of greatest popular interest and to publish from time to time bulletins or circulars of a non-technical nature.

6. To maintain in Yosemite Valley a library containing works of historical, scientific, and popular interest.

7. To study the living conditions, past and present, of the remaining Indians of the Yosemite region, for the purpose of preserving their arts, customs, and legends.

8. To strictly limit the operations, business, property, and assets of the association to purposes which shall be scientific and educational, in order that the association shall not be organized, constituted, or operated for profit, and so that no part of the net income of the association shall inure to the benefit of any member or other party thereto.

These objectives in almost every particular are also the objectives of the Naturalist Department of Yosemite National Park. In 1937 the Congress authorized park naturalists and other government employees to devote their regular working hours to the program of the Yosemite Natural History Association and similar "cooperating societies" in national parks which might be designated by the Secretary of the Interior. In effect, the Yosemite Natural History Association is an auxiliary of the naturalist department. Since its inception in 1924 it has adhered to its defined purposes, and the support it has given to the interpretive program has furthered research in the park, enriched the collections of the Yosemite Museum, and promoted the dissemination of the Yosemite story.

The function of the interpreters has been, and their purpose must be, to enrich the mountain experience of the Yosemite traveler and thereby demonstrate that a national park is far more than a tourist's way station. Upon today's visitor and his full awareness of national-park values the future of the national-park concept must depend. A public which, in its enjoyment of the parks, comprehends the importance of "the scenery and the natural and historic objects and the wildlife therein," will insist that they remain unimpaired.

CHAPTER XI

GUARDIANS OF THE SCENE

*I*n the body of Indian fighters who first entered Yosemite Valley, there appears to have been but one man who sensed the possibilities of public good to be derived from the amazing place just discovered. A year prior to the entry of the Mariposa Battalion, L. H. Bunnell, in climbing the trail from Ridley's Ferry (Bagby) to Bear Valley, had descried in the eastern mountains an immense cliff which, apparently, loomed, column-like, to the very summit of the range. He looked upon the "awe-inspiring sight with wonder and admiration and turned from it with reluctance to resume the search for coveted gold."

When, on March 25, 1851,[g] Bunnell stood at Inspiration Point with other members of Savage's command and gazed upon the extravagance of natural wonders, he recognized "the immensity of rock" which had, the previous year, astonished him from afar. He writes:

> Haze hung over the valley—light as gossamer—and clouds partially dimmed the higher cliffs and mountains. This obscurity of vision but increased the awe with which I beheld it, and as I looked, a peculiar exalted sensation seemed to fill my whole being, and I found my eyes in tears with emotion.

He withdrew from the trail and stationed himself on a projecting rock, where he might contemplate all that was spread before him. Major Savage, bringing up the rear of the column, brought him out of his soliloquy in time to join the battalion in its descent to the floor of the valley.

The party that night discussed the business of naming the valley as they sat about their first campfire, near the foot of Bridalveil Fall.

Bunnell comments:

> It may appear sentimental, but the coarse jokes of the careless, and the indifference of the practical, sensibly jarred my more devout feelings, while this subject was a matter of general conversation; as if a sacred subject had been ruthlessly profaned, or the visible power of Deity disregarded.

Bunnell's later discussions with residents of the Mariposa hills and his very tangible evidence in the form of personal funds expended on the Coulterville trail to Yosemite, indicate that he was the first to strive for public recognition of the assets available in the new scenic wonderland. Other men of the region were understandably slow to develop aesthetic appreciation for that which only thrilled and produced no gold.

By 1855 rumor and conjecture regarding the mysteries of the valley had created sufficient interest among the old residents and the many newcomers in the mining camps to prompt fascination in J. M. Hutchings and his story when he returned to Mariposa after his first "scenic banqueting" under Yosemite walls. With the publication of the Hutchings articles and the Ayres drawings, curiosity may be said to have become general, and the trek to the valley was started.

The entire mountain region was, of course, public domain, and, though it had not been surveyed, it was generally conceded that preemption claims could be made upon it. Homesteaders were establishing themselves in numerous mountain valleys above the gold region, and such "squatting" was done with the assent of state and federal officers. It is hardly surprising that some local aspirants laid claim to parts of Yosemite Valley. The company that expected to develop a water project in 1855 was apparently the first to attempt to establish rights. Then came the series of would-be hotel owners, whose activities have been described. James C. Lamon was a mountaineer who came to Yosemite in 1859 and aided in the building of the Cedar Cottage. While so engaged, he established himself in the upper end of Yosemite Valley and there developed the first bona fide homestead by settlement. For many years his log cabin was a picturesque landmark in the valley, and today two orchards near Camp Curry serve as reminders of his pioneering.

With the advent of the 'sixties California began to recognize the aesthetic value of some of her mountain features. The acclaim of leaders from the East and the expressed wonder of notables from abroad played a part in the development of a state pride in the beauties of Yosemite, and, gradually, it became apparent that only poor statesmanship would allow private claims to affect an area of such world-wide interest.

On March 28, 1864, Senator John Conness,[1] of California, introduced in the U. S. Senate a bill to grant to the State of California tracts of land embracing the Yosemite Valley and the Mariposa Grove of Big Trees. On May 17, his bill was reported out of committee. On the occasion of the debate which followed, Senator Conness entered into the record of American conservation the first evidences of national consciousness of park values as we conceive of them today. He started the long train of legislative acts which have given the United States the world's greatest and most successful system of national parks. It is a fact, of course, that the Senate action of 1864 did not create a national park but it did give Federal recognition to the importance of natural reservations in our cultural scheme, and charged California with the responsibility of preserving and presenting the natural wonders of the Yosemite.

Senator Conness explained to the Senate that it was the purpose of his bill "to commit them [Yosemite Valley and the Mariposa

1. Mount Conness, one of the outstanding peaks in the Tuolumne Meadows region, was named for Senator John Conness by Clarence King, later first director of the United States Geological Survey, but at the time a member of the Whitney Survey. King and James T. Gardiner were the first to climb the peak, making the ascent in 1864. Referring to the mountain, King said that because of its "firm peak with titan strength and brow so square and solid, it seems altogether natural we should have named it for California's statesman, John Conness."

Grove of Big Trees] to the care of the authorities of that State for their constant preservation, that they may be exposed to public view, and that they may be used and preserved for the benefit of mankind ... The plan [of preservation] comes from gentlemen of fortune, of taste, and of refinement ... The bill was prepared by the commissioner of the General Land Office, who also takes a great interest in the preservation both of the Yosemite Valley and the Big Trees Grove."[2]

The bill was passed by the Senate on May 17, referred to the House Committee on Public Lands on June 2, debated and passed by the House on June 29, and signed by President Lincoln on July 1, 1864.[h] These deliberations, which designated the first scenic reservation for free public use, were consummated under the stress of waging war.

In order to eliminate friction and delays in the operation of legislative machinery, proponents of the Yosemite bill secured its passage without recognition of the private claims made by Yosemite settlers. Lamon, clearly a bona fide homesteader; Hutchings, who had a short time before the passage of the act purchased the Upper Hotel property; Black, the owner of Black's Hotel; and Ira Folsom, interested in the Leidig property, pressed their claims and involved the new state park in prolonged litigation.

The State Park Act provided that the Yosemite Grant and the Mariposa Big Trees should be managed by a board of commissioners, of whom the governor of the state was to be one. On September 28, 1864, three months after the grant was made, Governor F. F. Low proclaimed that trespassing upon the tracts involved must desist. His board of Yosemite commissioners was appointed in the same proclamation.

Frederick Law Olmsted, even then an accomplished landscape architect, was made chairman of the board. As Brockman (1946, p.

2. *Congressional Globe*, May 17, 1864, p. 2301.

106) has revealed in his article on Olmsted, the chairman was also the first administrative officer of the Yosemite Grant. Olmsted's statement of 1890 substantiates this fact: "I had the honor to be made chairman of the first Yosemite Commission and in that capacity to take possession of the Valley for the State, to organize and direct the survey of it and to be the executive of various measures taken to guard the elements of its scenery from fires, trespassers and abuse. In the performance of these duties I visited the Valley frequently, established a permanent camp in it and virtually acted as its Superintendent."

Legal acceptance of the gift could not be made until the next session of the state legislature. On April 2, 1866, the necessary provisions for administration were secured. The board of commissioners made the best possible selection of a guardian, the Yosemite pioneer, Galen Clark, and invited the settlers of the valley to vacate their holdings.

J. M. Hutchings, as might be expected, was wrathy. It is probable that James Lamon, after eight years of permanent residence on his land, saw no justice in the act. The other claimants held out for what might be in it. Hutchings and Lamon refused to surrender their property, and a test suit was brought against Hutchings, which was decided in his favor. This was carried to the supreme court of the state and then to the federal Supreme Court. In these last actions the commissioners were sustained. That Hutchings and Lamon were deserving of consideration and remuneration cannot be denied, but millions of Americans are today indebted to the board of commissioners who pursued the case to a settlement favorable to the people. Private titles of the type held by the Yosemite Valley settlers would have been disastrous to all administration in the years that were to come.

On the other hand, Hutchings and Lamon were deserving of certain sympathy. No man had done more than J. M. Hutchings to call attention to the fact that the Yosemite was a wonderland, eminently worthy of the distinction bestowed upon it by the state. For a decade prior to the creation of the state park, he had devoted himself to disseminating knowledge on its "charming realities." Much of this was done through his *California Magazine* and the lithographic reproductions of the Ayres drawings. Some of it was accomplished with his volume *Scenes of Wonder*, which ran through several editions. The many published testimonials of his worth as guide and informant while operating his Hutchings House in Yosemite Valley indicate that his efforts to engender a public love for the place were not spared even after his difficulties arose with the state. And, finally, during the ten-year fight for reimbursement he lectured throughout the country, bringing home to the dwellers in Eastern cities the fact that a phenomenally beautiful California was worthy of their visit. Some of the manuscripts of these Eastern lectures are possessed by the Yosemite Museum. Their text reveals none of the commercialism and selfishness with which Hutchings sometimes has been charged.

The earnest efforts which Hutchings had expended in interesting the public in Yosemite had not failed to create an interest in him as well. The court had refused further consideration of the claims of the settlers, but the state legislature, influence by public feeling and the expressed approval of the Yosemite commissioners, appropriated $60,000 to compensate the four claimants. Hutchings received $24,000; Lamon, $12,000; Black, $13,000; Folsom, $6,000, and the remaining $5,000 was returned to the State Treasury. Because of this prolonged litigation, the commissioners did not secure full control of the grant until 1875.

To what extent such troubles would dissipate the best directed efforts of a board of managers of any business can well be imagined. Further difficulties developed when road privileges were granted. The state legislature failed to sustain the position of the commissioners in the matter of exclusive rights for a road on the north side of the valley, and again a controversy arose which directed heated criticism upon the management of the state park. Public hostility alternated with general indifference. The state failed to provide adequate funds with which to accomplish the important work before the commissioners, and the lack of a well-defined policy handicapped the administration to a point of ruin. In 1880 a new law removed the first board and appointed a new one.

The next decade saw important developments take place in the park, but policies adopted were sure to displease someone or some faction. Criticism still prevailed. Gradually the seethings of the press brought about the development of intelligent public interest in Yosemite affairs. Indifference was replaced by discriminating attention, and Yosemite administration arrived in a new era.

In these pages not enough has been said about John Muir. His contributions to the preservation of Yosemite National Park, to the determination of scientific facts regarding it, and to public understanding of its offerings place him in the front rank of conservationists who have been instrumental in saving representative parts of the American heritage. The role he played as explorer, researcher, interpreter, and defender of the public interests in the Yosemite may well become the subject of another book of Muiriana; however, at this juncture, it is only possible to relate him rather inequitably to the field of Yosemite administrative history.

John Muir arrived in Yosemite for the first time in 1868. Intent upon making deliberate studies of all that fascinated him, he determined to remain a resident of the Yosemite region. In order to do so, he attached himself to a sheep ranch. He gave the first winter to work on the foothill ranch and the next summer to herding in the Yosemite Sierra. With the intimate acquaintance so made with sheep and their ways, he was destined to create a wave of public interest in Yosemite that would eclipse all former attentions and revolutionize the administrative scheme.

For eight years after his first Sierra experience, John Muir rambled over his "Range of Light." He tarried for some time in Yosemite Valley and was employed by J. M. Hutchings, at times, to operate a sawmill, which Muir immortalized merely by inhabiting it.

Some impression of his first employment in Yosemite Valley and his early outlook upon the Yosemite scene may be gained from these memoirs published by Badè.[3]

"I had the good fortune to obtain employment from Mr. Hutchings in building a sawmill to cut lumber for cottages, that he wished to build in the spring, from the fallen pines which had blown down in a violent wind-storm a year or two before my arrival. Thus I secured employment for two years, during all of which time I watched the varying aspect of the glorious Valley, arrayed in its winter robes; the descent from the heights of the booming, out-bounding avalanches like magnificent waterfalls; the coming and going of the noble storms; the varying songs of the falls; the growth of frost crystals on the rocks and leaves and snow; the sunshine sifting through them in rainbow colors; climbing every Sunday to the top of the walls for views of the mountains in glorious array along the summit of the range, etc.

"I boarded with Mr. Hutchings' family, but occupied a cabin that I built for myself near the Hutchings' winter home. This cabin I think, was the handsomest building in the Valley, and the most useful and convenient for a mountaineer. From the Yosemite Creek, near where it first gathers its beaten waters at the foot of the fall, I dug a small ditch and brought a stream into the cabin, entering at one end and flowing out the other with just current enough to allow it to sing and warble in low, sweet tones, delightful at night while I lay in bed. The floor was made of rough slabs, nicely joined and embedded in the ground. In the spring the common pteris ferns

----

3. *The Life and Letters of John Muir*, I: 207-208.

pushed up between the joints of the slabs, two of which, growing slender like climbing ferns on account of the subdued light, I trained on threads up the sides and over my window in front of my writing desk in an ornamental arch. Dainty little tree frogs occasionally climbed the ferns and made fine music in the night, and common frogs came in with the stream and helped to sing with the Hylas and the warbling, tinkling water. My bed was suspended from the rafters and lined with libocedrus plumes, altogether forming a delightful home in the glorious Valley at a cost of only three or four dollars, and I was loath to leave it."

When he was not running Hutchings' mill, he was making lonely trips of discovery or guiding visitors above the valley walls. Perhaps Muir knew of the use he would make of the natural history data he was gathering, but few of his associates sensed the fact that he would soon make the nation quicken with new views of Yosemite values.

He first made his influence felt in the early 'seventies, when he began publishing on Yosemite in journals and periodicals. His material awakened responses everywhere. On February 5, 1876, he published an article in the *Sacramento Record Union* which was one of the initial steps in his forceful appeal to America to save the Yosemite high country from the devastations of sheep and the incendiary fires of sheepherders.

It is likely that few who today enjoy the Yosemite High Sierra realize that sheep, "hoofed locusts," were responsible for the creation of Yosemite National Park. The people of California, awakened to the danger by the warnings of Muir and others, attempted to secure an enlargement of the state park. Selfish local interests frustrated the plan. In 1889, John Muir allied himself with the *Century Magazine*, and a plan was launched which was designed to arouse a public sentiment that could not be shunted. Muir produced the magic writings, and Robert Underwood Johnson, editor of the *Century*, secured the support of influential men in the East. On October 1, 1890, a law was enacted which set aside an area, larger than the present park, as "reserved forest lands." Within this reserve were the state-controlled Yosemite and Mariposa Grove grants.

The reactions of residents of the regions adjacent to the new national park to this legislation was typical of the period. Citizens of the counties affected could not foresee the coming of unbroken streams of automobile traffic, which eventually would bring millions of dollars to their small marts of trade. The thought of losing some thousands of acres of taxable land caused county seats to seethe with unrest. The local press painted pictures of dejected prospects and near ruin. The following summary of a lengthy wail from a contemporary paper reveals the fears that prevailed:

> Let us summarize the result of our analysis. On the one side, we have 932,600 acres of land taken away from the control and use of the people at large, and of the people of Mariposa, Tuolumne, Mono, and Fresno counties in particular, for the ostensible purpose of preserving timber, mineral deposits, and natural curiosities or wonders within said reservation—for whose benefit the act does not say, but presumably for the benefit of tourists.
>
> On the other side, we find: That the avowed object of preserving forests appears to be only a false pretense to cover up the real object of the scheme, whatever it may be—that to preserve mineral deposits will prevent untold treasures from being employed in industry and commerce, and prevent the employment of thousands for many years to come in the exploration of these mineral deposits—that to preserve natural curiosities and wonders, it is not necessary to fling away nearly a million acres of land, when all that is necessary can be accomplished by attaching to each wonder as much land, as, through natural formation, contributes in any measure towards its maintenance—that, if on the one hand, these claims are respected, it will condemn hundreds of American settlers to poverty, if on the other hand, these claims are brought out, it will entail an expense of many millions on the country, whilst the claimants, themselves, will never receive anything like the amount their properties would be worth, in the course of time, if this part of the country is left to its own development

without Government interference, and all the settlements now existing will
be left to fall into decay and ruin, or will have to be worked by a system of
tenantry, a curse, as contemporary history shows, which ought never be allowed to take root in our country.

   The preservation of the full watershed of the Yosemite Valley is not
only a legitimate, but a desirable object; the same holds good with the
Hetch-Hetchy Valley, or any other grand work of nature. Every alien-
ation of land, beyond this, is of evil.

This local feeling resulted in immediate attempts to change the
park boundaries. The first attempt was frustrated largely through
the efforts of the Sierra Club. This organization came into existence
shortly after Yosemite National Park was created and has always
been one of the most important agencies that have promoted the
safety of Yosemite treasures. Its publication, the *Sierra Club Bulletin*,
which first appeared in 1893, is a rich source of Yosemite history.
For twenty-two years John Muir was the president of the club. His
vim in leaping to the defense of the great natural preserve was no
less than had been his vigor in working for its creation. Muir aided
in the preservation of national monuments as well. In early May,
1903, Theodore Roosevelt, then president, visited Yosemite via
Raymond and the Mariposa Grove. Governor George C. Pardee,
Benjamin Ide Wheeler, president of the University of California,
and John Muir were among those who interpreted the scene for the
President. Conservation matters were discussed by Muir and the
legislation which was to become famous as the Antiquities Act of
1906 was given some definition at this time. It was truly an important occasion.

   Chief among the Sierra Club defenders of Yosemite who have
carried on since the death of Muir is William E. Colby. He served
forty-four years as secretary of the organization, two years as president; as honorary president he is an oft-sought source of council.
He led the club's summer outings for more than three decades.
Throughout this period Colby has unceasingly built the Sierra
Club's prestige in the field of conservation. For some sixteen years

he was an active member of the Yosemite Advisory Board, and has been in close touch with past and current park problems.

The failure of the national government to provide funds with which to extinguish private claims within the park involved the administration in difficulties which are being felt even yet. By 1904 relations between administrative officers and the large number of owners of private holdings had become so strained that legal action was imperative. Boundary revisions were required. Major Hiram M. Chittenden headed the commission appointed to investigate possible boundary changes. Upon the recommendation of this commission large areas on the east and west were lopped off. In 1906 a tract on the southwest was cut off, and since that time small changes have been rather numerous. Private lands still exist within the park and constitute an ever-present source of trouble.

From the first the control of Yosemite National Park has been vested in the Secretary of the Interior. Immediately after the passage of the act of creation, military units were detailed to take charge of all national park lands. The state retained its plan of administration of the original Yosemite Grant, and so came about the dual control which for sixteen years colored the Yosemite administration with petty misunderstandings and hindered progress in the maintenance of the entire region.

Galen Clark's old ranch (Wawona) became headquarters for the Acting Superintendent of the federal preserve. From this eccentric hub, patrols of cavalrymen were sent into the unbounded wilderness area of the new preserve. A trail system and accurate maps did not exist. One of the first undertakings of the early superintendents was to make the rough country accessible by horse trail. The topography was studied, and a good map was prepared. Following the practice established in Yellowstone National Park, patrolling·stations were established, and the United States Army had the safety of Yosemite's fauna and flora fairly within its keeping.

Since pioneer days, sheep and cattlemen had enjoyed unrestricted use of the excellent range which was now forbidden them. Naturally they were reluctant to abandon it. Their trespass was the most formidable threat with which the troopers were confronted, and concerted, ingenious work was necessary to expel the intruders. When the first culprits were taken into custody, it was found that no law provided for their punishment. Congress had failed to provide a penalty for the infraction of park rules. Nothing daunted, the superintendents put the captured herders under arrest and escorted them across the most mountainous region to a far boundary of the park. There they were liberated. The herder's sheep were driven out of the reserve at another distant point. By the time the herder had located his animals, his losses usually were so great as to represent a more severe punishment than could have been meted out by the court had the law applied. Several years of this practice caused neighboring ranchers to keep their animals out of the forbidden territory.

Captain Abram Epperson Wood was the first superintendent. With detachments from the Fourth Cavalry he arrived in the park on May 19, 1891, and continued in charge until his death in 1894. Each year the troopers came in April or May and withdrew in the fall. During the winter two civilian rangers attempted to patrol the area. With such inadequate winter protection, it is small wonder that poachers grew to feel that the wild life of the reserve was their legitimate prey. It was not until 1896, in fact, that a determined effort was made to keep firearms out of the park at any time of the year.

For twenty-three years the Department of the Interior continued to call upon the War Department for assistance in administering Yosemite National Park. Eighteen army officers took their turn at the helm. Some of them assumed leadership after some years of Yosemite experience as subordinate officers. Others were placed in command with no previous service in the park. Lieutenant (later Colonel) Harry C. Benson and Major W. W. Forsyth were perhaps the most distinguished of the superintendents. Benson was certainly more than a superintendent; he was an explorer, map maker, trail builder, fish planter, and nemesis of the sheepmen. Among the subordinate officers and enlisted men a number left their mark by way of accomplishments. N. F. McClure and Milton F. Davis are remembered for their explorations and excellent map making. William F. Breeze and W. R. Smedberg worked with McClure and Benson in stocking the headwaters of the Yosemite rivers with trout. A. Arndt pioneered in exploration of some of the northern sections of the park. Many others in the military organizations are remembered in place names throughout the Yosemite High Sierra.

Yosemite was fortunate in having within its National Park Service personnel one man, Gabriel Sovulewski,[4] who pioneered with these army units and who was acting superintendent of the park in 1908-1909 and again in 1914. For thirty-five years Mr. Sovulewski was actively engaged in caring for Yosemite. An unpublished manuscript on his National Park Service experiences is preserved in the Yosemite Museum. Within it he comments upon the Yosemite work of United States troops.

> National Parks in California, and Yosemite especially, owe much to the late Colonel H. C. Benson. No one who has not participated in those strenuous years of hard riding and incessant fighting of natural and human obstacles can ever realize the need for indomitable spirit and unselfish devotion to a cause that existed during those first years in Yosemite National Park. Sheep and cattle overran the country. They were owned by men who knew every foot of the terrain. We were ordered to eliminate them. There were few or no trails, and maps did not exist. Reliable guides were unobtainable, and we had more than a thousand square miles to cover.

....

4. Gabriel Sovulewski was born in Poland in 1866; he died Nov. 29, 1938. For a synopsis of his work and the activities of others in the military administration, see "Administrative Officers of Yosemite," by C. Frank Brockman, *Yosemite Nature Notes* (1944).

Officers with detachments set out upon patrols that would keep them away from our base of supplies for thirty days at a time. Many times rations were short, and sixteen to twenty hours of action per day, covering sixty miles in the saddle was not unusual. Constant hammering at the offending cattlemen continued for several years, and at last they were convinced that they must vacate the territory set aside for National Park purposes. The would-be poachers and the entire countryside were taught a moral lesson which still has its effect today. Some of the present-day administrative problems are made easier because of the foundation laid in those first years of the park's existence.

The duplication of effort and expense which resulted from the anomaly of state and federal administration within the reserve brought about controversies which finally caused many Californians to conclude that their Yosemite State Grant of 1864 might well be placed in the hands of the federal government, to be managed by the same officers who controlled the surrounding national park. The Sierra Club and many civic organizations took the lead in urging recession. Not a few citizens felt that the proposed move was an affront to state pride. This group proved to be an obstacle but was overcome in 1905, when the state legislature re-ceded to the United States the Yosemite Valley and the Mariposa Big Tree Grove. A formal acceptance by Congress brought the Yosemite State Park to an end on August 1, 1906. Major Benson removed military headquarters from Camp A. E. Wood (Wawona), and Fort Yosemite came into existence on the site of the present Yosemite Lodge.

For seven years the administrative organization set up by the military continued to function. The succeeding superintendents found their responsibilities increased considerably. Other national parks were coming into existence, and a national conscience was beginning to recognize the value of wilderness preserves. In 1910 the American Civic Association had launched a campaign for the creation of a national park bureau. President Taft favored central administration of the parks, and bills were introduced creating such a bureau. Major William T. Littebrant was in command in Yosemite when Dr. Adolph C. Miller, a civilian, became assistant to Secretary Lane and was placed in charge of the national parks. The next year troops did not come to Yosemite. Mark Daniels was made superintendent, and civilian employees undertook the work that had been done by the troopers.

A few civilian rangers had assumed the care of the park each winter when troops were withdrawn. Archie O. Leonard had been the first of these and he remained in the service when the administrative change was made. In 1914 "park rangers" came into existence under authorization of Secretary Lane. They patrolled the park as had the troopers, but, unlike the troopers, they remained in touch with their problems throughout the year.

In 1916 Congress created the National Park Service. Dr. Miller, in the meantime, had been called to other work, and Stephen T. Mather, who had followed Dr. Miller as assistant to the secretary, was made Director of the National Park Service. He was authorized by law to "promote and regulate the federal areas known as the national parks, monuments, and reservations." Conservation of scenery and wild life of the area was declared by Congress to be a fundamental purpose of the new organization. Mr. Mather's first undertaking was to balk exploitation schemes. Unfortunately, Yosemite had already been raided. In 1913 Congressman John E. Raker had introduced a bill granting to San Francisco rights to the Hetch Hetchy as a water reservoir. Secretary Garfield had opened the way to this move in 1908. In spite of much opposition, the Raker Bill was passed by the House and Senate and approved by President Wilson. Since that time the Hetch Hetchy dam has become a reality and provides all the administrative difficulties and troubles that were expected.[5]

Private holdings in Yosemite were rather large even after the

5. Taylor, Mrs. H. J. "Hetch Hetchy Water Flows into San Francisco," *Yosemite Nature Notes* (1934), pp. 89-91; Badè, W. F. "The Hetch Hetchy Situation [Editorial]," *Sierra Club Bulletin*, 9 (1914): 3, 174.

boundary changes of 1905 and 1906 were made. Timber companies possessing tracts of choice forest constituted the greatest menace. Some of these private lands have been bought up, and others have been exchanged.

During 1930 much progress was made in the acquisition of private holdings in the national park. There were 15,570 acres of land involved, which cost approximately $3,300,000. Half of the cost of purchasing these lands was defrayed by John D. Rockefeller, Jr., the remainder coming from the fund provided by Congress for the acquisition of private holdings in national parks.

The following statements regarding timber holdings in and near Yosemite National Park are taken from the Report of the Director of the National Park Service for 1930:

> It is impossible to overestimate the importance of this Yosemite forest acquisition. It brought into perpetual Government ownership the finest remaining stands of sugar-pine timber in the area and reduced the total area of private holdings in that park to 5,034 acres. This total will be materially reduced when two pending deals are consummated. A tract containing 640 acres is now in course of acquisition with funds contributed by George A. Ball, of Muncie, Indiana, as is another of about 380 acres, half the funds for the latter transaction being contributed through the co-operation of Dr. Don Tresidder, president of the Yosemite Park and Curry Company.
>
> Additional timber holdings in the Tuolumne River watershed—fine stands of sugar and yellow pine—remain in private ownership outside the park. One cannot help regretting that they are imperiled, and it is hoped by all friends of these majestic forests that they may yet be saved.
>
> In order that the beauty of the Big Oak Flat Road may be unimpaired, arrangements have been made between the Sugar Pine Lumber Co., the Forest Service, the State, and the Park Service to preserve the roadsides through selective cutting of the larger trees and careful removal of any trees that are taken out. Particularly interesting and valuable stands of timber which should be preserved untouched will be made the subject of exchanges between the Forest Service and the Sugar Pine Lumber Co.

This land acquisition program was finally assured of success in

July, 1937, when legislation authorized the Secretary of the Interior
to acquire the Carl Inn tract, comprising some 7,200 acres of magnificent sugar pine forest bordering the western boundary of the
park. After a year and a half of negotiations with the Yosemite
Sugar Pine Lumber Company, owner of most of the tract, agreement
was reached on a price of $1,495,500 to be paid by the United
States. The purchase was consummated early in 1939. Senator
William Gibbs McAdoo and Representative John S. McGroarty,
both of California, were the ardent supporters who introduced the
bills, S. 1791 and H.R. 5394, in their respective houses.

Policies regarding the toll roads by which tourists could enter
the park constituted another perplexing problem with which the
young National Park Service was confronted. The routes had been
privately constructed and were privately owned and controlled by
turnpike companies. Government funds were not available with
which to purchase them outright. One company was persuaded to
turn the Wawona Road over to the public in exchange for a grant
for the exclusive rights to the route during a certain number of
years. The government assumed responsibility for the maintenance
of the road during this period. The owners of the Coulterville Road
could not be persuaded to agree to such a plan. As a result, that
part of it which is within the park has not been maintained and, because of erosion, has fallen into disuse.

The Tioga Road, first called the Great Sierra Wagon Road, was
built in one summer — 1883, by the Great Sierra Co. for the purpose
of serving the Tioga Mine. The mining venture terminated in 1884
after an expenditure of $300,000 had been made. The road had be-
come impassable during the many years of neglect, but it was still
the property of private owners when the region through which it
passes became a national park. Stephen T. Mather and some of his
friends bought it privately and in 1915 turned it over to the federal

government.[6] The state of California purchased the portions of the route which were outside of the park and extended the road eastward, down Lee-vining Canyon, so giving Yosemite a remarkable high mountain highway, free from toll, which connects Yosemite Valley with the routes of the Mono basin. Tolls were also removed from the Big Oak Flat route. Every effort was made to put all recognized routes in the best of condition consistent with government appropriations. Travel to the park grew apace, and Yosemite had, indeed, entered a new era.

The first scheme of centralized administration of the national park system was promising in theory but proved faulty in practice. More than a few difficulties appeared on the parks horizon. The national preserves were regarded in Washington somewhat as orphans and were not receiving the specialized attention so necessary for their proper administration. The introduction of Mather ideals and methods was required to bring about coordination.

The story is told that one day in 1915 Stephen Mather walked into the office of Secretary Lane and expressed indignation over the way things were run in Sequoia and Yosemite.

"Steve," said Lane, "if you don't like the way those parks are run, you can run them yourself."

"Mr. Secretary, I accept the job," was Mather's rejoinder.

The genial Secretary of the Interior showed him into a little office and said, "There's your desk, Steve; now go to work." With that Lane went out and closed the door, but presently opened it and said, "By the way, Steve, I forgot to ask what your politics are."

With such brief preliminaries did Stephen T. Mather assume directorship of the national parks. He served through the presidential administrations of Wilson, Harding, and Coolidge, but the matter of his politics was never inquired into by any party.

----

6. Present plans call for retention of portions of the old road as historic exhibits even when complete realignment has taken place.

Stephen Mather was born on the Fourth of July, 1867, in San Francisco. His ancestry traces back to Richard Mather, a Massachusetts clergyman of the days of the Pilgrim Fathers. Stephen T. Mather was not a scion of wealth. As a young man, he made his way through college by selling books. He graduated from the University of California in 1887 and for several years was a newspaper reporter. Thereafter, he entered the employ of the Pacific Coast Borax Company and was identified with the trade name, "Twenty Mule Team Borax," that became well known around the world. For ten years he engaged in the production of profits for his employers and then organized his own company. It was in borax that he built up his business success and accumulated the fortune which "he later shared so generously with the nation through his investments in scenic beauty on which the people received the dividends."

For more than twenty-five years Stephen Mather resided in Chicago, Illinois, but his loyalty to his native state, California, never waned. He was the leading spirit in the organization of the California Society of Illinois and, as its secretary, always secured donations of a carload of choice California fruits to be served at the Society's annual banquets. Mather then saw to it that these affairs were well written up by the press and telegraphed throughout the country on the Associated Press wires. In this publicity the spirit and motives of the present Californians, Inc., had their birth.

As might well be expected, Mather was a member of the Sierra Club and participated in many of its summer outings. (See Farquhar, 1925, pp. 52-53). He became acquainted with national park areas on these trips, and it is said that his ideal of a unified administration of the parks resulted from the intimacies so acquired. It was his ambition to weld the parks into a great system and to make them easily accessible to rich and poor alike.

At the time Mather undertook his big task, there were thirteen parks. Some of them were difficult of access and provided few or no facilities for the accommodation of visitors. Government red tape stood in the way of action in the business of park development, but Mather cut the red tape. When government appropriations could not meet the situation, he usually produced "appropriations of his own." It was such generosity on his part which gave the Tioga Road to the government and saved large groves of Big Trees in the Sequoia National Park. In his own office it was necessary for him personally to employ assistants. Because of the lack of government funds, he expended twice his own salary in securing the personnel needed to set his parks machine in operation. The national benefits derived from the early Mather activity in the parks were recognized by Congress, and that body took new cognizance of national park matters. Larger appropriations were made available, and Mather's plans were put into effect.

For fourteen years he gave his initiative and strength, as well as his money. His ideas took material form, and the park system came into being as he had planned. His work was recognized and appreciated. In 1921 George Washington University bestowed upon him the honorary degree of Doctor of Law. His alma mater, the University of California, conferred the same degree in 1924. President W. W. Campbell on that occasion characterized him as follows:

"Stephen Tyng Mather, mountaineer and statesman; lover of Nature and his fellow-men; with generous and farseeing wisdom he has made accessible for a multitude of Americans their great heritage of snow-capped mountains, of glaciers and streams and falls, of stately forests and quiet meadows."

In 1926 he was awarded the gold medal of the National Institute of Social Sciences for his service to the nation in national parks development. The American Scenic and Historical Preservation Society awarded the Pugsley gold medal in recognition of his national and state park work, and he was made an honorary member of the American Society of Landscape Architects.[7]

In the fall of 1928, Mather's health failed. He suffered a stroke of paralysis which forced his retirement from public service in January, 1929. For more than a year he fought to regain his strength but in January, 1930, he was suddenly stricken and died quickly. Indeed, "the world is much the poorer for his passing, as it is much the richer for his having lived."

One of Mather's first acts as Director of the National Park Service was to appoint a strong man to the superintendency of Yosemite National Park. On the staff of the Geological Survey was an engineer of distinction, Washington B. ("Dusty") Lewis. Mather appointed him to the Yosemite task and he became the first park superintendent on March 3, 1916. The Yosemite problems were complicated and trying from the beginning. The park was, even then, attracting more visitors than had been provided for. Public demands kept steadily ahead of facilities that could be made available through the government appropriations. For more than twelve years W. B. Lewis expended his energy and ingenuity in bringing the great park through its formative stages.

Under his superintendency practically all the innovations which today characterize the public service of a national park were instituted in Yosemite. Motor buses replaced horse-drawn stages; tolls were eliminated on all approach roads; the operating companies were reorganized and adequate tourist accommodations were provided at Glacier Point and Yosemite Valley; a modern school was provided for the local children; the housing for park employees was improved; the best of electrical service was made available; the park road and trail system was enlarged greatly and improved upon; the construction of an all-year highway up the canyon of the Merced

7. See Report of the Secretary of the Interior, 1933, pp. 158-159, for account of the Stephen T. Mather Appreciation and the dedication of Mather Memorial Plaques, presented by that organization. See also *Steve Mather of the National Parks* by Robert Shankland, Knopf, 1951.

made the park accessible to a degree hardly dreamed of; provision of all-year park facilities met the demands of winter visitors; a new administrative center was developed; the Yosemite High Sierra Camps were opened; and an information service was devised. The ranger force was so organized as to make for public respect of national park ideals and personnel. The interpretive work, which makes for understanding of park phenomena and appreciation of park policies, was initiated in Yosemite and has taken a place of importance in the organization of the entire national park system.

In short, the present-day Yosemite came into existence under the hands of Lewis and his assistants. How well the demands of the period were met and future requirements provided for is evidenced by the continued healthy growth and present success of the Yosemite administrative scheme.

In the fall of 1927 Lewis was stricken by a heart attack. He later returned to his office, but in September, 1928, it became apparent that he should no longer subject himself to the strain of work at the high altitude of Yosemite Valley. He removed to West Virginia, and there partly regained his strength. Director Mather then sought his services as Assistant Director of the National Parks, and in that capacity he functioned until the summer of 1930. His physical strength, however, failed to keep pace with his ambitious spirit, and after another attack, he died at his home in a Washington suburb on August 28, 1930.

Soon after Lewis accepted his Washington appointment, Director Mather experienced the breakdown which brought about his resignation as Director. There was but one man to be thought of in connection with filling the difficult position. That man was Horace M. Albright, who had been Mather's right-hand man since the National Park Service had existed. A native of Inyo County, California, and a graduate of the University of California, he became an assistant attorney in the Department of the Interior,

Washington, D. C., in order to advance his learning, and there took a keen interest in plans then developing for the establishment of the National Park Service. He was detailed to work in connection with park problems and had already become familiar with them when Stephen T. Mather assumed their directorship. The Secretary of the Interior assigned him to Mather as a legal aid, which position quickly grew in responsibilities as the two men became acquainted. From the first, Albright was the Director's chief reliance, and when the National Park Service was organized in 1916, he was made Assistant Director. In 1917, 1918, and 1919 he aided in the creation of Mount McKinley, Grand Canyon, Acadia,[8] and Zion national parks. At twenty-nine, he was made superintendent of the largest of all parks, Yellowstone, and in addition shouldered the job of Field Director of the Park Service. In that capacity he compiled budgets, presented them to congress, and handled general administrative problems in the West.

Outstanding among his special interests in park problems was his vigorous participation in programs launched to conserve and reestablish the native fauna of national parks. He gained an intimate understanding of the needs of American wildlife and actively engaged in attempts to supply its wants. He allied himself with such organizations as the National Geographic Society, the American Game Protective Association, the American Forestry Association, the American Bison Society, the American Society of Mammalogists, the Boone and Crockett Club, the Save-the-Redwoods League, and the Sierra Club. He became an expressive factor in American conservation and in his own domain, the national parks, practiced what he preached. He recognized the importance of ecological study of the great wilderness areas, with the safety of which he was charged, and pressed into service a special investiga-

---

8. At that time called Lafayette National Park and since re-named when it was extended to include a portion of the mainland.

tor to work on Yellowstone mammal problems. Later he seized upon the opportunity to extend this research to all parks. In keeping with his desire to assemble scientific data for the preservation of fauna and flora, he had an ambition to popularize the natural sciences as exemplified in the varied park wonderlands. He engaged actively in the development of plans for the museum, lecture, and guide service which today distinguishes the national parks as educational centers as well as pleasure grounds.

Upon the resignation of Director Mather in 1929, it was but natural that Albright should succeed him. He entered into the Yosemite administrative scheme by actual residence in the park and study of its problems. From the Yosemite personnel he drew new executives for other parks, field officers for the service at large, and administrative assistants for his Washington Office. He turned to Crater Lake National Park to obtain a superintendent who would succeed Lewis. Colonel C. G. Thomson had distinguished himself as the chief executive of Crater Lake and in 1929 was called to Yosemite.

Some of the developments in Yosemite for which Thomson was largely responsible included the construction and improvements of the Wawona Road and Tunnel, improvement of the Glacier Point Road, commencement of the Big Oak Flat Road and Tioga Road realignment, the installation of improved water systems at the Mariposa Big Trees, Wawona, and Tuolumne Meadows, construction of the new Government Utility Building, and many smaller projects. Such important land acquisition programs as the Wawona Basin project and the Carl Inn sugar pine addition constituted heavy administrative responsibilities imposed upon the superintendent's office during his regime. The establishment of "emergency programs," C.C.C., C.W.A., W.P.A., and P.W.A., greatly expanded the developmental activities in the park after 1933, and the inclusion of the Devils Postpile National Monument and Joshua Tree National

Monument in the Yosemite administrative scheme increased the duties of the superintendent.

In 1937, Colonel Thomson was stricken by a heart ailment and died in the Lewis Memorial Hospital on March 23. In eulogy, Frank A. Kittredge said:

"Colonel Thomson has, through his dynamic personality and energy and the wealth of his experience, been an influence and inspiration not only to the thousands of Park visitors with whom he has had personal contact, but especially to the Park Service itself. His keen sense of the fitness and desire for the harmony of things in the national parks has made itself felt in the design of every road, every structure, and every physical development in the Park. He recognized the importance and practicability of restricting and harmonizing necessary roads and structures into a natural blending of the surroundings. He has set a standard of beauty and symmetry in construction which has been carried beyond the limits of Yosemite into the entire National Park system. The harmony of the necessary man-made developments and the unspoiled beauty of the Yosemite Valley attest to the Colonel's injection of his refinement of thought and forceful personality, into even the everlasting granite itself of the Yosemite he loved so well."

In June, 1937, Lawrence Campbell Merriam, a native Californian, was transferred to the superintendency of Yosemite National Park. He had received a degree in forestry from the University of California in 1921, had become a forest engineer, and had later gone into emergency conservation work in the state parks throughout the United States. Upon the death of Thomson, Secretary of the Interior Harold L. Ickes appointed Merriam Senior Conservationist in the National Park Service and designated him Acting Superintendent of Yosemite.

During his four years as the chief executive of the park he renewed the service's efforts to restore the natural appearance of the valley, and modified the master plan to provide suitable areas for the operators' utilities.

In August, 1941, Merriam became Regional Director of Region Two, National Park Service, with headquarters at Omaha, Nebraska. Frank A. Kittredge succeeded him in Yosemite.

During World War I, Kittredge served as an officer in the Army Corps of Engineers and saw service in France. Afterward, while with the Bureau of Public Roads, he was identified with park work; he made the location survey of the Going-to-the-Sun Highway in Glacier National Park, did the first road engineering in Hawaii National Park, and devoted his attention to national park road matters handled by the Bureau.

In 1927, Kittredge was appointed chief engineer of the National Park Service and continued in that capacity for ten years, when he was made Regional Director, Region Four, a position involving supervision over Park Service programs in Washington, Oregon, California, Idaho, Nevada, and Utah; Glacier National Park in Montana; and the territories of Alaska and Hawaii. In August, 1940, he was made Superintendent of Grand Canyon National Park, from which position he was transferred in 1941 to the chief executive position in Yosemite National Park. In all this varied experience with the scenic masterpieces of the national park system, Frank Kittredge maintained a sincerity of purpose in safeguarding the natural and historic values of the parks.[9]

As was true of Mather and Albright, succeeding directors of the National Park Service have taken personal interest and active part

9. On December 10, 1954, Frank A. Kittredge died at his Palo Alto home. For 25 years he had distinguished himself as an executive in the National Park Service. On the occasion of his retirement from government service on May 31, 1952, Oscar L. Chapman, Secretary of the Interior, stated: "He...met challenging engineering problems with both brilliance and practicability; with unimpeachable integrity; with a driving ability to work long hours far beyond those of the usual hard worker; and with an idealism and an enthusiasm for his work and for his bureau that are an example to others...Mr. Kittredge's value to the Government has not been confined to technical phases of his work. He had studied every phase of National Park Service activity, acquiring knowledge that has served him and the Service well in administrative capacities."

in the management of Yosemite National Park. On July 17, 1933, Arno B. Cammerer, formerly Associate Director, succeeded Albright in the Washington post. During his incumbency, 1933-1940, the national park system increased from 128 areas to 204 units, and in addition to regular appropriations, nearly 200 million dollars was expended by the Service in connection with the programs of the Civilian Conservation Corps, the Public Works Administration, and the Emergency Relief appropriation acts. Under Cammerer's directorship, five C.C.C. camps were established in Yosemite National Park. With the help of C.C.C., C.W.A., and P.W.A., many management and construction projects in the park were advanced far ahead of regular schedule. The Wawona Road tunnel project was completed, and notable progress was made in constructing the Tioga and Big Oak Flat roads on modern standards. Winter use of the park increased mightily, and the Yosemite Park and Curry Company developed the Badger Pass ski center in accordance with Service plans.

Because of failing health, Cammerer resigned as Director in 1940, and Newton B. Drury, a Californian and a member of the Yosemite Advisory Board, was appointed to the position on June 19, 1940. Since 1919, Drury had been a leader in the movement to preserve distinctive areas for park purposes. As executive head of the Save-the-Redwoods League, he had become a nationally recognized authority on park and conservation affairs and was intimately acquainted with the problems of Yosemite National Park through personal study. The normal problems of the park and of the Service, generally, were greatly complicated by the circumstances resulting from World War II, and the years 1942-1945 were probably the most critical in the history of national parks. But in spite of pressure exerted by production interests and those who sought to capitalize on the park's assets under the guise of "war necessity," the natural values of Yosemite were held inviolate. And it is to the everlasting credit of Director Drury and his staff and associates in central offices and the field that during the years of all-out warfare serious inroads were nowhere made upon national park values.

When Dr. Drury resigned from the Directorship at the end of March 1951, representatives from 19 conservation organizations honored him at a special meeting at the Cosmos Club in Washington. One of the discerning appraisals of Drury and his methods of work was uttered by Dr. Waldo G. Leland of the Advisory Board on National Parks:

> Mr. Drury's great service has been the complete dedication of himself to his task. He has expressed his ideals in inspiring words...and he has justified faith by his works. He has identified himself with his staff so that together they have seemed to have one voice. He has been a leader among equals; not their boss. He has inspired the loyalty of the staff to the ideals that they have held in common, but he has never demanded a personal loyalty to himself. He has been eager to obtain the best possible judgment on problems, and his decisions have been reached after conscientious consultation and mature deliberation. He has not dramatized himself or his position...He has not pounded the desk...or broadcast epithets to the front pages.

Drury's successor was Arthur E. Demaray, who had been with the National Park Service since its beginnings and who had served as Associate Director for 18 years. In 1926, Mr. Demaray was for a time Acting Superintendent of Yosemite National Park. At this time he made the preparation for the visit of the Crown Prince and Princess of Sweden and took charge of the royal tour in the park, a responsibility which he met so successfully as to elicit from the King of Sweden the Order of the Knight of Vasa.

Mr. Demaray became thoroughly familiar with every aspect of Park Service work and he ascended from the position of topographic draftsman to the top administrative jobs in Washington. The responsibilities of all Directors had been shouldered, in part, by him, and in recognition of his able service he was awarded the Cornelius

Amory Pugsley silver medal in 1942. Upon his retirement in the fall
of 1951, the Secretary of the Interior said of him:

> His keen judgment, fairmindedness, vision, and unselfish devotion to
> his many tasks influenced countless actions taken by the National Park
> Service. He contributed guidance to each new phase of its work—the de-
> velopment of professional branches, its interpretive programs, its historical
> and archeological activities, its program of state cooperation, and its na-
> tion-wide interest in parks and recreation. Scores of younger employees
> have benefited from his counsel and encouragement. His stability and
> poise in all emergencies and under all pressures contributed greatly to the
> progress of the Service.

In 1947 the writer was sent to Yosemite as superintendent. I
had spent six and a half years in the park as park naturalist during
the Lewis and Thomson regimes and I welcomed the assignment.
My post as Chief Naturalist in Washington was turned over to John
E. Doerr, and in the fall of 1947 I moved to Yosemite.

During my five-year tour of duty the park program returned to
the normalcy of peace-time operation, if one regards the surge of
postwar travel to be a part of normalcy. The tremendous increase in
travel hurried the initial steps in renewal of concessioner facilities
and the expansion of public campgrounds. A "travel study" was organized in order that park planning might be aligned with the more
immediate needs for added physical facilities. Personnel was increased so far as possible within the limits of "insufficient funds."
Probably the most significant contribution made at this time to park
management was the continuous demonstration of the need for better support to be accorded to the protection programs and to the development of facilities needed for the safety of both visitor and the
features that attract the visitor.

In 1950 Yosemite was host to the service-wide National Park
Service Conference. In the fall of that year the flooding Merced
River wreaked damage in and below Yosemite Valley to the extent
of a million dollars. The Yosemite Centennial was observed in 1951,

and new contracts with the park concessioners were negotiated. In the long-time view, the most important accomplishment was the notable acquisition of private lands within the park, a program in which Mr. Bernard F. Manby of the Region Four Office and Director Conrad L. Wirth participated personally.

Associate Director Conrad Wirth had succeeded to the Directorship when Arthur Demaray retired at the end of 1951. He had entered federal service in 1928 as a landscape architect with the National Capital Park and Planning Commission and joined the branch of Lands, National Park Service, in 1933. Upon the inception of the Park, Parkway, and Recreational Area Survey in 1936 he directed that program. After a year abroad with the United States Allied Council he returned again to the Service in 1946 as Assistant Director in charge of land planning functions. The five years of Wirth's administration as Director have been marked by improved public consciousness of the dire needs of Service areas and programs. Mr. Wirth's invention of "Mission 66" provided a magic formula needed to correct the adverse effects of years of neglect. Under the new plan, park appropriations were justified as a "10-year package" with the expectation that facilities needed for the use of some 80 million visitors who were expected to enter National Park Service areas in 1966 will have been provided.

In Yosemite, John C. Preston succeeded Russell as superintendent in November 1952. Preston joined the National Park Service in 1926 as a ranger in Rocky Mountain National Park and rapidly rose to the position of Assistant Superintendent. He served as Superintendent of Lassen Volcanic National Park, Mount Rainier National Park, and Great Smoky Mountains National Park from which area he was transferred to the Yosemite position. Under his direction the steadily increasing numbers of visitors have been accommodated and the park master plan has been refined. In 1955 another devastating flood caused damage as to persuade park planners to give new scrutiny to development plans.

Each year more than a million people benefit by the great
park's offerings, and each year witnesses new demands for expansion of public facilities provided by the concessioners and the
Government. Park travel projections indicate increasing demand
for use of Yosemite both by day and overnight. To meet these demands and at the same time guarantee the continued availability of
Yosemite values for future generations is one of the exacting tasks
shouldered by the National Park Service personnel.

TWO HUNDRED YEARS

More than 120 years have passed since the hardy explorers in
Joseph Walker's party first made their way to some point on the
north rim of Yosemite Valley and beheld a tremendous scene beneath them. It is to be hoped that the Yosemite visitor today will
have his enjoyment of Yosemite National Park somehow enhanced
by the recorded story of the human events during the past century,
particularly by the story of the human effort that made Yosemite accessible to him, but not too accessible.

Yosemite, like other national parks, has its master plan. Upon
it is set down in rather definite form the conception of the park staff
of needs for physical improvements. This prescription is reviewed
by technicians and executives in central offices and made to delimit
the maximum development necessary to meet the requirements of
staff and public. The master plan also contains an analysis of the in-
spirational and recreational experiences which attract the multitude
of visitors to the park. As might be expected this analysis of
Yosemite's offerings points to the fact that one of the notable values
of the reservation is found in its capacity to stimulate pride in and
understanding of the heritage of natural beauty preserved within the
park's boundaries. Another important value is indicated in the capacity of the park to serve as a repository of scientific treasures. In

this last-named role as "museum of the out-of-doors," Yosemite National Park reasonably may be expected to become increasingly important as the less protected areas of the Sierra Nevada are more and more encroached upon by exploiters. The exploiters are not always concerned with live-stock, minerals, or timber. The aggressiveness of recreation-seekers constitutes a force to be reckoned with. This group in particular lays siege to the structure of National Park Service policy.

It is well that the visitor to this and other national parks extend his ken. We know something of what has happened since 1833. But what will have happened to the Yosemite region by the year 2033 A.D., two hundred years after white man's first glimpse of the valley? Will the men of great enterprise have built "ladders touching the sky, changing the face of the universe and the very color of the stars?" Or will there still be a remnant of mountain sanctuary, where the handiwork of today's and tomorrow's visitors will be as hard to discern as Joe Walker's footsteps are to trace?

ANNOTATIONS
BY HANK JOHNSTON

CHAPTER I

a. Whether or not Walker's men actually looked down into Yosemite Valley is a matter of debate among historians. The opinion that the Walker party did not see the Valley is cogently expressed by Irene Paden in *The Big Oak Flat Road to Yosemite*, 5th ed., Fredericksburg, Texas, Awani Press, 1986, pp. 261-264. There is also now overwhelming evidence that Walker's middle name was "Rutherford" not "Reddeford" as it appeared for years. See Bil Gilbert's *Westering Man — The Life of Joseph Walker*, Norman, University of Oklahoma Press, 1983, p. 299.

CHAPTER III

b. For a brief but interesting description of James Savage, see *The Mariposa Indian War, 1850-51, Diaries of Robert Eccleston*, edited by C. Gregory Crampton, Salt Lake City, University of Utah Press, 1957, pp. 106-107.

c. Three attendants <u>were</u> murdered at Savage's Fresno River store (a fourth escaped), but I cannot verify Russell's statement that three attendants were killed at his Mariposa store. In Savage's claim to the State for damages from the Indian raids, reprinted on page 193 in this book, he says only that he lost 16 mules and 40 head of cattle from his tent on the little Mariposa. I believe Russell is mistaken about there being any raid on the Mariposa store beyond the stealing of livestock.

d. Wiley B. Cassity, from Mississippi, operated a ferry on the San Joaquin River. According to Eccleston, *op. cit.*, p. 31 and p. 40, Cassity (the name was variously spelled Cassidy, Cassady, etc.) was found three miles from his ranch shot through with arrows, his tongue cut out, and one of his legs cut off. The remains were discovered by Captain John Kuykendall and Company A of the newly formed Mariposa Battalion.

e. Russell took the discovery date of March 25, 1851, from a letter written by Judge J. G. Marvin, Quartermaster of the Mariposa Battalion, to the *Daily Alta California* newspaper in San Francisco, published April 23, 1851. Marvin's account, obtained from a conversation with Adjutant Lewis and a Lieutenant Brooks, called "a letter from 'M,'" is reprinted as Document V. in the Appendix of this book. Some of the facts related by Lewis (who was not even with the discovery group according to Lafayette H. Bunnell, *Discovery of the Yosemite and the Indian War of 1851 Which Led to That Event*, Yosemite Association, 1990, p. 58) and Brooks are hard to accept: for example, the continuous march of 45 miles over a snowy mountain without food, which is contradicted by other accounts. The discovery of the *Eccleston Diary, op. cit.*, published in 1957, established the correct discovery date: March 27, 1851. Eccleston's entry for that date begins, "Today about noon Major Savage started for the Yoosemita Camp with 57 men & an Indian Guide."

CHAPTER IV

f. The correct date is March 27, 1851 (see above).

g. The murder of the prospectors by Yosemite Indians in May, 1852, is examined in detail in Hank Johnston's "The Mystery Buried in Bridalveil Meadow," *Yosemite*, Vol. 54 No. 2, Spring 1992. Grover's story, written many years after the event, is difficult to believe. It seems unlikely that his party passed through the Mariposa Grove of Big Trees, which was well out of the way, both going and coming from Coarsegold. It is also highly doubtful that Chief Tenaya, who had already had two painful experiences with punitive expeditions, would have conspired with Rose to provoke a third. The ambush was most likely the work of a small band of irresponsible Indians who then foolishly lingered near the scene of the crime until captured and executed by Lieutenant Moore's soldiers.

h. According to Bunnell, *op. cit.*, pp. 266-267, two parties of miners, totalling eight men, entered the Valley in 1853. In 1854, James Capen "Grizzly" Adams passed through Yosemite Valley with a companion named Solon on a bear-hunting expedition. "The Valley," Adams said, "produced impressions on my mind that are ineffaceable." Theodore H. Hittell, *The Adventures of James Capen Adams, Mountaineer and Grizzly Bear Hunter of California*, 1860. Russell himself twice mentions Adams' 1854 visit later in the book. A possible explanation for his omitting it here is that Bunnell erroneously said that no one had entered Yosemite in 1854. Russell may have simply repeated Bunnell's statement at this point in his story.

i. Russell took the date of June, 1855, from Hutchings' own account of his visit, published in his book, *In the Heart of the Sierras, op. cit.*, pp. 80-92. Hutchings, writing some 30 years after the fact, apparently either mislaid or forgot the diary he had kept during the year 1855 while traveling around California seeking material for his forthcoming magazine. (Hutchings was not yet publishing the magazine, as Russell states; the first issue was July, 1856.) Fortunately for historians, Hutchings' daughter, Gertrude Hutchings Mills, located the 1855 journal, along with two other Hutchings' diaries, and presented them to the Library of Congress in 1945. The diary gives a brief but unquestionably authentic day-by-day account of Hutchings' historic excursion. He entered Yosemite Valley on July 27, and left to go back to Mariposa on July 30 after spending two full days exploring the Valley "end to end." Artist Thomas Ayres made five pencil sketches on this trip; he returned the following year to make more drawings on his own behalf. See Hank Johnston, *Yosemite's Yesterdays - Volume II*, Yosemite, Flying Spur Press, 1991, pp. 16-18.

CHAPTER V

j. Once again Russell understandably took Hutchings at his word about the article in the *Mariposa Gazette* appearing "about July 12, 1855." Hutchings, *op. cit.*, p. 92. Although no copy seems to exist today, the *Gazette* of Friday, August 3, 1855, was most likely the issue that carried the Hutchings' account, which the *San Francisco Chronicle* reprinted on August 18, 1855. Johnston, *ibid.*, pp. 17-18.

k. The horse trail built by brothers Milton, Houston, and Andrew Mann, operators of a Mariposa livery stable, actually began at Mormon Bar, the end of the existing road, and ran 40 miles over Chowchilla Mountain past present Wawona to Yosemite Valley.

l. The Coulterville Free Trail ran for 50 miles past Bower Cave, Bull Creek, Deer Flat, Hazel Green, and Crane Flat to the Valley. While it is true that a rough mine road covered the first 17 miles to Black's Ranch on Bull Creek, horses and guides could be procured only at Coulterville. For more information on early Yosemite trails, see Johnston, *op. cit.*, pp. 31-34.

m. Big Oak Flat, which is actually about 10 miles northwest of Coulterville, was the starting point of the Big Oak Flat Trail blazed in 1857 by Tom McGee, a local pack train operator. It passed by Hardin's Ranch (since corrupted to "Harden"), named after "Little Johnny Hardin," an eccentric Englishman who had a ranch and sawmill. The junction of the Coulterville and Big Oak Flat Trails was at Crane Flat, not between Crane and Tamarack Flats. Paden, *op. cit.*, pp. 120, 202, and 219.

n. In 1870 Galen Clark had a three-seat wagon packed in by mules. He used it as a "taxi" to carry tourists to points of interest in the Valley. Not to be outdone, James Hutchings packed in a small stage on August 4, 1871. The vehicle Beadle refers to here was probably the Hutchings' conveyance, since he used the term "stage." Clark's wagon still exists and is presently on loan to the Fresno Metropolitan Museum. See Johnston, *op. cit.*, pp. 37-38.

o. Hutchings was again Russell's source for the statement that Weed's first Yosemite subject was the Upper Hotel. Hutchings, *op. cit.*, p. 101. Some Yosemite historians now believe, however, that Weed's photograph of Yosemite Falls may have preceded his picture of the Upper Hotel. A discussion of this occurs in David Robertson's *West of Eden: A History of the Art and Literature of Yosemite*, Yosemite Association, 1984, p. 14.

p. The Big Tree Room was built in 1870-71, some six years after the log cabin Russell describes in the next paragraph, not in 1865 as Russell implies. For further information on Muir, Hutchings, and the "Big Tree Room" see Linnie Marsh Wolfe, *Son of the Wilderness: The Life of John Muir*, 1945, pp. 128-129, and Johnston, *op. cit.*, p. 23.

q. Emily Ann Hutchings was the third wife of James Hutchings, not the second wife as Russell says. Hutchings had three wives: Elvira, the mother of his three children, from whom he was later divorced; Augusta Ladd Sweetland, whom he married in 1879; and Emily. Second wife Augusta died in 1881 in Yosemite, probably from tuberculosis. She is buried in the Hutchings plot in the cemetery in Yosemite Valley.

CHAPTER VI

r. Russell's reliance on Hutchings once more resulted in wrong data. Hutchings, *op. cit.*, p. 287. The Coulterville and Yosemite Turnpike Company was not incorporated until October 6, 1870. Work on the toll road from Bower Cave to Crane Flat began in 1870, not 1859. Dr. John Taylor McLean was not involved with the road until the summer of 1872. For information on the early toll roads to Yosemite, see Johnston, *op. cit.*, pp. 30-63.

s. For some reason Dr. McLean, writing some years later, made a mistake as to the date of the opening of the Coulterville Road. The activity he describes occurred on June 18, not June 17. Johnston, *op. cit.*, p. 42.

t. The stage road from present Wawona to Yosemite Valley was completed on June 24, 1875. The dedication and celebration took place on July 22, after three postponements. Johnston, *op. cit.*, pp. 45-46.

u. Contrary to Russell's statement, the completion of the stage roads did not increase Yosemite tourism as everyone expected. A severe depression between 1875 and 1880 resulted in a considerable drop in visitation. From a record high of 2,711 persons in 1874, visitation fell to only 1,183 in 1878. Not until 1883, in fact, did travel to the Valley exceed the 1874 total. Johnston, *op. cit.*, p. 47.

v. Russell is confused about the Milton railroad. It never ran to Copperopolis as he says. The Stockton and Copperopolis railroad built 25.8 miles of track between Stockton and Milton in 1866-70. On May 14, 1888, the line became part of the Southern Pacific Company. The 11.78-mile section from Peters to Milton was abandoned in 1940. Guy L. Dunscomb, *A Century of Southern Pacific Steam Locomotives*, Modesto, Private Printing, 1963, pp. 418-419. For a description of the Stockton-Yosemite route via Milton during staging days, see Hutchings, *op. cit.*, pp. 311-335.

w. A detailed description of the many holdups on the Yosemite roads can be found in Hank Johnston, *Yosemite's Yesterdays-Volume I*, Yosemite, Flying Spur Press, 1989, pp. 20-35.

x. The first car to enter Yosemite Valley was a 1900 Locomobile driven by Oliver Lippincott, a Los Angeles photographer, and his companion Edward Russell. Their entry over the old Wawona Stage Road on June 23, 1900, occurred 33 days before the Holmes brothers arrived on July 26, 1900. Automobiles entered Yosemite legally until June, 1907, when they were banned, as Russell later describes. On August 23, 1913, cars were once again permitted in the park. Johnston, *ibid.*, pp. 7-19.

CHAPTER VII

y. Many other informative books and maps have become available since Russell wrote this book. The Yosemite Valley Visitor Center book store and other park outlets carry a wide assortment of Yosemite material.

z. This is the same Reverend James Woods that Russell earlier mentioned as being associated with James Savage at Woods Creek near present Jamestown. Savage moved his operations to "Savage's Diggins," soon to be known as Big Oak Flat, in the fall of 1848. Paden, *op. cit.*, p. 97 and pp. 121-124.

a. The Coulterville Road within the Yosemite Grant was purchased by the State in 1885; the Big Oak Flat Road within the Grant became State property in 1886. The Wawona Road within the Grant was acquired by the State in 1888. Johnston, *Yosemite's Yesterdays-Vol. II*, p. 52.

CHAPTER VIII

b. The first structure, a shack, was actually built in 1855, which Russell said earlier in the book. Bunnell, *op. cit.*, p. 276.

c. Hutchings hired John Muir to operate his water-powered sawmill in November, 1869. During 1870 and the first six months of 1871, Muir and others built the Rock and River Cottages for Hutchings. The Oak Cottage, however, was not constructed until some years after Hutchings was ousted from his hotel by the State in 1875. Johnston, *Yosemite's Yesterdays-Vol. II*, p. 23.

d. The name "Wawona" did not replace "Big Tree Station" until 1882. Wah-wo-nah is the Indian name for the great sequoia tree, a word supposedly formed in imitation of the hoot of an owl. Shirley Sargent, *Yosemite's Historic Wawona*, Yosemite, Flying Spur Press, 1979, p. 39.

e. The Yosemite Park and Curry Co. owns only the furnishings, equipment, and inventory of the Wawona Hotel. The Federal Government purchased the real property (2,665 acres plus structures) from the Washburn interests in 1932. Sargent, *ibid*, p. 69.

f. James McCauley advertised his hotel for sale in the August, 1876, *Mariposa Gazette*, so his structure was built by at least 1876. His advertisement listed the house as "just complete, with fourteen bedrooms, sitting room, dining room, kitchen, etc. It is furnished in first-class style, and is a rare opportunity for anyone who wishes to engage in the hotel business."

CHAPTER XI

g. The correct date is March 27, 1851 (see note "e.," Chapter III).

h. President Lincoln signed the bill on June 30, 1864, not July 1. United States Statutes at Large, 13 (1864), 325.

APPENDIX
DOCUMENTS
CHRONOLOGY
BIBLIOGRAPHY

DOCUMENTS

I.   EVENTS LEADING TO THE MARIPOSA INDIAN WAR
     Letter from Adam Johnston, United States Sub-Agent, to L. Lea, Commissioner
     of Indian Affairs. Dated March 7, 1851. Published in *Senate Executive Document
     No. 4*, Special Session, 1851.

II. PEACE TREATY MADE WITH INDIANS OTHER THAN YOSEMITES,
     APRIL 29, 1851
     Thirty-second Congress, First Session, "Message from the President of the United
     States Communicating Eighteen Treaties Made with Indians in California,"
     Washington, 1905.

III. DEPOSITIONS REGARDING OPENING EVENTS IN THE MARIPOSA
     INDIAN WAR
     Claim of J. D. Savage for remuneration of losses sustained through Indian
     depredations. Published in *Senate Executive Document No. 4*, Special Session,
     1851.

IV. MUSTER ROLL OF VOLUNTEERS IN INDIAN WAR
     Muster Roll of Mariposa Battalion. From Elliott's *History of Fresno County*, 1881.

V.   SAVAGE'S ENTRY INTO YOSEMITE VALLEY
     A letter from "M," dated April 22, 1851, and published in the *Daily Alta
     California*, April 23, 1851.

VI. BOLING'S CAPTURE OF TENAYA
     Boling's letter of May 15, 1851, published in *Daily Alta California*, June 12, 1851.

VII. BOLING'S CAPTURE OF THE YOSEMITES
     Boling's letter of May 29, 1851, published in *Daily Alta California*, June 14, 1851.

VIII. CERTIFICATE OF DISBANDMENT, MARIPOSA BATTALION,
     JUNE 29, 1851
     From Elliott's *History of Fresno County*, 1881.

IX   VIOLATION OF THE PEACE TREATY
     Item in *Daily Alta California*, August 12, 1852.

CHRONOLOGY AND BIBLIOGRAPHY

I.   HISTORY OF HUMAN EVENTS IN YOSEMITE
     Chronological outline of the history of the Yosemite region, with sources.

II. BIBLIOGRAPHY

DOCUMENTS

I. EVENTS LEADING TO THE MARIPOSA INDIAN WAR

ADAM JOHNSTON TO HON. L. LEA, COMMISSIONER OF INDIAN AFFAIRS, WASHINGTON CITY[1]

MARIPOSA, CALIFORNIA
March 7, 1851

SIR: Since my last communication to the department I have spent most of my time among the Indian tribes of the San Joaquin valley and those located on the tributaries of that river, along the western side of the Sierra Nevada.

On my return from a tour through the valley of the Sacramento, I received information that the Indians of the San Joaquin valley were exhibiting feelings of discontent, and occasionally committing depredations on the persons and property of the whites. The mining region was threatened, and fears were entertained that serious consequences would ensue if something was not immediately done to quiet the Indians, and put a stop to their thefts, which were becoming daily more frequent and daring. I was solicited to go to that part of the country at the earliest possible day. It was thought that a few presents and fair promises might quiet them for a time—at least until I could communicate with the department and obtain instructions for future action. I was then without funds, and thought the circumstances would justify me in drawing for a small amount, and accordingly on the 15th day of November, 1850, I negotiated a draft on the Department of the Interior for the sum of eight hundred dollars. A few days were occupied in selecting and purchasing proper articles for presents and in making other necessary arrangements, previous to leaving for their location. On the 21st of November I left San Francisco intending to push as rapidly as possible to the camp of James D. Savage, situated in the mountains, on the headwaters of the Mariposa. Mr. Savage has been for some years with the Indians of California, speaks the language of several tribes fluently, and possesses a powerful influence over them. I therefore viewed his camp as the most favorable location for effecting my purpose, and especially for obtaining facilities in opening a communication with the wild Indians of the mountains. Difficulty in obtaining transportation from Stockton to Mariposa delayed me in reaching his camp until the first of December. Mr. Savage was then at another camp or trading post which he had recently established yet further in the mountains, on a river or stream called the Fresno.

I remained at his camp on the Mariposa for a few days; but, as he did not return, I procured an Indian guide and proceeded to the Fresno, where I found him in the midst of numerous wild and rather war-like Indians. The Indians in that region are quite numerous and rather war-like, quite fine looking, especially the"Chowchille" and "Chook-chancy" tribes. The most of them are wild, though they have among them

....

1. *Senate Executive Document No. 4*, Special Session, 1851

many who have been educated at the missions, and who have fled from their real or supposed oppressors to the mountains. These speak the Spanish language as well as their native tongue, and have intermarried with the wild tribes. Many of the tribes are therefore in a rather doubtful state—rather inclined toward barbarism, than to cherish such ideas of civilization as they may have acquired. This may be said of all the tribes inhabiting the western side of the Sierra Nevada, along the whole valley of the San Joaquin.

Mr. Savage has done much to open communication with the Indians of California, and to keep them on terms of friendship with the Americans. He had often told them before I reached Mariposa, of the Great Father at Washington; that he had sent a man to see them, who would talk with them and make them a few presents. They were therefore expecting me for some time before I reached them. On my arrival on the Fresno the Indians there seemed greatly gratified, and dispatched couriers to the other tribes announcing the fact that I had reached them. I remained on the Fresno several days during which time I had various interviews with the chiefs, braves, and men of authority among their respective tribes, the most powerful of which is the Chouchille. In an interview with the chief of that tribe on one occasion, he said to me:

"This is our country; why do the Americans come here? They are good and brave, but they come upon the land of my people. What do they intend to do? I want to know, and must know, *right now*."

I was not exactly prepared for so imperious a demand, but made such explanations as seemed to satisfy his majesty. After some time he said,

"Heretofore my people did not permit any stranger to pass over our country or stop in it, except Mr. Savage—he made us many presents;" and he added, "If you will make us presents, too, you may remain in our country *awhile*."

I endeavored to explain my mission; told him that the Great Father had sent me to talk with them, and to make them some presents as a token of his friendship and regard for them, but that they must not expect many presents at this time.

At the close of our *talk* the chiefs seemed fully satisfied, and assured me that their people should not steal or commit any depredations on the Americans. At the same time, they told me they should not control others. I set Christmas day as the time for a general meeting; and as my presents were limited, it was my intention to procure some beef cattle and make a feast for them.

I left Fresno with the prospect of at least being able to arrest hostilities until the commissioners (of whose appointment I had then heard) should arrive. In the meantime I visited the rancherias or villages, of other surrounding tribes. They all professed great friendship for the Americans, when at the same time they contemplated hostilities, as I had before been secretly informed. I of course conferred with them in such manner as seemed to me best calculated to arrest their designs. My efforts, however, were of no avail, as there was doubtless a general understanding among the various tribes that they should commence a predatory war, at an appointed time, all along the valley of the San Joaquin, if not along the entire base of the Sierra Nevada, from the northern to the southern boundary of the State. As an evidence of this, murders and robberies were committed simultaneously at various points.

The first serious depredations committed in this region were on the Fresno, and in the very camp which I had but a few days before left. On the 17th of December about five hundred Indians assembled at the camp on the Fresno, and murdered Mr. Savage's clerk and two other men — one alone escaping, through the efforts of the chief. I was then at the Mariposa. Soon after hearing of this outbreak we also discovered that all of the Indians in that vicinity had suddenly disappeared. Every day brought news of thefts and murders in various parts of the valley. This established beyond doubt the fact that a general hostility existed. I had obtained information that the Indians declared open war upon the whites, and every day's report confirmed the fact.

On the 20th day of December I left the Mariposa, with thirty-five men to bury the murdered men on the Fresno, and, if possible, to punish the Indians. We expected to meet them there, not only in considerable numbers, but to some extent fortified. Our force being small, we thought it necessary to take them by surprise. In order to do so, we must travel all night, which we did, and reached the Fresno about daylight, but found no Indians there. The destruction of property, however, and the bodies of the dead before us, filled with arrows, presented a horrible scene. We immediately proceeded to inter the remains of the deceased. Our force being small, we concluded not to pursue the Indians further into the mountains, but to return that evening on our way back to Mariposa. This determination was perhaps fortunate for us, as I have since learned the Indians were not far distant, knew of our arrival, and intended to attack us that night, had we remained on the ground.

On reaching Mariposa we learned that most of the Indians in the valley had hurriedly taken their women and children to the mountains. This is always looked upon as a sure indication of hostilities

Knowing the meager force of the United States troops here and having no authority to call upon them, I immediately repaired to the seat of government to ask aid from the State.

My communication to the governor (a copy of which I herewith transmit) was laid before the legislature, and that body acted as promptly as possible in furnishing aid and protection to the mining region of this country. Two hundred volunteers, under authority of the State, are at this time encamped within a few miles of this place. They are ordered by the governor to await the arrival of the commissioners, who desire to make an effort for peace before opening the campaign. I have been in company with the commissioners for the last few days, during which time we met several of the more friendly Indians, of the few who yet remain in the valley. Some of them have been induced to go to the mountains for the purpose of inducing the wild tribes to meet the commissioners near this point. I fear, however, even if they can be induced to come in, which I doubt, no good can be accomplished with the hostile Indians until they are severely dealt with. In the first place, they are entirely ignorant as to the strength of the Americans. So rapidly have the whites emigrated into this country, that but few of the mountain Indians have any idea of their number. They see the miners among them, and believe the whites have moved their camps from the old camping grounds upon their own. Others who know something of the numbers in various towns and cities here, look upon San Francisco, Sacramento, and the United States, as about the same size. The commissioners entertained some hopes of effecting a peace, but I am satisfied that nothing can be done, for some time to come, with many of the mountain tribes. They are now in the valleys and cañons of the mountains, living on animals and provisions plundered from the whites and if not subdued before the snows leave the Sierra Nevada, they will doubtless give the government much trouble, and in all probability a protracted war.

Again: if a treaty could be effected, my opinion is, it will not be respected by either Indians or Americans. The Indians are notoriously treacherous and thievish, and doubtless will continue their depredations. On the other hand, many of the whites in this region have lost either property or friends by the Indians, and openly declare they will shoot down any and all Indians they meet with, whether a treaty be made or not.

There is one way, and one alone, by which peace can be maintained between the whites and the Indians here; and that is, by establishing a line of small fortifications along the valley of the San Joaquin. Let the Indian agent of such district reside at a post of this kind, and punish the white man who murders an Indian, as promptly as an Indian who would commit the same crime. In my opinion, about five posts of this kind, with from ten to twenty soldiers and a few extra stands of arms, would be sufficient to maintain order and peace throughout this border. Some such regulation, under the present state of society here, is in my opinion indispensable.

I have obtained some of the Indian language of the San Joaquin valley, and other matters of interest, which I will transmit with the present mail.

I have the honor to remain, your most obedient servant, &c.

ADAM JOHNSTON

II. PEACE TREATY [2] MADE WITH INDIANS OTHER THAN YOSEMITES

A TREATY OF PEACE AND FRIENDSHIP, APRIL 29, 1851

Made and concluded at Camp Barbour, on the San Joaquin River, California, between Redick McKee, George W. Barbour, and O. M. Woozencraft, commissioners thereto especially appointed on the part of the United States, and the undersigned

----

2. *Thirty-second Congress, First Session*, "Message from the President of the United States Communicating EighteenTreaties Made with Indians in California," Washington, 1905, pp.1-69. Read June 7, 1852, and, with the documents and treaties, referred to the Committee on Indian Affairs, and ordered to be printed in confidence for the use of the Senate; injunction of secrecy removed January 18, 1905; ordered reprinted January 19, 1905.

chiefs, captains, and head men of the tribes or bands of Indians now in council at this camp, known as the Howechees, Chookchances, Chowchillas, Pohoneechees, and Nookchoos, which five tribes or bands acknowledge Naiyakqua as their principal chief; also the Pitoatchees, Cansons, Toomnas, Tallinches, and Poskesas, which five tribes or bands acknowledge Tomquit as their principal chief; also the Wachaets, Itachees, Choenemnees, Chokimenas, Wewahches, and Notonotos, which six tribes or bands acknowledge Pasqual as their principal chief.

ARTICLE 1.—The said tribes or bands acknowledge themselves jointly and severally, under the exclusive jurisdiction, authority, and protection of the United States, and hereby bind themselves to refrain hereafter from the commission of all crimes of hostility or aggression toward the Government or citizens thereof, and to live on terms of peace and friendship among themselves and all other Indian tribes, which are now, or may hereafter come, under the protection of the United States.

ART. 2—Lest the peace and friendship hereby established between the United States and the said tribes should be interrupted by the misconduct of individuals, it is expressly agreed that for injuries on either side no private revenge or retaliation shall take place or be attempted; that instead thereof complaint shall be made by the party aggrieved to the other, through the Indian Agent of the United States in their district, whose duty it shall be to investigate, and if practicable, to adjust the difficulty; or in case of acts of violence being committed upon the person or property of a citizen of the United States, by an Indian or Indians, belonging to, or harbored by, either of said tribes or bands, the party or parties charged with the commission of the crime, shall be promptly delivered up to the civil authorities of the State of California for trial; and in case the crime has been committed by a citizen or citizens of the United States, upon the person or property of an Indian or Indians of either of said tribes, the agent shall take all proper measures to bring the offender or offenders to trial in the same way.

INDIANS QUITCLAIM THEIR LANDS

ART. 3—The said tribes or bands here by jointly and severally relinquish and forever quitclaim to the United States all the right, title, claim, or interest of any kind, they or either of them have, or ever had, to lands or soil in California.

ART. 4—To promote the improvement of said tribes or bands, it is hereby stipulated and agreed, that the following district of country in the State of California shall be, and is hereby set apart forever for the sole use and occupancy of the aforesaid tribes of Indians, to wit: Beginning at a point in the middle of the Chowchilla River, near an old Indian rancheria, called Tahaleel, and immediately at the junction of the first two mainforks of said river, in the foot-hills, running thence in a straight line in a southwesterly direction to the top of the point of the Table Mountains, on the San Joaquin River, being the first high hill or mountain above and adjoining the valley in which the camp known as Camp Barbour is established, on the southside of the San Joaquin River; continuing thence a straight line in the same southwesterly direction to the eastern base of what is known as the Line or Lost Mountain, on the south side of King's River; continuing thence in a line in the same direction to the middle of the Cowier River, generally known as the first of the Four-creeks; thence down the middle of said stream to a point fifteen miles distant, in a straight line from where the first line strikes it; thence back to the middle of the Chowchilla River, to a point fifteen miles distant, in a straight line from where the first line strikes it; thence back to the middle of the Chowchilla River, to a point fifteen miles distant in a straight line from the starting point as aforesaid, on said river, the said line from the Cowier River, or first of the Four-creeks, to be so run as to cross King's, San Joaquin, and Fresno Rivers, at the distance of fifteen miles in a straight line from where the first-mentioned line herein crosses each one of said rivers, and from where the last-mentioned line strikes the Chowchilla River, up the middle of said stream to the beginning. To have and to hold the said district of country, for the sole use and occupancy of said Indian tribes forever. *Provided*, that there is reserved to the Government of the United States, the right of way over any portion of said territory, and the right to establish and maintain any military post or posts, public buildings, school-houses, houses for agents, teachers, and such others as they may deem necessary for their use or the protection of the Indians; and provided further that said tribes of Indians, or any portion of them, shall at all times have the privilege of the country east of the aforesaid district and between the waters of the Chowchilla and Cowier Rivers, or first of the Four-creeks, to the foot of the Sierra Nevada Mountains, to hunt, and to gather fruit, acorns, etc., but in no event are they, or any of them to remove or settle their families beyond the limits of the first described district or boundary of lands, without the permission of the Government of the United States through their duly authorized agent, and also that the said tribes shall never sell or dispose of the right or claim to any part thereof, except to the United States; nor shall they ever lease to, or permit, white men to settle, work or trade on any part thereof, without the written permission of the Indian Agent for the district; and it is also expressly understood that the Mono or wild portion of the tribes herein provided for, which are still out in the mountains, shall, when they come in, be incorporated with their respective bands, and receive a fair and equal interest in the lands and provisions hereinafter stipulated to be furnished for the whole reservation; and the tribes above named pledge themselves to use their influence and best exertions to bring in and settle the said Monos at the earliest possible day; and when the Yosemite tribe comes in, they shall in like manner be associated with the tribes or bands under the authority of Naiyakqua.

ART. 5—To aid the said tribes or bands in their subsistence while removing to, and making their settlement on, said reservation, the United States, in addition to the numerous and valuable presents made to them at this council, will furnish them, free of charge, 500 head of beef cattle, to average in weight 500 pounds, and 260 sacks of flour, 100 pounds each, during each of the years 1851 and 1852, to be divided among them by the agent, according to their respective numbers.

ART. 6—As early as convenient, after the ratification of this treaty by the

President and Senate, in consideration of the premises, and with a sincere desire to encourage said tribes in acquiring the arts and habits of civilized life, the United States will also furnish them with the following articles to be divided among them by the agent according to their respective numbers and wants, during each of the two years succeeding the said ratification, viz:

Two pairs strong pantaloons and two red flannel shirts for each man and boy; one linsey gown for each woman and girl; 3,000 yards calico and 3,000 yards brown sheetings; 30 pounds Scotch thread; 6 dozen pairs scissors, assorted; 1 gross thimbles and 5 needles, assorted; one 2½ pt. Mackinaw blanket for each man and woman over 15 years of age; 3,000 pounds iron and 800 pounds steel. And in like manner in the first year for the permanent use of the said tribes and as their joint property, viz: 75 brood mares and 3 stallions; 150 milch cows and 3 bulls; 12 yoke of work cattle, with yokes, chains, etc.; 12 work mules and horses; 30 plows (10 large and 20 small); 30 sets plow harness for horses or mules; seeds of all proper kinds for planting and sowing; 100 chopping axes; 100 hatchets, 300 mattocks or picks; 300 garden or corn hoes, 100 spades; 15 grindstones; 3 United States flags (one for each principal chief).

The stock enumerated above and the product thereof shall be marked or branded with such letters as will at all times designate the same to be the property of the said tribes, and no part or portion thereof shall be killed, exchanged, sold, or otherwise parted with, without the consent and direction of the agent.

ART. 7.—The United States will also employ and settle among said tribes, at or near their town or settlement, one practical farmer, who shall act as superintendent, or director of agricultural operations, to reside at some central point and to have two assistants, also of practical knowledge and industrious habits; one carpenter, or worker in wood, to direct and aid in the construction of houses, repairing floors, etc.; one blacksmith, to reside at some central point; three principal school-teachers, and as many assistant teachers as the President may deem proper, to instruct said tribes in reading, writing, etc.; and in the domestic arts of sewing, house-keeping, etc., upon the manual labor system; all the above-named workmen and teachers to be maintained and paid by the United States, for the period of five years and as long thereafter as the President may deem advisable; the United States will also erect suitable school-houses, shops, and dwellings for the accommodation of the school-teachers and mechanics above specified, and for the protection of the public property.

These articles to be binding on the contracting parties when ratified and confirmed by the President and Senate of the United States.

In testimony whereof the parties have hereunto signed their names and fixed their seals this 29th day of April, Anno Domini 1851.

Signed and sealed and delivered, after being fully explained in presence of

JOHN McKEE, *Secretary*
JOHN HAMILTON, *Interpreter*
ADAM JOHNSTON, *Agent*

C. D. KEYS, *Capt. 3d Art'y, Escort*
W. S. KING, *Ass't Surg. U.S.A.*
I. H. LANDRAM, *Lieut. 3d Art'y*
H. J. G. GIGSON, *2nd Lieut. 3dArt'y*
N. H. M. LEAN, *Lieut. 2nd Inf't*
T. H. A. MARS

(*Signed*), REDICK MCKEE, G. W. BARBOUR, O. M. WOOZENCROFT

For and in behalf of the Howechais — Nai-yak-qua, No-cheel, Chal-wak-chee, Por-sa, Po-qui.

For and in behalf of the Chookchaney — Co-tum-si, Tim-oh, Sa-wa-lui, A-chat-a-wa, Mi-e-wal.

For an in behalf of the Chowchillas — Po-ho-leel, E-keen-o, Kay-o-ya, A-pem-shee, Cho-no-hal-ma.

For and in behalf of the Pohonoeeches — Po-tol, Chee-ko, Mooch-ca-te, Ho-has-see, Cow-wal.

For and in behalf of the Nookchoos — Pan-wach-ee, Ket-ta, Mullu-ee, Taw-wich, Wal-lin.

For and in behalf of the Pitcachees — Tom-quit, Ya-ko-wal, Too-tro-mi, Cho-lul, Ne-sa-plo.

For and in behalf of the Capoos — Domingo Perez, Tom-mas, Jose Antonio.

For and in behalf of the Toomaneh — Hat-chu-too, Tap-pa, Po-sha.

For and in behalf of the Tallinchy — Cho-kate, Pal-lo-koosh, How-il-me-na, So-kuch.

For and in behalf of the Poskesas — Ko-shish, Ko-itch, Cop-pi, Wo-wal.

For and in behalf of the Wachahets — Pasqual, Wa-keen, Jose Antonio.

For and in behalf of the Itaches — Wa-too, A-por-trai, To-hai-chee.

For and in behalf of the Choenemnes — Wau-toi-ki, Ho-let-tee, Ta-ween.

For and in behalf of the Chokimenas — Ko-heel, Tra-ta-it-se, Woh-ton.

For and in behalf of the Notohotos — Pasqual.

For and in behalf of the Narmelches — Pasqual.

The above Indian names are signed by an "X," his mark.

III. DEPOSITIONS REGARDING OPENING EVENTS IN THE MARIPOSA INDIAN WAR

ADAM JOHNSTON, UNITED STATES SUB-AGENT FOR THE VALLEY OF SAN JOAQUIN, TO COMMISSIONER OF INDIAN AFFAIRS [3]

SAN FRANCISCO, CALIFORNIA
December 3, 1851

SIR: In accordance with the laws and regulations in regard to "depredations of Indians on the property of white persons," I herewith transmit a claim of Major James D. Savage for remuneration. The facts set forth in the application are known to me to be true. I was near to the place at the time the murders and robbery were committed among the Indians residing on the Little Mariposa. On hearing of this outbreak on the Fresno, I immediately repaired to the spot, where I found the bodies of the murdered men and had them interred. The house was stripped of everything valuable, and safe broken open and robbed of its contents. Major Savage had applied to me some time previous for a license to trade with those Indians. I did not then give him formal license, but gave him permission to go on and erect his trading-house in Fresno, and to trade with the Indians until I could visit that part of the country. I therefore supposed he was "lawfully within the Indian country." I had only reached the neighborhood at the time of the outbreak and was visiting the Indians on the Little Mariposa. On this occurrence all the Indians of that region fled to the mountains, and a predatory war was the result. Since treaties have been entered into in that region, I have inquired of the Indians engaged in the robbery in regard to the cause. They acknowledge the act, but say they were "hungry, and their heads got bad." I submit the claim for consideration and directions.

Respectfully, your obedient servant,

ADAM JOHNSTON
United States Sub-Agent for the Valley of the San Joaquin

JAMES D. SAVAGE TO ADAM JOHNSTON, [4] UNITED STATES SUB-AGENT, VALLEY OF SAN JOAQUIN

October, 1851

To ADAM JOHNSTON,
U. S. Indian Agent, Valley of San Joaquin:

The undersigned respectfully represents to you that on or about the 6th day of

3. *Senate Executive Document No. 4*, Special Session, 1851.
4. *Ibid.*

October, A. D. 1850, after obtaining your consent to erect a trading-house on the headwaters of the Fresno river, for the purpose of trading with the Indians on said stream, I have erected a house for my goods, and a corral for my cattle, and continued to do business on said stream until about the 17th day of December, A. D., 1850, when the Chouchilla, Chookchuney, and Pohuniche tribes or bands of Indians broke out, killing my clerk, Mr. Greely, a Mr. Stiffner, and Mr. James Kennedy, and robbed my store of all goods, broke open my iron safe and abstracted a large amount of money and valuable papers, and destroyed all of my furniture and property.

The losses sustained by me were as follows:

Goods and provisions actually on hand, which were taken and destroyed by the Indians	$13,000
Money in my safe	5,000
Iron safe	150
Two riding-mules, at $150 each	300
Twelve head of work-oxen	900
Two fine horses	300
One house, furniture and fixtures	1,000
Two canvas tents and fixtures	500
At the same time at my tent on the Little Mariposa, sixteen mules, at $100 each	1,600
Forty head of beef cattle, at $60 each	2,400
Making in all the sum of	25,150

The undersigned further represents that all of the above-named property was taken by force, with an intent to steal, and that the property was appropriated by the said Indians to their own use.

JAMES D. SAVAGE

I, James D. Savage, being duly sworn, do solemnly aver that all of the matters and things set forth in the foregoing statement are true, and that neither myself, representative, attorney, nor agent, has violated the provisions of the law by seeking or attempting to obtain private satisfaction or revenge in the premises.

J. D. SAVAGE

Subscribed and sworn to before me, this 21st day of October, A. D. 1851.

ADAM JOHNSTON,
United States Sub-Agent, Valley of the San Joaquin

I, Anthony Brown, do solemnly swear in the presence of Almighty God, that I was at the house of James D. Savage, on the Fresno river, on or about the 17th day of December, A. D. 1850, when the Indians of the Chouchilla, Chook-chuney, and Pohuniche tribes or bands commenced the robbery and massacre as above stated by James D. Savage; that Mr. Greely, Mr. Stiffner, and Mr. Kennedy were killed by said Indians in my presence, and that I narrowly escaped with my life after having my arm broken, my head fractured, and being elsewhere hurt; that the attack was unprovoked, and the property was taken by force, with an intent to steal, or be otherwise maliciously destroyed; that all of the matters and things set forth in the statement of Mr. James D. Savage are true in every particular.

A. S. BROWN

Subscribed and sworn to before me, this 21st day of October, 1851.

ADAM JOHNSTON,
United States Sub-Indian Agent

I, William H. Hays, being duly sworn, depose and say: That I was at the house of James D. Savage, on the Little Mariposa, about the 17th day of December, A. D. 1850, and know that the forty head of beef cattle and nine mules mentioned in the claim of James D. Savage were stolen by the Indians, as stated by him. Deponent further states that he was familiar with the business of Mr. James D. Savage, and has been at his store, on the Fresno, before the robbery and massacre alluded to above; that he is satisfied that the attack and robbery were unprovoked, and that the goods were taken by force, with an intent to steal, and that his property was maliciously destroyed by the Indians.

WILLIAM H. HAYS

Subscribed and sworn to before me, this 21st day of October, A. D. 1851.

ADAM JOHNSTON,
U. S. Sub-Indian Agent, Valley of San Joaquin

IV. MUSTER ROLL OF VOLUNTEERS IN INDIAN WAR

MUSTER ROLL, MARIPOSA BATTALION [5]

Muster Roll of a Volunteer Battalion under the command of Major James D. Savage, mustered into the service of the State of California by James Burney, Sheriff of Mariposa, pursuant to an order from his excellency, the Governor of the State of California, bearing date January 24, 1851, at Aqua Frio, February 10, 1851:

1. James D. Savage, *Major*
2. M. B. Lewis, *Adjutant*
3. A. Brunston, *Sergeant*
4. Robert E. Russell, *Sergeant-Major*
5. Francis Laumiester, *Quartermaster and Commissary*
6. Theodore Wilson, *Quartermaster Sergeant*
7. Vincent Haylix, *Guide*

COMPANY A

1. Kuykendall, John I., Captain, 36, Harris County, Texas
2. Scott, John I., First Lieutenant, 30, Clark County, Alabama
3. Rodgers, Thomas T., Second Lieutenant, 46, Red River County, Texas
4. Smith, Elisha M., Second Brevet, 25, Steuben County, New York
5. Hector, M. Forbz, Ordnance Sergeant, 40, Monterey, California
6. Aldrich, Julius, Private, 24, Southwich, Massachusetts
7. Bell, George, Private, 26, Camdon County, Massachusetts
8. Blanchard, Aaron, Private, 29, Calais, Vermont
9. Brison, James, Private, 21, Boston, Massachusetts
10. Brundidge, V. D., Private, 21, Steuben County, New York
11. Burnham, H., Private
12. Barrett, Joseph, Private, 20, New York City
13. Burgess, Joseph, Private, 34, Erie County, New York
14. Criper, Henry, Private, 34, St. Louis, Missouri
15. Crookshank, Wm. T., Private, 28, Troy, New York
16. Cheoiles, Henry, Private, 27, New York City
17. Dudley, Wm., Private, 34, City of York
18. Davis, Walter L., Private, 28, District of James Town[Jamestown], U.C.
19. Ellis, John, Private, 23, Boston, Massachusetts
20. Fulton, Francis, Private, 21
21. Folsome, Daniel, Private, 21, Norfolk County, Massachusetts
22. Freeman, Wm. F., Private, 21, Charles Town, Massachusetts
23. French, Clent, Private, 25, Steuben County, New York
24. Fearon, Samuel, Private, 23, New York City
25. Green, Wm., Private, 29, Covington, Rhode Island
26. Gidian, Charles, Private, 23, Philadelphia (a black boy)

....

5. From Elliott's *History of Fresno County*, 1881.

27. Gosmer, Joseph, Private, 29, St. Louis, Missouri
28. Hugh, Martin, Private, 25, Neward [Newark], New Jersey
29. Hill, Richard, Private, 32, Australia
30. Hill, R. E., Private, 32, Australia
31. Huffman, Henry A., Private, 25, Clark County, Ohio
32. Hunter, Bob, Private, 38, Lion [Leon] County, Texas
33. Herman, John, Private, 30, Philadelphia
34. Hazelrig, Charles, Private, 20, Genesee, Iowa
35. Hunter, William C., Private, 26, St. Louis, Missouri
36. Isham, Claburn, Private, 30, Faning [Fannin] County, Texas
37. James, John, Private, 29, St. Landre Parish, Louisiana
38. Leach, Lewis (Dr.), Private, 28, St. Louis, Missouri
39. Leander, Joseph, Private, 25, Albany, New York
40. Luker, Wm., Private
41. Lewis, Samuel H., Private, 22, Jasper County, Texas
42. Loyd, Sim M., Private, 30, Leon County, Texas
43. McSlay, Andrew, Private, 38, Harris County, Texas
44. McKey, Thomas, Private, 28, New Orleans, Louisiana
45. McFadden, O. P., Private, 24, Cass County, Texas
46. Myers, Charles P., Private, 26, Monmouth, New Jersey
47. Milhouse, Gustavis, Private, 25, Santa Barbara, California
48. Miller, R. F., Private, 18, Lamar County, Texas
49. McKenzie, David, Private, 21, Travis County, Texas
50. McCloud, Wm., Private
51. O'Donel, Joseph, Private, 30, California
52. Pilkington, Mathew, Private, 34, Buffalo, New York
53. Puples, A. H., Private, 28, Cado [Caddo] Parish, Louisiana
54. Potter, James W., Private, 32, Hanson, Maine
55. Petchford, Washington, Private, 19, Holms [Holmes] County, Mississippi
56. Robertson, W. W., Private, 25, Cass County, Texas
57. Rheem, Charles W., Private, Carlisle, Pennsylvania
58. Riley, John S., Private, 30, Franklin, Mississippi
59. Stone, Samuel S., Private, 22, Lexington, Missouri
60. Seybola, Conrad, Private, 23, Newton, Texas
61. Selar, John, Private, 28, Natchez, Mississippi
62. Smith, Hyram C., Private, 18, Genesee, New York
63. Stone, John E., Private, 19, Henderson County, Kentucky
64. Small, Wm. B., Private, 32, Boston, Massachusetts
65. Still, Vendell, Private, 28, New Orleans, Louisiana
66. Sutton, John D., 34, [Lawrence] County, Ohio
67. Thomas, Isaac P., Private, 25, Dallas County, Texas
68. Wilson, Robert, Private, 26, New Orleans, Louisiana

69. Wright, Wm., Private, 28, Morgan County, Illinois
70. Westcott, Varnum, Private, 25, Jefferson County, New York

COMPANY B

1. Bowling [Boling], John, Captain
2. Chandler, Reuben T., First Lieutenant
3. Gilbert, Thomas J., Second Lieutenant
4. Hancock, Thomas J., Second Brevet
5. Hawkins, John J., First Sergeant
6. Gray, James, First Corporal. All the time.
7. Adams, Edward S., Second Corporal. All the time.
8. Allen, Joseph A., Private
9. Anderson, Philip, Private
10. Bradly, Thomas N., Private
11. Black, Norman, Private
12. Black, John C., Private
13. Burnell, Lafayette H., Private
14. Brooks, Israel H., Third Corporal. All the time.
15. Brown, Wm. P., Private
16. Blakey, Everett C., Private
17. Berdon, Joseph S., Private
18. Chambers, James H., Private
19. Crenshaw, George H., Private
20. Crenshaw, Wm. A., Private
21. Cameron, Alexander M., Third Sergeant. All the time.
22. Clark, Francis B., Private. Place taken by R. McKee Mar. 20th.
23. Chase, George, Private
24. Drinkwater, Nelson, Private
25. Davis, Wm. H., Private
26. Edmunson, John C., Private
27. Fermon, Edward, Private
28. Flanegan, Patrick, Private
29. Folsome, Joseph B., Private
30. Ford, George M., Private
31. Fisher, Wm. P., Private
32. Fairchilds, John, Private
33. Gordon, Ennis B., Second Sergeant. All the time.
34. Graham, Jesse J., Private. A. D. Fireball [Firebaugh] substituted Mar. 10th.
35. Gray, Augustus A., Private
36. Hill, Pembleton, Private. Place taken by G. W. Camron
37. Howard, Wm. H., Private
38. Hall, Robert L., Private. Time served out by P. Hussery

39. Houghton, Edward W., Private
40. Hale, Johnson B., Private
41. Hunt, John L., Private
42. Hayes, Wm H., Private
43. Kerr, John C., Private
44. Kerney, James, Private
45. Lendrum, George, Private
46. Lyles, Isaac, Private
47. Lloyd, George W., Private
48. Lustor, Sterling H., Private
49. Lowring, James, Private. Time served out by Clint French.
50. McKenney, Andrew, Private
51. McKenney, James M., Private
52. McGarrah, James, Private
53. Miller, John I., Private
54. Morris, Thomas, Private
55. Mallard, Charles W., Private. Time served out by Joseph Young.
56. Nolin, Joseph, Private
57. O'Neill, John, Private
58. Peirpont, Daniel L., Private
59. Perry, Willis C., Private
60. Roundtree, Wm., A., Private
61. Rankin, John I., Private
62. Rainbolt, Peter A., Private
63. Roane, James H., Fourth Corporal
64. Stracy, Alpha H., Private
65. Slaughter, Edward J., Private
66. Spencer, Champion H., Private
67. Starkey, Jesse S., Private
68. Shaw, John B., Private
69. Stone, Thomas H., Private
70. Shepherd, Joseph, Private. (Feb. 10th)
71. Tannihill, Benjamin H., Fourth Sergeant
72. Thompson, Robert H., Private

COMPANY C

1. Dill, William, Captain, 30, Texas
2. Ferrell, Hugh W., First Lieutenant, 21, Beauford [Beaufort] District, South Carolina
3. Russell, F. W., Second Lieutenant, 22, Fulton, Missouri
4. Fletcher, Crawford, Second Brevet, 26, Jackson, Mississippi
5. Bishop, S. A., First Sergeant, 25, Halloway [Callaway] County, Missouri

6. Taylor, George, Second Sergeant, 27, Augusta, Virginia
7. Wingfield, A. A., Third Sergeant, 25, Johnson County, Missouri
8. Durlle, R. G., Fourth Sergeant, 24, Antonia County, New York
9. Lee, H., First Corporal, 24, Fulton County, New York
10. Kirkpatrick, I., Second Corporal, 29, Will County, Illinois
11. Carson, William, Third Corporal, 21, Augusta County, Virginia
12. Reynolds, I. S., Fourth Corporal, 25, Columbia County, New York
13. Burry, E. J., Private, 22, England
14. Bachman, B. F., Private, 21, Lancaster, Pennsylvania
15. Barrow, Julian, Private, 35, France
16. Coy, J., Private, 23, San Jose, California
17. Canfield, C. T., Private, 39, New York City
18. Coy, Mathew, Private, 21, San Jose, California
19. Chandelera, Private, 40, Santa Fe, New Mexico
20. Draper, William, Private, 21, Johnson County, Missouri
21. Ecleston, Robert, Private, 21, New York City
22. Fifer, M. W., Private, 28, New York City
23. Gray, J. F., Private, 22, Fulton County, Missouri
24. Godkin, Thomas, Private, 25, New York City
25. Hart, James W., Private, 20, Callaway County, Missouri
26. Hodgson, John, Private, 32, York, England
27. Huchett, A. C., Private, 39, France
28. Jones, J. W., Private, 24, England
29. John, A., Private, 19, France
30. Kenny, Thomas B., Private, 28, Petersburg, Virginia
31. Long, Thomas A., Private, 20, Jackson County, Missouri
32. Lewis, Henry D., Private, 29, Henry County, Missouri
33. McGathy, James C., Private, 24, Bonce County, Illinois
34. McGathy, James S., Private, 25, Bonce County, Illinois
35. McEwing, Felix, Private, 24, Montgomery County, Missouri
36. McVicker, Henry, Private, 40, Pennsylvania
37. Prather, George, Private, 19, Linn County, Missouri
38. Pate, Francis, Private, 27, Harrison County, Texas
39. Poittesin, Arista, Private, 37, France
40. Parkinson, John, Private, 29, New York
41. Randolph, Wm. F., Private, 20 [Fauquier] County, Virginia
42. Rail, Edmond, Private, 20, Cooper County, Missouri
43. Rodgers, Charles A., Private, 24, Fulton County, Missouri
44. Soto, Jose, Private, 19, Calaway [Callaway] County, Missouri
45. Sims, Parris, Private, 48, St. Clair County, Missouri
46. Slavin, Charles S., Private, 27, Patterson County, Virginia
47. Smith, James, Private, 23, New York

48. Saucer, Ferdinand, Private, 43, France
49. Stevens, Elbert C., Private, 24, Collinville City
50. Simeon, Augustus, Private, 29, France
51. Talbott, Thomas J., Private, 22, Cooper County, Missouri
52. Valentine, Charles T., Private, 30, Aberdeen County, Mississippi
53. Varney, George, Private, 26, Perkatgues County, Missouri
54. Winfield, Charles R., Private, 25, LaFayette County, Missouri
55. Winters, John D., Private, 31, York County, Pennsylvania

RECAPITULATION

Staffs, Surgeon, Quartermaster, and Adjutant.. 7
Company A... 70
Company B... 72
Company C... 55

Battalion rank and file... 204

P.S. Russell and Hayhr detached from Captain Dills' Company.

V. SAVAGE'S ENTRY INTO YOSEMITE VALLEY
A LETTER[6] FROM "M," PUBLISHED APRIL 23, 1851

SAN JOSÉ, April 22, 1851

MESSRS. EDITORS: I have just had a conversation with Judge Lewis, the Adjutant of Maj. Savage's Battallion of mounted Volunteers, and Lieut. Brooks of the same Battallion, who are recently from the seat of the Indian war in Mariposa County. From them I learn the following particulars: On the 19th of March Major Savage, with Captains Bowling and Dill's Companies started from Camp No. 3 for the head waters of the Merced river to subdue the Yo Semites and Neuch-Teus who refused to come into the treaty made with the tribes in that vicinity by the Indian Commissioners at Camp Frémont. The volunteers after three days march arrived in the neighborhood of the Indians and on the morning of the fourth day surprised the Neuch-Teus and took them prisoners. The march was over rugged mountains and through deep defiles covered with snows and was one of considerable exposure and hardship. The command upon the 21st marched all day and during the night until about 4 o'clock on the morning of the 22d, some forty-five miles, when the troops arrived at the South Fork of the Merced river about seven miles above the rancheria of the Neuch-Teus. During the march the volunteers were without food and marching continually through the

6. *Daily Alta California*, San Francisco, April 23, 1851.

snow. Upon arriving at the stream above mentioned, the pack train was left with a guard who succeeded by removing the snow in procuring a few rushes for the animals. The volunteers, after resting a few moments took up the line of march for the rancheria, where they arrived about seven in the morning of the 23d.

This part of the march was exceedingly difficult and dangerous. It lay along a deep canyon and a part of it had to be made through the water and a part over precipitous cliffs covered with snow and ice. Major Savage had with him an Indian boy from the Chowchilla tribe who had married a Neuch-Teus wife who was living in the rancheria at this time. He told the boy that in case the Neuch-Teus attempted to run from the rancheria the whole of them would be killed. The boy was much alarmed at this, went a short distance ahead of the volunteers, and by creeping on his hands and knees through the bushes managed to get within a short distance of the rancheria before being discovered by the Indians. He communicated to them what Savage had told him and finding themselves entrapped surrendered without showing any disposition to fight and without a gun being fired. Almost the first question asked by Pan-Wache, their Chief, was whether Savage was there? When Savage answered in their own language that he was, the Chief came out and met the Major who told the Chief the object for which they had come. The Major told him that he had before said that some day the white people would come for them and that now since his Indians were enemies of the whites he had come to kill them all unless they could consent to live like good Indians.

These Indians as well as most of the tribes on this side of the Sierra's believe in wizards and witches. A man distinguished for his superior knowledge and power is regarded as a wizard. The Major told the Chief that three wizards had been sent to the Indian country by the great wizard of the white men to make the Indians presents, to learn them how to till the soil and live like the whites, and that the great wizard wanted all the Indians to be good and honest and to come out of the mountains and reside on the plains, and that the white people were very numerous, and if the Indians did not do as the three wizards desired the great wizard would tell the white men to kill all of the Indians. The chief replied that he had heard at different times the same thing that was now told him but that he did not believe it was true—since he (Savage) had come and told him he believed it true and would go with him. The volunteers having selected camping ground about two miles from the rancheria, sent up for the mules, and the next day made preparation to march against the Yo Semitees, living about twenty-five miles distant, on the middle fork of the Merced. In the mean time an Indian courier had been dispatched by Maj. Savage to the Indians informing them of his approach to their country and the objects of his mission, with a request that the chief, Yo Semite [Tenaya], together with his tribe should come into the camp. The chief obeyed the summons but brought none of his tribe with him except two sons. Upon arriving he made many excuses for not bringing with him his people, among which were that they were all good Indians—that they never stole animals nor killed white men—that it was now in the dead of winter and the snows deep—that they were well supplied with acorns and living happy and contented. These Indians, nevertheless, have committed numerous depredations about Burn's Diggings and Mariposa and the assertions of their goodness and peaceable intentions obtained no credence, and the chief and his people were peremptorily ordered to be in camp within three days. Major Savage, doubting whether Yo Semitee would obey the order, started on the morning of the 25th with a part of his command and three days' provisions for the Middle Fork. On the way he met the Yo Semitees coming in, but still doubting whether they were all on the road, he pushed forward through the snows, and a snow storm, to the rancheria, taking with him the chief. Upon arriving there he found a large quantity of acorns put up in cribs which he destroyed, as well as their huts. He found also a very old Indian and his wife, the father and mother of Yosemitee, who had been left behind to perish or to take care of themselves as best they could. They were living in a cave in which was kindled a small fire, but will doubtless perish during the winter. The Major had a large pile of wood carried to them, and acorns, but they were old, decrepid, and Yo-Semitee [Tenaya] remarked that he had thrown them away and must leave them since they could not travel and take care of themselves.

Quite a number of Indian tracks led toward the Sierras and upon inquiry it was ascertained that they were those of some Monas, a tribe of Indians living the other side of the Sierras, and whilst on a visit last fall were caught this side by early snows, and unable to return. Upon learning that the Yo Semitees were likely to have difficulties, they became alarmed and started for their tribe. The Monas are nearly white and are much superior, mentally and physically, to the Indians this side of the mountains. Maj. Savage despatched Yo Semitee [Tenaya] on their trail to bring them back, but after traveling several hours he was unable to overtake them. During the night the snow fell to the depth of three or four feet which obliterated all trace of their footsteps. Being satisfied that no more Indians were in that quarter, the command commenced the march back. The snows impeded their progress very much, and the volunteers were obliged to go in advance of their animals and break a path in order to get them along. On the march several animals became exhausted from the want of food and from fatigue, and were left on the road. Upon returning for them the next day, they were found dead. Upon arriving in camp, the Volunteers with the Indians started for the headquarters on the Fresno, on the 29th. The rancheria of the Yo Semitees is described as being in a valley of surpassing beauty, about 10 miles in length and one mile broad. Upon either side are high perpendicular rocks, and at each end through which the Middle Fork runs, deep cañons, the only accessible entrances to the Valley. The forest trees, such as pine, fir, red wood and cedar, are of immense height and size. There is a species of pine tree here from which exudes a sacharine substance nearly resembling in looks and taste brown sugar. The Indians gather and use it as an article for food, and Judge Lewis informs me that excepting a slight piney taste, it cannot be distinguished from common brown sugar. On the first day of April the whole command arrived at the head quarters of the regulars on the Fresno, and the Indians were turned over to the Commissioners. The Commissioners declined treating with them until the Chow-Chillas came in, but furnished them with a supply of food and some clothing.

Judge Lewis and Lieut. Brooks left Camp No. 4 on the Fresno on the 13th of April, upon which day the regulars started for Cassady's on the San Joaquin, and Maj. Savage with his command on an expedition against the Chow-chillas. This, the most powerful of the Indian tribes in California, is believed to have at its command 1,000 warriors. A portion of the Pyanches [Piutes] from the other side of the Sierras are known to be allied with them and other tribes this side of the mountains. A hard fight is anticipated with them since they have refused all overtures of peace and have committed the most daring robberies and unprovoked murders in the neighborhood of fine and coarse Gold Gulches. Large quantities of snow have fallen since the expedition started, which will render the march exceedingly difficult, and perhaps defeat the ultimate success of the troops. However, the Major and the officers and the men under him will not turn back for any ordinary difficulties, and we may expect soon to hear of the complete subjection of the Chow-chillas. The next treaty will be made with the Indians at some point on the San Joaquin. The best of feeling exists between the regular and volunteer forces, and in the course of a month it is believed that the Indian difficulties will be satisfactorily settled from the Calaveras to the Tulare Lake, opening to miners some of the best mining and agricultural districts in the State. May future success attend the negotiations with the Indians, and the volunteers receive the meed of praise which they deserve, and the money which they have earned by numerous hardships incident to a border warfare carried on in the snow hills in mid-winter.

M.

VI. BOLING'S CAPTURE OF TENAYA

BOLING'S LETTER ABOUT MAJOR SAVAGE'S BATTALION [7]

We publish below two more letters touching the movements of the battalion of State troops under Major Savage—one from Captain Bowling and the other from the Sergeant Major of the command.

MERCED RIVER, YO-SEMETY VILLAGE
May 15, 1851

Major Savage

SIR: On reaching this valley, which we did on the 9th inst. I selected for our encampment the most secluded place that I could find, lest our arrival might be discovered by the Indians. Spies were immediately despatched in different directions, some of which crossed the river to examine for signs on the opposite side. Trails were soon found, leading up and down the river, which had been made since the last rain. On

7. *Daily Alta California*, San Francisco, June 12, 1851.

the morning of the tenth we took up the line of march for the upper end of the valley, and having traveled about five miles we discovered five Indians running up the river on the north side. All of my command, except a sufficient number to take care of the pack animals put spurs to their animals, swam the river and caught them before they could get into the mountains. One of them proved to be the son of the old Yo-Semety chief. I informed them if they would come down from the mountains and go with me to the United States Indian Commissioners, they would not be hurt; but if they would not, I would remain in their neighborhood as long as there was a fresh track to be found; informing him at the same time that all the Indians except his father's people and the Chou-Chillas had treated, and that you were then after the Chou-chillas with two companies of volunteers, determined upon chasing them as long as a track could be found in the mountains, and that all the Indians which had been treated with were well satisfied with their situation. He then informed me that we had been discovered by their spies and that we would not have got so close had they have known we could run over the river so quick on horseback, and that if I would let him loose with another Indian, he would bring in his father and all his people by twelve o'clock the next day. I then gave him plenty to eat and started him and his companion out. We watched the others close intending to hold them as hostages until the despatch-bearers returned. They appeared well satisfied and we were not suspicious of them, in consequence of which one of them escaped. We commenced searching for him, which alarmed the other two still in custody, and they attempted to make their escape. The boys took after them and finding they could not catch them, fired and killed them both. This circumstance connected with the fact of the two whom we had sent out not returning, satisfied me that they had no intention of coming in. My command then set out to search for the Rancheria. The party which went up the left towards Canyarthia found the rancheria at the head of a little valley, and from the signs it appeared that the Indians had left but a few minutes. The boys pursued them up the mountain on the north side of the river, and when they had got near the top, helping each other from rock to rock on account of the abruptness of the mountains; the first intimation they had of Indians being near was a shower of huge rocks which came tumbling down the mountain, threatening instant destruction. Several of the men were knocked down, and some of them rolled and fell some distance before they could recover, wounding and bruising them generally. One man's gun was knocked out of his hand and fell seventy feet before it stopped, whilst another man's hat was knocked off his head without hurting him. The men immediately took shelter behind large rocks, from which they could get an occasional shot, which soon forced the Indians to retreat, and by pressing them close they caught the old Yo-semity chief, whom we yet hold as a prisoner. In this skirmish they killed one Indian and wounded several others.

You are aware that I know this old fellow well enough to look out well for him, least by some stratagem he makes his escape. I shall aim to use him to the best advantage in pursuing his people. I send down a few of my command with the pack animals for provisions; and I am satisfied if you will send me ten or twelve of old Pon-watchez' best men I could catch the women and children and thereby force the men to come in. The Indians I have with me have acted in good faith and agree with me in this opinion.

I have the honor to be, very respectfully,
Your most obedient servant,
JOHN BOWLING*

*Mr. Hal Barnett of Stockton, relative of John Boling, writes under date of December 4, 1931: "As far as we know, John Boling always spelled his name and signed his name "Boling," and his grandchildren spell their name "Boling."

VII. BOLING'S CAPTURE OF THE YOSEMITES

ANOTHER LETTER ABOUT SAVAGE'S BATTALION [8]

Subjoined is the last of the letters descriptive of the expedition of the State troops against the Indians. It is a letter from Captain Bowling to Colonel Barbour, Indian Commissioner:

FRESNO RIVER, May 29, 1851

SIR: You will no doubt have learned from my report of the 12th inst., to Major Savage, that we were at that time in close pursuit of the Yosemitie tribes of Indians, that in a slight brush with them we captured their famous chief, and that at this stage of the proceedings the further success of our proceedings was materially affected from the necessity of having to replenish our stock of provisions, which was at a distance of over one hundred miles from our encampment. Notwithstanding the number of our party being reduced to twenty-two men, by the absence of the detachments necessary to escort with safety the pack train, we continued the chase with such rapidity, that we forced a large portion of the Indians to take refuge in the plains with friendly Indians, while the remainder sought to conceal themselves among the rugged cliffs in the snowy regions of the Sierra Nevada.

Thus far I have made it a point to give as little alarm as possible. After capturing some of them I set a portion at liberty, in order that they might assure the others that if they come in they would not be harmed. Notwithstanding the treachery of the old chief, who contrived to lie and deceive us all the time, his grey hairs saved the boys from inflicting on him that justice which would have been administered under other circumstances. Having become satisfied that we could not persuade him to come in, I

8. *Daily Alta California*, San Francisco, June 14, 1851.

206

determined on hunting them, and if possible running them down, lest by leaving them in the mountains, they should form a new settlement and a place of refuge for other ill disposed Indians, who might do mischief and retreat to the mountains, and finally entice off those who are quiet and settled in the reserve. On the 20th the train of pack animals and provisions arrived, accompanied by a few more men than the party which went out after provisions, and Ponwatchi, the chief of the Nuch-tucs tribe with twelve of his warriors.

On the morning of the 21st we discovered the trail of a small party of Indians traveling in the direction of the Mono's country. We followed this trail until 2 o'clock next day, 22d when one of the scouting parties reported a rancheria near at hand. Almost at the same instant a spy was discovered watching our movements. We made chase after him immediately, and succeeded in catching him before he arrived at the rancheria, and we also succeeded in surrounding the ranch and capturing the whole of them. This chase in reality was not the source of amusement which it would seem to be when anticipated. Each man in the chase was stripped to his drawers, in which situation all hands ran at full speed at least four miles, some portion of the time over and through snow ten feet deep, and in the four mile heat all Ponwatchi gained on my boys was only distance enough to enable them to surround the rancheria while my men ran up in front. Two Indians strung their bows and seized their arrows, when they were told if they did not surrender they would be instantly killed.

They took the proper view of this precaution and immediately surrendered. The inquiry was made of those unfortunate people if they were then satisfied to go with us; their reply was, they were more than willing, as they could go to no other place. From all we could see and learn from those people we were then on the main range of the Sierra Nevada. The snow was in many places more than ten feet deep, and generally where it was deep the crust was sufficiently strong to bear a man's weight, which facilitated our traveling very much. Here there was a large lake completely frozen over, which had evidently not yet felt the influence of the spring season. The trail which we were bound to travel lay along the side of a steep mountain so slippery that it was difficult to get along barefoot without slipping and falling hundreds of yards. This place appeared to be their last resort or place where they considered themselves perfectly secure from the intrusion of the white man. In fact those people appear to look upon this place as their last home, composed of nature's own materials, unaided by the skill of man.

The conduct of Pon-watchi and his warriors during this expedition, entitled him and them to much credit. They performed important service voluntarily and cheerfully, making themselves generally useful, particularly in catching the scattered Indians after surprising a rancheria. Of the Yosemities, few, if any, are now left in the mountains. Our prisoners say they have all gone down to Cypriano's people.

It seems that their determined obstinacy is entirely attributable to the influence of their chief, whom we have a prisoner, among others of his tribe, and whom we intend to take care of. They have now been taught the double lesson, that the white man would not give up the chase without the game, and at the same time, if they would come down from the mountains and behave themselves, they would be kindly treated.

Since I have had those Indians in the service with me, and seen the interest they take in trying to bring all others to terms, taking into consideration the good faith in which they have acted, all the men with me who have been witnesses to their good conduct, are satisfied that if the general government furnishes them promptly, as agreed, and bad-disposed white men are kept from among them, peace and quiet will soon be restored and maintained by the Indians.

I have the honor to be, very respectfully,

Your most obed't serv't,
JOHN BOWLING, *Capt. Comp'y B*

TO COL. G. W. BARBOUR

VIII. CERTIFICATE OF DISBANDMENT
MARIPOSA BATTALION

AT THE CAMP OF DISBANDMENT [9]

June 29, 1851

I certify on honor, that the entire force of volunteers under command of Major James D. Savage, was honorably discharged on the evening of the aforesaid first day of July, 1851. By order of James D. Savage, Major Commanding. Pursuant to the previous order of his excellency, John McDougal.

Given under my hand,
M. B. LEWIS, *Mustering Officer*

The Camp of Disbandment was at Buckeye Creek, about halfway between Bridgeport and Mariposa.

IX. VIOLATION OF THE PEACE TREATY

SAN JOAQUIN NEWS [10] (BY TODD'S EXPRESS)

The *Stockton Journal* says that Maj. Fitzgerald arrived at that city last Sunday, with ninety dragoons from Benicia, and left the same day for the neighborhood of the Four Creeks. His object is to be present at the grand council of Indians summoned to meet on the 15th of this month, low down on the Tulare Valley, for the purpose of having a talk. This council was convoked by Dr. Wozencraft to adjust and settle the difficul-

---

9. From Elliott's *History of Fresno County*, 1881.
10. *Daily Alta California*, San Francisco, August 12, 1852.

ties between the whites and Indians, caused by the doings of a certain Mr. Harvey who recently attacked a rancheria of Indians and killed a number of them. The war belt has been sent to all the tribes, and a general spirit is exhibited by all Indians to join and prosecute a war against the whites. It is to avoid this melancholy result, as it surely would be deplorable, that Dr. Wozencraft has summoned this council of the Indians together. It is not to be denied that a few restless spirits in Mariposa county have fomented this state of things, by not only disregarding the treaties made with the Indians, but by also trampling on their acknowledged rights, and setting at naught every principle of justice and humanity.

CHRONOLOGY, WITH SOURCES

The following outline of the history of the Yosemite region cites the original sources of information used in preparing this book. References are to the pages of publications and manuscripts appearing in the bibliography which follows. Items cited frequently are abbreviated:

SCB   *Sierra Club Bulletin*, 1893 to date.

USNPS   *Annual Report*, United States National Park Service.

USWD   *Annual Report of the Chief of Engineers*, United States War Department.

YNN   *Yosemite Nature Notes*, Yosemite Natural History Association, 1922 to 1962.

YNP   *Report of the Acting Superintendent*, 1892-1914, Yosemite National Park.

YSR   *Yosemite Superintendent's Annual Report*, 1916-present, Yosemite National Park.

YVC   *Biennial Report*, Yosemite Valley Commissioners, 1867-1904.

   * Denotes change or addition by the editors.

1776

Garces entered Tulare Valley and named the interior range "Sierra de San Marcos." (Bancroft, 1884, p. 291; Farquhar, 1928, p. 56.)

Name "Sierra Nevada" applied to mountains that now carry the name, by Padre Pedro Font. (Font, map; Farquhar, 1928, p. 55.)

1806

Moraga Expedition explored lower course of Merced River and gave it the name "Merced." (Richman, p. 465; Farquhar, 1928, p. 58.)

1826

Jedediah Smith brought first party of trappers from the East. Crossed near Cajon Pass in November. (Dale, p. 183; Merriam, 1923, p. 228.)

1833

J. R. Walker crossed present Yosemite National Park with a party of trappers. (Leonard, Z., p. 174; Bancroft, 1885, p. 390; Farquhar, 1942, pp. 35-49; Watson, p. 57.)

1841

Bartleson party was first of immigrants. Crossed Sonora Pass and probably saw Calaveras Grove. (Bidwell, 1890; Bancroft, 1886, p. 268.)

1844

First wagons brought across the Sierra by Stephens-Townsend-Murphy party. (Bancroft, 1886, p. 445.)

1847

J. B. Alvarado conveyed "Mariposa Grant" to J. C. Frémont for $3,000. (California Supreme Court.)

1848

Sierra gold discovery. (Tinkham, p. 59.)

1849

William Penn Abrams and U. N. Reamer looked down into Yosemite Valley from southwestern rim. (SCB, 1947.)*

1850

Rush to "Southern Mines" (Mariposa region). (Bunnell, 1880, p. 315.)

Tuolumne County organized. (Coy, 1923, p. 288.)

Mariposa County established. (Coy, 1923, p. 161.)

Joseph Screech discovered Hetch Hetchy Valley. (Hoffmann, p. 370.)

J. D. Savage forced to abandon trading station at mouth of South Fork of Merced. (Bunnell, 1880, p. 15.)

Indians attack Savage's Fresno River store and his Mariposa Creek Station, Dec. (Bunnell, 1880, pp. 22, 23.)

1851

Mariposa Battalion organized at Agua Fria under James Savage, Feb. 12. (Eccleston, p. 26—see Annotation "b," page 177; Bunnell, 1880, p. 29.)*

Battalion left Camp Frémont, March 19. (Eccleston, p. 45—see Annotation "b," page 177.)*

Battalion met 72 Yosemite Indians coming in to surrender; obtained first view of Yosemite Valley at Inspiration Point; camped in Bridalveil Meadow; name "Yosemite Valley" applied, March 27. (Eccleston, p. 48—see Annotation "b," page 177; Bunnell, 1880, pp. 43-56; Marvin.)*

Battalion explored Valley; found no Indians except an elderly woman; squad discovered Vernal and Nevada Falls, March 28. (Eccleston, p. 48—see Annotation "b," page 177; Bunnell, 1880, pp. 72-85; Marvin.)*

Battalion withdrew from Valley after destroying acorn stores, March 29. (Eccleston, p. 48—see Annotation "b," page 177; Bunnell, 1880, p. 91; Marvin.)*

Second entry to Yosemite made by Capt. John Boling's Company, May 9. (Bunnell, 1880, p. 142; Boling, June 12; Kuykendall, p. 9.)

First letter dispatched from valley, May 15. (Boling, June 12; Kuykendall, p. 9.)

Boling captured band of Yosemite Indians at Tenaya Lake, May 22. (Boling, June 14; Bunnell, 1880, p. 230; Kuykendall, p. 10.)*

Indians escorted to Fresno Reservation. (Bunnell, 1880, p. 238.)*

Tenaya and family allowed to return to Yosemite during winter. (Bunnell, 1880, p. 273.)*

1852

Eight prospectors entered valley in May, and two or three were killed by Indians. (Bunnell, 1880, p. 247.)

Lt. Tredwell Moore entered Yosemite with detachment of 2d Infantry in June. (Bunnell, 1880, p. 275; Elliott, p. 172; Hutchings, 1862, p. 75.)

Yosemite Indians took refuge with Mono Indians and were not found by soldiers. (Elliott, p. 172.)

In August Lt. Moore found promising mineral deposits east of Sierra crest. (Bunnell, 1880, p. 277.)

Mariposa Grove discovered by party of prospectors. (Elliott, p. 172; Russell, 1926, p. 332; YNN, 1929, p. 51.)

1853

Yosemite Indians left Monos and returned to Yosemite, but stole horses, and Monos nearly annihilated the Yosemites for their treachery. (Bunnell, 1880, pp. 275, 291; Hutchings, 1862, p. 75. Eyewitness account at variance with Bunnell's - see page 46 of this book.)

Two parties of prospectors entered Yosemite Valley in the fall of 1853. (Bunnell, 1880, p. 295.)*

1854

James Capen Adams visited Yosemite to capture grizzlies, which he trained. (Hittell, T. H., 1860, p. 196.)

1855

J. M. Hutchings organized first party of sightseers to enter Yosemite. First Yosemite sketches made by Thomas A. Ayres in July. (Hutchings diary, 1855.)*

Trail from Mormon Bar built to Yosemite Valley by Milton, Houston, and Andrew Mann. Finished in 1856. (Bunnell, 1880, p. 304; Brockman, 1943, pp. 53-54.)*

Galen Clark engaged in surveying ditch to supply water to Mariposa Frémont Grant. (Foley, p. 108.)

First house, a shack with no roof, built in Yosemite Valley by surveyors, including Bunnell. (Bunnell, 1880, p. 304.)*

1856

"Coulterville Free Trail" from Bull Creek to Yosemite built by G. W. Coulter and Bunnell. (Bunnell, 1880, p. 315.)

T. A. Ayres made second trip to Yosemite and made more pencil drawings. (Bunnell, 1880, p. 310; Farquhar, 1926, p. 111; Ayres.)

"Lower Hotel," first permanent structure, built by Walworth and Hite at base of Sentinel Rock. (Bunnell, 1880, p. 309.)

1857

Rush of miners from Tuolumne, over Mono Trail, to Mono Diggings; Tom McGee, of Big Oak Flat, blazed open part of old Mono Trail. (*Bodie Standard*, March 1, 1879; Wasson; Hodgdon.)*

Beardsley and Hite put up canvas-covered house at later Cedar Cottage site. (Bunnell, 1880, p. 310.)*

Galen Clark provided overnight stop for tourists at Clark's Station on site of present Wawona Hotel, and with Milton Mann explored Mariposa Grove. (Sargent, Shirley, *Galen Clark, Yosemite Guardian*, 1964, p. 57.)*

1858

"Upper Hotel" (Cedar Cottage) built. Operated by Mr. and Mrs. John H. Neal. (Bunnell, 1880, p. 310; Hutchings, 1886, p. 101.)

J. L. Cogswell party visited Tuolumne Grove of Big Trees. (YNN, 1937, pp. 60-63.)

1859

W. S. Body located mineral deposits in region that later became famous as Bodie. (Wasson, p. 5.)

First photographs made in Yosemite by C. L. Weed. (Hutchings, 1886, p. 101.)*

James C. Lamon preempted claim and took up summer residence in Yosemite Valley. Recorded claim on May 17, 1861. (Mariposa County Records, Land Claims K, p. 63; Hutchings, 1886, p. 136.)*

1860

"Sheepherder Mine" (Tioga Mine) located. (*Bodie Daily Free Press*, September 10, 1881.)

California State Geological Survey established, with Prof. Josiah Dwight Whitney in charge. (Whitney, 1865, p. ix; Farquhar, March, 1925, pp. 15-23.)

1861

Nine Bactrian camels taken to Nevada mines. Stopped in Calaveras Grove en route. (Farquhar, March, 1925, p. 26.)

C. E. Watkins, pioneer photographer, visited Yosemite Valley. (YNN, 1936, pp. 17-18.)

1862

James Lamon took up permanent residence and spent first winter in Yosemite entirely alone (1862-63). (Hutchings, 1886, p. 135.)*

1863

State Geological Survey made expedition to region between upper Merced and Tuolumne rivers. (Whitney, J.D., 1865, p. 13.)

Artist Albert Bierstadt made first trip to Yosemite. (YNN, 1944, pp. 49-51.)

1864

J. M. Hutchings took over Upper Hotel, and it became known as "Hutchings House." (Calif. Legis., p. 323; Hutchings, 1886, p. 102.)

Sonora Pass wagon road improved to serve Bodie, etc. (Wasson, p. 59.)

Florence Hutchings was the first white child to be born in Yosemite. (Hutchings, 1886, p. 144.)

I. W. Raymond, of Central American Steamship Transit Co., New York City, advocated to Senator Conness of California that the Yosemite Valley and the Mariposa Grove be reserved as a State Grant for public enjoyment. The members of a proposed board of commissioners were recommended by Raymond and Conness jointly. (Raymond, 1864; Farquhar, 1926, p. 77.)

Yosemite Valley and Mariposa Big Trees granted to California as public trust on June 30. Grant contained 60.4 square miles. Board of eight commissioners created, Frederick Law Olmsted, chairman. (U. S. Congress, 1864, p. 3444; YVC, 1877, p. 5; Matthews, 1906, pp. 382-387; YNN, 1946, p. 107.)*

1866

First appropriation made for administration of Yosemite Grant. (*Calif. Statutes*; YVC, p. 7.)

Galen Clark appointed first guardian, May 21. (Sargent, Shirley, *Galen Clark, Yosemite Guardian*, 1964, p. 70.)*

1868

John Muir made his first trip to Yosemite. (Badè, 1924, I: 185; YNN, 1938; Wolfe, 1945, pp. 117-122.)

1869

George F. Leidig built "Leidig's Hotel" near Lower Hotel. (Churchill, 1876, p. 138; Vivian, p. 376; Calif. Legis., pp. 164, 208, 210; Leidig; YNN, 1930, p. 4.)

Mr. and Mrs. A. G. Black removed Lower Hotel and built "Black's Hotel" on its site. (Hutchings, 1886, p. 101.)

Edwin Moore acquired half interest in Clark's Station, and it became known as "Clark & Moore's." (Ellsworth, p. 44; Greenwood, p. 313; Lester, Boston, p. 170.)

Mountain View House (Peregoy's) built on Wawona-Yosemite Valley trail. (YNN, 1929, p. 71.)

Central Pacific built from Sacramento to Stockton. (Ingram.)

1870

Albert Snow built trail to flat between Vernal and Nevada falls. (Calif. Legis., p. 170; Minturn, p. 264; Lester, Boston, p. 197.)

Central Pacific built to Modesto. (Ingram.)

Copperopolis branch of Central Pacific built. (Ingram.)

Joseph LeConte made his first trip to Yosemite. (LeConte, 1903, p. 247.)

La Casa Nevada was built by Albert Snow above Vernal Fall. (Buckley, p. 25; YNN, 1930, p. 4.)

John Muir explored the Grand Canyon of the Tuolumne. (SCB, 1924; Farquhar, 1926, pp. 96-97.)

1871

Peregoy built a stopping place at Glacier Point. (Peregoy Hotel Register.)

John Conway built trail from La Casa Nevada to Little Yosemite; he attempted the ascent of Half Dome. (Russell, 1926, p. 340.)

Central Pacific built to Berenda. (Ingram.)

Conway started work on Four Mile Trail to Glacier Point (completed in 1872). (Russell, 1926, p. 340; Kneeland, p. 82.)

J. C. Smith opened his Cosmopolitan bath house and saloon, May 1. (*Sonora Union Democrat*, Nov. 5, 1870.)*

Mount Lyell climbed by J. B. Tileston, Aug. 29 (first ascent). (Tileston, pp. 89-90.)

1872

Central Pacific built to Merced. (Ingram.)

Stage road built on north side of Yosemite Valley by Conway. (Calif. Legis., p. 198; Russell, 1926, p. 340.)

Earthquake in Yosemite. (Kneeland, p. 88.)

Harlow Street erected telegraph line from Sonora to Yosemite Valley. A line was built from Yosemite to Bodie also. (*Bodie Daily Free Press*, January 29, 1881; Hutchings, 1886, p. 358; Morris, Paul.)

1873

Eagle Peak Trail built to foot of Upper Yosemite Fall by Conway. (Russell, 1926, p. 340.)

1874

Coulterville Road built to valley floor. (Know as "J.T McLean's Road.") (Hutchings, 1886, p. 288; U.S. Senate; YNN, 1930, pp. 73-74; 1943, pp. 59-60.)

Big Oak Flat route completed to Yosemite Valley by Yosemite Turnpike and Road Company. (Hutchings, 1886, p. 335; U.S. Senate; YNN, 1943, p. 60.)

Wood road built from "Hutchings" up the south side of the valley. (Calif. Legis., p. 340.)

State of California purchased private claims in Yosemite Valley. (Calif. Legis., p. 351; YVC, 1877-78, p. 16.)

1875

George W. Coulter and A.J. Murphy leased former Hutchings property. (YVC, 1877-78, p. 10.)

Wawona Road built to floor of Yosemite Valley. (U.S. Senate; YVC, 1874-75; YNN, 1943, pp. 60-61.)

George G. Anderson made first ascent of Half Dome. (Hutchings, 1886, p. 457; Leonard, R.M., et. al., 1937, p. 40.)

Public School provided for Yosemite. (Mariposa County, May, 1875; YNP, 1909, p. 10; Hutchings, 1886, p. 355.)

Washburn Brothers purchased Clark & Moore's. Place has been called "Wawona" since 1882. (Vivian, p. 370; Stornoway, p. 72.)*

1876

Sentinel Hotel built by Coulter and Murphy. Known as Yosemite Falls Hotel for many years. (Calif. Legis., p. 238; Jones.)

John Muir's first article on devastation of Sierra by sheep was published. (Farquhar, March, 1925, p. 30; Badè, 1923-24, 2: 58-59.)

Mountain House built at Glacier Point. (*Mariposa Gazette*, 1876.)*

1877

J.K. Barnard took over "Coulter and Murphy's" (Sentinel Hotel). (Blake, p. 119; YVC, 1877-78, p. 14; Jones.)

1878

John L. Murphy settled at Tenaya Lake (exact date doubtful). (Jackson, pp. 109-171; Hutchings, 1886, p. 481.)

High Sierra country surveyed by Lieut. M.M. Macomb of Wheeler Survey. (USWD.)

Bodie and Lundy mining excitement reached height. Tioga came into prominence. (*Bodie Daily Free Press*, Dec. 29, 1880; Whitney, H.A.)

A. Harris established first public campgrounds in Yosemite Valley. (Harris Register; Calif. Legis., p. 232; Hutchings, 1886, p. 355.)

Tunnel in Big Tree of Tuolumne Grove made in June. (Marshall, p. 341.)

1879

Homer District (Lundy) organized. Was discovered by C.H. Nye. (*Mammoth City Herald*, Sept. 24, 1879; *Homer Mining Index*, 1880.)

Yosemite chapel built by Sunday School Union. (Hutchings, 1886, p. 355; Glass, pp. 114-118.)

1880

Legislation ousted Board of Yosemite Commissioners. New board appointed J.M. Hutchings guardian. (YVC, 1880, p. 3.)

Charles D. Robinson, artist, maintained studio in the valley (1880-1890). (YNN, 1944, pp. 38-40.)

L.H. Bunnell, of Yosemite discovery party, published *Discovery of the Yosemite.*

1881

Silver found on Mount Hoffmann. Mount Hoffmann Mining District organized, but amounted to nothing. (YNN, 1925, p. 83.)

Tunnel cut through Wawona Tree. (YNN, 1925, p. 83.)

1882

"Anderson Trail" (Happy Isles to bridge below Vernal Fall) built. (Calif. Legis., pp. 311, 367; YVC, 1880-82, p. 5.)

Construction of Tioga Road started. (Completed in 1883 at cost of $62,000.) (Calif. State Mineralogist; U.S. Senate.)

Great Sierra Consolidated Silver Mining Company (Tioga Mine) incorporated. (Calif. State Mineralogist.)

John Conway built road to Glacier Point. (Conway.)

1883

Former President Rutherford Hayes with party of twelve visited Yosemite Valley.*

1884

Tioga Mine closed after expenditure of $300,000 and no production. (Calif. State Mineralogist.)

Mr. and Mrs. John Degnan established bakery and store, the oldest business among Yosemite concessions. (USNPS, 1941, p. 9; Degnan, p. 1.)

Hutchings removed as guardian, and W.E. Dennison appointed. (YVC, 1883-84, p. 14.)

1885

Legislature appropriated $40,000 to build Stoneman House. (YVC, 1885-86, p. 6.)

John B. Lembert took up homestead in Tuolumne Meadows. (Stornoway, p. 64; Farquhar, March, 1925, pp. 40-41; YNP, 1903, p. 23.)

"Echo Wall Trail" (Nevada Fall to Glacier Point) built. (YVC, 1885-86, p. 9.)

Log Cabin built in Mariposa Grove. (YVC, 1885-86, p. 10.)

1886

John L. Murphy preempted 160 acres at Tenaya Lake. (YNP, 1903, p. 23.)

1887

Mark L. McCord made guardian. (YVC, 1887-88.)

A tramway to Glacier Point considered and surveyed. (Calif. Legis., p. 341.)

1888

Stoneman House leased to J.J. Cook. (YVC, 1887-88, p. 14; Calif. Legis., pp. 263, 336; Stornoway, p. 24.)

Commissioners removed Black's and Leidig's hotels. (Calif. Legis., p. 210; YVC, 1887-88, p. 17.)

1889

Galen Clark again made guardian. (YVC, 1889-90, p. 5.)

Mirror Lake dam built to increase area of lake. (YVC, 1889-90, p. 5.)

1890

Reserved forest lands totalling 1,452 square miles, later to be called Yosemite National Park, created Oct. 1. John Muir's writings were instrumental in bringing this about. (YVC, 1889-90, p. 27.)*

1891

Capt. A.E. Wood, first Acting Superintendent, arrived with federal troops to administer park, May 19; headquarters at Wawona. (YNP, 1891, p. 3; YNN, 1944, p. 54.)

First telephones installed in Yosemite Valley. (YVC, 1891-92, p. 6.)

1892

Sierra Club organized, with John Muir as president, to aid effort to secure federal administration of entire Yosemite region. (SCB, 1893.)

First plant of trout (rainbow) made in Yosemite by California Fish and Game Commission. (YNP, 1893, p. 8; YNN, 1934, p. 58.)

1893

Sierra Forest Reservation established, Feb. (SCB, 1896, pp. 257-259.)

1894

Capt. G.H.G. Gale made Acting Superintendent. (YNP, 1894.)

1895

Capt. Alex Rodgers appointed Acting Superintendent. (YNP, 1895.)

Wawona fish hatchery erected. Operated by state. (YNP, 1895, p. 5.)

1896

Stoneman House destroyed by fire, Aug. 24. (YVC, 1895-96, p. 9.)

Lt. Col. S.B.M. Young appointed

Acting Superintendent. (YNP, 1896; Farquhar, 1926, p. 109.)

First effort made to keep firearms out of park. (YNP, 1896, p. 4.)

Galen Clark resigned as guardian, Oct. 19. (Sargent, Shirley, *Galen Clark, Yosemite Guardian*, 1964, p. 150.)*

1897

Miles Wallace made guardian. (YVC, 1897-98.)

Wooden stairs at Vernal Fall removed and replaced by rock steps. (YVC, 1897-98, p. 6.)

Capt. Alex Rodgers again made Acting Superintendent. (YNP, 1897.)

1898

Camps rented to visitors by state. (YVC, 1897-98, p. 5.)

Archie O. Leonard, first civilian park ranger. (YVC, 1897-98, p. 12; YNP, 1898, p. 3.)

Both J.W. Zevely, special inspector, and Capt. J.E. Caine were Acting Superintendents. (YNP, 1898.)

1899

Lt. Wm. Forse and Capt. E.F. Wilcox were Acting Superintendents. (YNP, 1899.)

Curry Camping Company established. (Tresidder, D.B.; Tresidder, M.C., MS;

YNP, 1908, p. 12.)

Chris Jorgensen maintained artist's studio in the valley (1899-1918). (YNN, 1944, pp. 94-97.)

1900

Major L.J. Rucker, Acting Superintendent. (YNP, 1900.)

Oliver Lippincott drove first automobile into Yosemite, June 23. (Johnston, Hank, *Yosemite's Yesterday's*, 1989, pp. 7-9.)*

1901

Camp Yosemite (Lost Arrow) established. (YVC, 1901-02, p. 6; YNP, 1908, p. 12; 1910, p. 12; Tresidder, D.B., p. 35.)

Major L.A. Craig, Acting Superintendent. (YNP, 1901.)

First of the annual outings of the Sierra Club took place in Tuolumne Meadows. (Farquhar, March, 1925, pp. 52-53.)

1902

Power plant at Happy Isles built by state. (YVC, 1901-02, p. 4.)

Major O.L. Hein, Acting Superintendent. (YNP, 1902.)

J.M. Hutchings killed on Big Oak Flat Road near Yosemite Valley, Oct. 31. (Foley, p. 6; Godfrey, 1941, MS, p. 14.)

Harry Cassie Best established artist studio in valley. (Maintained business until his death, 1936.) (YNN, 1945, pp. 42-44.)

1903

LeConte Memorial Lodge built in Yosemite Valley by Sierra Club. (SCB, 1904, pp. 66-69; 1905, pp. 176-180.)

San Francisco's first application for use of Hetch Hetchy denied by Secretary Hitchcock. (U.S. Dept. of Interior, 1908, 1910, 1914.)

George T. Harlow, guardian. (YVC, 1903-04.)

U.S. Weather Bureau installed instruments in Yosemite. (YVC, 1903-04, p. 7.)

Lt. Col. Jos. Garrard, Acting Superintendent. (YNP, 1903.)

John Muir, Theodore Roosevelt, and Gov. George C. Pardee discuss Yosemite Grant recession in Yosemite. (Badè, 1923-1924, 2: 355.)

1904

Major John Bigelow became Acting Superintendent. (YNP, 1904.)

Arboretum established, and first plans for a Yosemite Museum made at Wawona. (YNP, 1904, p. 20; YNN, 1930, pp. 17-18.)

1905

Area of Yosemite National Park reduced. Mount Ritter region and Devils Postpile eliminated. (Yosemite Park Commission; YNP, 1905, p. 5; 1906, p. 8.)

Capt. H.C. Benson, Acting Superintendent. (YNP, 1905; SCB, 1925, pp. 175-179.)

1906

Yosemite Valley and Mariposa Grove re-ceded to United States. Superintendent's headquarters (Major H.C. Benson) moved to Yosemite Valley. (YNP, 1905, pp. 5-6; 1906, p. 6; Badè, 1923-1924, 2: 355; Colby, 1938, pp. 11-19.)*

1907

Yosemite Valley Railroad opened to travel. Del Portal, the railroad hotel at El Portal, shown in Williams, p. 143. (YNP, 1907, p. 5; Radcliffe; Bartlet.)

Extensive telephone system installed in park. (YNP, 1907, p. 8.)

Yosemite cemetery given permanent marking with boundary of trees. (YNN, 1932, pp. 1-4.)

Automobiles banned from Yosemite National Park by Acting Superintendent Major H.C. Benson, June. (*Mariposa Gazette*.)*

1908

Hetch Hetchy rights granted to San Francisco. (YNP, 1908, p. 14.)

Camp Ahwahnee established at foot of Sentinel Rock by W.M. Sell. (YNP, 1908, pp 11,12; Tresidder, D.B., p. 37.)

Pacific Telephone and Telegraph Co. built telegraph line from El Portal to Sentinel Hotel. (YNP, 1908, p. 9.)

Supervisor Gabriel Sovulewski, Acting Superintendent, Oct. 25 (to April 27, 1909). (YNP, 1909, p. 5.)

1909

Major W.W. Forsyth, Acting Superintendent. (YNP, 1909.)

1910

Death of Galen Clark, March 24, age 96. (YNP, 1910, p. 15; 1911, p. 8.)

1911

Tenaya Lake Trail completed. (YNP, 1910, p. 10; 1911, p. 8.)

Devils Postpile made a national monument by President Taft. (SCB, 1912, pp. 170-173, 226-227.)

Galen Clark Memorial Seat built. (YNP, 1911, p. 12.)

1912

Yosemite hospital built by U.S. troops. (YNP, 1912, p. 12; Tresidder, D.B., p. 157.)

Sierra Club purchased Soda Springs property at Tuolumne Meadows. (Farquhar, 1926, p. 58.)

1913

Major William T. Littebrant, Acting Superintendent. (YNP, 1913.)

Automobiles admitted to Yosemite Valley. (YNP, 1913, p. 12.)

Raker Act authorized use of Hetch Hetchy Valley as reservoir; approved by President Wilson, Dec. 19. (Farquhar, 1926, p. 39; Johnson, R.U., pp. 307-313; Wolfe, 1945, pp. 339-346.)

1914

Civilian employees replaced the military in administration of Yosemite. Mark Daniels, first superintendent. (USNPS, 1916, p. 4; Calif. State Mineralogist, p. 61.)

Museum of Vertebrate Zoology, University of California, began 5-year field study of animal life in Yosemite, which culminated in publication of 752-page treatise. (Grinnell and Storer; YNN, 1924, p. 2.)

John Muir died in a Los Angeles hospital, December 24. (Badè, 1923-1924, 2: 390-391.)

1915

Parsons Lodge built by Sierra Club in Tuolumne Meadows. (SCB, 1916, pp. 84-85.)

First appropriation for the John Muir Trail approved by Governor Johnson. (Rensch, 1933, p. 484; Wolfe, 1945, p. 364.)

Yosemite Lodge established in Yosemite Valley. (Tresidder, D.B., p. 37.)

Stephen T. Mather purchased Tioga Road and presented it to U.S. Government. (Farquhar, 1926, p. 94.)

Mather became assistant to Franklin K. Lane, Secretary of the Interior. (Albright, 1929, pp. 10-11; Cramton, 1929, p. 13.)

Yosemite horse-drawn stages replaced by motor stages. (Tresidder, D.B., p. 33.)

R.B. Marshall made superintendent of all national parks. (USNPS, 1916, p. 5.)

1916

National Park Service Act passed August 25. Stephen T. Mather made Director. (USNPS, 1916, p. 81; 1917, p. 1; Farquhar, 1926, p. 63.)

W.B. Lewis made Superintendent of Yosemite National Park. (USNPS, 1916; Farquhar, 1926, p. 114.)

Tuolumne Meadows Lodge installed; also Tenaya and Merced Lake camps opened. (Tresidder, D.B., p. 76.)

1917

Glacier Point Hotel completed. (USNPS, 1917, p. 59; Tresidder, D.B., p. 61.)

Wawona Road and Glacier Point

Branch turned over to federal government. (USNPS, 1917, p. 62.)

Parts of park opened to grazing. (USNPS, 1917, p. 153.)

Modern school buildings constructed. (USNPS, 1920, p. 237.)

David A. Curry dies; Mrs. Curry continues operation of Camp Curry. (Tresidder, Mary C., MS.)

1918

Cascade power plant completed at cost of $215,000. (USNPS, 1917, pp. 61, 143; 1919, pp. 45, 134.)

Ledge Trail built to Glacier Point. (USNPS, 1918, p. 47.)

1919

First airplane landed in Yosemite Valley, May 27. Lt. J.S. Krull, pilot, alone. (USNPS, 1919, pp. 183, 190.)

LeConte Memorial Lectures instituted. (USNPS, 1919, p. 194.)

1920

Construction started on all-year highway up Merced Canyon. (USNPS, 1920, p. 110.)

Rangers' Club House built. (USNPS, 1920, p. 250.)

Yosemite National Park Co. founded. (USNPS, 1920, p. 248.)

Yosemite educational work started by H.C. Bryant, A.F. Hall, L.H. Miller, and Enid Michael. Yosemite Museum planned. (USNPS, 1920, pp. 113, 245, 253; Hall, 1930; YNN, 1932, pp. 2-3.)

California valley elk brought to Yosemite. (USNPS, 1920, p. 250; 1921, p. 196.)

Big Trees Lodge built at Mariposa Grove. (Tresidder, D.B., p. 72.)

1921

First Yosemite Museum installations made. (USNPS, 1921, pp. 72, 196, 202; Yosemite Park Naturalist, July, 1921; Hall, 1930.)

1922

Yosemite Educational Department created. (USNPS, 1922, pp. 113, 115; 1923, p. 20.)

Yosemite Nature Notes first published (mimeographed through 1924, then printed). (YNN, 1925, p. 1.)

1923

Hikers' camps installed. (USNPS, 1923, p. 54; 1924, pp. 37, 109; YNN, 1923; Tresidder, D.B., p. 80; Adams, 1940, pp. 79-83; Russell, 1925.)

Educational Department for all national parks created. (Yosemite Park Naturalist; USNPS, 1923, p. 20; 1925, p. 10; 1926, p. 7; Burns, N.J., pp. 4-25.)

1924

Hoof and mouth disease epidemic in Yosemite deer. (USNPS, 1924, pp. 36, 108; 1925, pp. 6, 93; 1926, p. 14.)

New administration center and village developed. (USNPS, 1924, pp. 37, 108; 1925, p. 87.)

1925

Yosemite Park and Curry Co. formed by consolidation of Curry Camping Co. and Yosemite National Park Co. (Tresidder, D.B., p. 37; UPNPS, 1925,p. 27.)

Yosemite School of Field Natural History organized. (USNPS, 1925, pp. 11, 90; YNN, 1925, pp. 9-10, 16, 66.)

Glacier Point branch of Yosemite Museum opened. (Yosemite Park Naturalist, June, 1925; YNN, 1925, p. 55.)

1926

All-year highway dedicated July 31. (USNPS, 1926, pp. 30, 102.)

Yosemite Museum opened, May 29. (USNPS, 1924, pp. 8, 105; 1925, pp. 12, 89; 1926, pp. 31, 99; YNN, 1924; 1926, p. 95.)

1927

Ahwahnee Hotel opened by Yosemite Park and Curry Co. (USNPS, 1926, pp. 31, 101.)

1928

Board of expert advisors, Frederick Law Olmsted, Duncan McDuffie, and John P. Buwalda, appointed by authority of Congress to study and assist in the solution of Yosemite problems. (USNPS, 1928, p. 173.)

Maria Lebrado, one of the last of the original Yosemite Indians, gives first-hand account of Yosemite Valley discovery. (YNN, 1928, pp. 41-46; 1929, pp. 69-70, 85-86.)

Wildlife research in national parks instituted by George M. Wright, of Yosemite naturalist organization. (YNN, 1929, p. 66; Russell, 1939, p. 10; Wright, Dixon, and Thompson.)

W.B. Lewis transferred to Washington; became Assistant Director, National Park Service. E.P. Leavitt designated Acting Superintendent. (YSR, 1929.)

1929

A hospital, which after the death of Assistant Director Lewis, 1930, was named the W.B. Lewis Memorial Hospital, was constructed in Yosemite Valley at cost of $50,000. (USNPS, 1929, p. 144.)

Col. C.G. Thomson appointed Superintendent. (YSR, 1929.)

1930

Stephen T. Mather dies, January 22. (Story.)

"Live Indian Exhibit" instituted on Yosemite Museum grounds; project made possible by the cooperation of the Yosemite Natural History Association. Maggie Howard, "Ta-bu-ce" of the Monos, was engaged to demonstrate modes of Indian life. (USNPS, 1930, p. 168; YNN, 1933, pp. 14-16.)

Sugar pine forest on west side of park acquired through private gift and government appropriation. (YNN, 1930, pp. 65-66.)

W.B. Lewis died August 28 in Chevy Chase, Maryland. (USNPS, 1931.)

High Sierra snow surveys organized on consolidated basis. (Brockman, 1946, pp. 105-109; YNN, 1927, p. 19; Russell, 1928, pp. 36-38.)

1931

Marjorie Montgomery Ward presented $4,000 with which to develop a living exhibit of native flowers at the rear of the Yosemite Museum. (USNPS, 1931; YNN, 1931, p. 64; 1932, pp. 4-5.)

Research Reserves established (White Mountain, Boundary Hill, and Swamp Lake). (USNPS, Master Plan, 1942, Sheet 7, map; YNN, 1927, pp. 46-48.)

Glacier measurements instituted in the Yosemite High Sierra. (YNN, 1934, pp. 44-46; 1935, pp. 93-96; 1942, pp. 89-91.)

1932

Wawona Basin, 8,785 acres, added to

Yosemite National Park. Half of the funds required were donated; the Department of Interior was authorized by Congress to match the donation with federal funds. (USNPS, 1932, p. 61.)

Mariposa Grove Museum established. (USNPS, 1932, p. 63; YNN, 1932, p. 4.)

Big Trees Lodge constructed in Mariposa Grove at Sunset Point. Earlier tent camp eliminated from upper grove. (USNPS, 1932, p. 64.)

Cosmopolitan House, built in 1870-71, destroyed by fire, Dec. 8. (YNN, 1933, pp. 1-2.)

Sierra Club Rock Climbing Section organized. (Leonard, R.M., 1938, p. ii.)

1933

Devils Postpile National Monument placed under supervision of the superintendent, Yosemite National Park. (YNN, 1935, pp. 45-57.)

Tule elk herd (27 animals) removed from Yosemite Valley to Owens Valley, east of Sierra. (YNN, 1933, pp. 107-109.)

Arno B. Cammerer made Director of National Park Service upon resignation of Horace M. Albright. (USNPS, 1933, p. 153.)

Wawona Road and tunnel dedicated June 10, 1933. (YSR, 1933, p. 1.)

"Emergency programs," C.C.C., C.W.A., and P.W.A. advanced the construction and management projects of the park. Five C.C.C. camps were established at Wawona, Crane Flat, and Eleven Mile Meadow. (YSR, 1933, pp. 26-32.)

1934

First ascent of Higher Cathedral Spire, April 15; Lower Cathedral Spire, August 25. (Leonard, R.M., 1934, p. 178.)

Hetch Hetchy water flows into San Francisco. (YNN, 1934, pp. 89-91; YSR, 1935, pp. 11-12.)

Radio replaced mountain telephone lines in Yosemite administration. (YSR, 1934, p. 11.)

Outdoor church bowl in Yosemite Valley improved by C.C.C. (YSR, 1934.)

1935

Ski house built at Badger Pass by Yosemite Park and Curry Co. (YSR, 1936, p. 6.)

1936

Thomas Moran art collection acquired by the Yosemite Museum. (YSR, 1936, p. 4; YNN, 1936, pp. 57-64, pp. 64-68.)

Yosemite Museum acquired 198 oil and water-color paintings by the Yosemite artist, Chris Jorgensen. (YSR, 1937, p. 7.)

First ski ascent of Mount Lyell, March 2, by Bestor Robinson, David R. Brower, Lewis F. Clark, Boynton S. Kaiser, and Einar Nilsson. (Brower, 1938, pp. 40-45.)

Harry Cassie Best dies in San Francisco, October 14. Virgina Best Adams and Ansel Adams take over operation of Best Studio, Yosemite Valley. (YNN, 1936, p. 88a, back cover; 1945, p. 44.)

1937

Lawrence C. Merriam appointed to superintendency in June following death of C.G. Thomson. (YSR, 1937, p. 2; YNN, 1937, pp. 36-38.)

1938

Hetch Hetchy Dam enlarged by addition of 85 feet to its height. (YSR, 1938, p. 9.)

Tenaya Lake High Sierra Camp removed and new camp established at May Lake. (YSR, 1938, p. 14.)

President Franklin D. Roosevelt visited Yosemite Valley and Mariposa Grove, July 15. (YSR, 1939, p. 6.)

Sentinel Hotel, River Cottage, and Ivy Cottage torn down in December. (YNN, 1939, p. 21.)

Gabriel Sovulewski died Nov. 29. (YSR, 1939, p. 11.)

1939

Vegetation type map of the park prepared by Branch of Forestry, National Park Service. (USNPS, Master Plan, 1942, two maps and key.)

Newton B. Drury appointed to Yosemite Advisory Board, Feb. 24. (YSR, 1939, p. 10.)

1940

Newton B. Drury appointed Director of the National Park Service in June, when Arno B. Cammerer requested that he be relieved of his duties as Director for reasons of health. (USNPS, 1940, p. 204.)

Tioga Road, Crane Flat to McSwain Meadows, and Big Oak Flat Road, from Crane Flat to El Portal Road, constructed on modern standards; opened with ceremonies, June 23. (YSR, 1940, p. 1; USNPS, Master Plan, 1942.)

Cedar Cottage (Upper Hotel) and Oak Cottage razed. (YSR, 1941, pp. 3-4; 1942, p. 6.)

C.A. Harwell vacated the Yosemite Park Naturalist position, Sept. 7. (YNN, 1941, p. 37.)

Ski-touring accommodations in the form of a rock ski hut provided at Ostrander Lake, under slopes of Horse Ridge. (YSR, 1941, p. 2.)*

William E. Colby appointed to membership on Yosemite Advisory Board effective November 15. (Maulding, Mrs. J. Atwood.)

Mrs. John Degnan, pioneer park operator, died Dec. 15. (YSR, 1941, p. 9.)

1941

Arno B. Cammerer, Director of National Park Service, 1933-1940, died April 30. (USNPS, 1942.)

C. Frank Brockman appointed Yosemite Park Naturalist, March 27. (YNN, 1941, p. 37.)

Bear-feeding programs in Yosemite Valley discontinued. (YSR, 1941, p. 3.)

Superintendent Lawrence C. Merriam appointed Regional Director, National Park Service, Region Two (Omaha, Nebraska), July 31. Frank A. Kittredge transferred from Grand Canyon National Park to the Yosemite superintendency, August 1. (YSR, 1942, pp. 1-5.)

Cosie Hutchings Mills visited Yosemite Valley, Aug. 20, after absence of 42 years. (YNN, 1941, p. 111; 1942, pp. 37-40.)

1942

Yosemite School of Field Natural History and Junior Nature School discontinued for duration of war. (YNN, 1942, p. 30; YSR, 1942, p. 7.)

Activities of C.C.C. in Yosemite National Park discontinued in July. (YSR, 1943, p. 1.)

U.S. Army Signal Corps utilized National Park Service facilities at Wawona and Badger Pass as special training schools. (YSR, 1943, p. 1; 1944, pp. 1-2; 1945, p. 2.)

Armed-forces men who came to Yosemite National Park for recreation or conditioning totaled 23,272 in the fiscal year ending June 30. (This total reached 89,686 during the war years.) (YSR, 1943, p. 1; 1944, p. 2.)

J.N. LeConte appointed Collaborator, Yosemite Advisory Board. (YSR, 1943, p. 2.)

1943

Ranger-naturalist program discontinued as a war measure. (YNN, 1943, pp. 46-47.)

Death of Dr. H.C. Bumpus, of the National Park Service Advisory Board, June 21. (YNN, 1943, pp. 97-101.)

Death of John Degnan, pioneer resident and operator, Feb. 27. Mary Ellen Degnan, daughter, continued operation of Degnan store. (YSR, 1943, p. 10.)

Death of Mrs. Mabel Sweetman Boysen, longtime operator and resident, May 10. (YSR, 1943, p. 11.)

Ahwahnee Hotel converted to hospital use by U.S. Navy, June 23 (to Dec. 15, 1945.) (YSR, 1944, p. 1; YNN, 1946, p. 75; Yosemite Park and Curry Co., 1946, pp. 1-76.)

Death of Chief Ranger Forest S. Townsley, August 11. (YSR, 1944, p. 6; YNN, 1943, p. 75.)

1944

Transfer of Acting Chief Ranger John H. Wegner to Sequoia and Kings Canyon national parks. (YNN, 1944, pp. 32-33.)

Oscar A. Sedergren appointed Chief Ranger. (YNN, 1944, pp. 37-38.)

M.E. Beatty, Associate Park Naturalist, transferred to Glacier National Park, Montana. M.V. Walker appointed *vice* Beatty. (YNN, 1944, pp. 58, 60.)

1945

First consideration given to the removal of some of the physical developments from Yosemite Valley and the establishment of new centers of operations in less precious localities. (Vint, 1945.)

Elizabeth H. Godfrey, a student and writer of Yosemite history, transferred from Yosemite to Region Four, National Park Service. (YNN, 1945, p. 97.)

Meadows and vista restoration program initiated in Yosemite Valley. (YSR, 1945, p. 10.)

Yosemite Valley Railway abandoned August 27. (YSR, 1946, p. 5.)

1946

Park Naturalist C. Frank Brockman

resigns from National Park Service. (YNN, 1946, pp. 110-111.)

Lost Arrow ascended by Jack Arnold, Anton Nelson, Fritz Lippmann, and Robin Hansen, September 2. (YNN, 1946, pp. 113-116; Brower, 1946, pp. 121-122.)

Constam T-bar lift for skiers constructed at Badger Pass in fall. (YSR, 1947.)

1947

Maggie Howard, "Ta-bu-ce," a principal character in Yosemite Indian demonstration, died at Mono Lake. (Kittredge, 1947.)

Travel begins sharp increase with gain of 20.9% over 1946 to 775,878 visitors. (YSR, 1948.)

Infestation of lodgepole pine needle-miner approached epidemic stage in Tenaya Lake and Tuolumne Meadows region. (YSR, 1947.)

Superintendent Frank Kittredge transferred to Washington Office as Chief, Engineering branch. (YSR, 1947.)

Dr. Carl P. Russell transferred from Chief Naturalist, Washington, to Superintendent, Yosemite. (YSR, 1947.)

1948

Dr. Donald B. Tresidder, President, Yosemite Park and Curry Co., died

January 28. (YSR, 1948.)

Death of Mrs. David A. Curry, pioneer resident and co-founder and operator of Yosemite Park and Curry Co. (YSR, 1948.)

Rancheria Mountain fire which started in Pate Valley, September 9, worst in park history, burned 10,000 acres and cost $90,000 to suppress. (YSR, 1949, p. 1.)

Yosemite School of Field Natural History for training of naturalists resumed after lapse during World War II. (YSR, 1949.)

Annual Yosemite Glacier Surveys resumed. (YSR, 1949.)

1949

Frog Creek Trout Egg Taking operation resumed at Lake Eleanor. (YSR, 1949.)

First use of helicopter for rescue in Yosemite brought out injured boy from Benson Lake area. (YSR, 1950.)

100th Anniversary of Department of the Interior observed. (YSR, 1950.)

1950

Flood on November 19 similar to flood of 1937 caused $454,000 damage to park roads, trails, buildings and utilities. (YSR, 1951.)

National Park Service Conference

held in Yosemite, October 16-20. (YSR, 1951.)

1951

Yosemite Centennial observed with numerous special studies, magazine articles, talks, press releases and other publicity. Much valuable history material received and tape recordings made of interviews with early pioneers. Centennial pageant staged on Ahwahnee Hotel grounds. (YSR, 1952.)

NPS acquired important parcels of private land at Gentry and at Wawona. (YSR, 1952.)

Newton B. Drury resigned, April 1, as Director of the National Park Service, and Arthur E. Demaray appointed as Director. Demaray retired in December.

Conrad L. Wirth succeeded Arthur E. Demaray as Director.

First airplane planting of trout in Yosemite. (YSR, 1951.)

1952

Heaviest winter since 1911 with twice the normal snowfall and 17 feet on ground at Badger Pass, 7,300 ft., on March 15. (YSR, 1952.)

Acquisition of 291.85 acres of private land in Aspen Valley. (YSR, 1952.)

Furlough of Superintendent Carl P. Russell to accept Guggenheim Fellowship for continuance of work on the history of the American fur trade. (YSR, 1953.)

John C. Preston transferred from Superintendent, Great Smoky Mountains National Park, to Superintendent, Yosemite. (YSR, 1953.)

1953

Worst fire season in park records with 79 forest fires burning at the same time as result of dry lightning storm in September. (YSR, 1954.)

First large scale control effort for lodgepole pine needleminer epidemic. 11,000 acres of the 45,000 acres of infested areas were sprayed with DDT from airplane. (YSR, 1954.)

White pine blister rust disease found 11 miles northwest of the park. (YSR, 1954.)

Yosemite School of Field Natural History suspended by order of the Director. (YSR, 1954.)

Park entrance fees increased. (YSR, 1954.)

1954

Park travel exceeds one million for the first time — 1,008,031. (YSR, 1954.)

Study of visitor impact on Mariposa Grove of Giant Sequoias. (YSR, 1955.)

Intensified vista clearing restoring many fine views obscured by recent tree growth. (YSR, 1955.)

Carl P. Russell returned to duty in interpretive planning, Western Office of Design and Construction, November.

1955

Mission 66 prospectus for Yosemite prepared as part of NPS conservation program to develop and staff all the areas to meet the anticipated requirements of an expected 1,800,000 visitors by 1966, the anniversary year of the establishment of the National Park Service. (YSR, 1955.)

Flood on December 23 which resulted in $767,000 damage to park facilities crested at 16 feet which exceeded the 1937 and 1950 floods. (YSR, 1956.)

Accelerated land acquisition in Foresta subdivision and acquisition of 160 acres at Johnson Lake. (YSR, 1956.)

1956

New Yosemite Lodge central buildings completed and old Lodge razed. (YSR, 1956.)

New telephone communication system for Yosemite installed by Pacific Telephone and Telegraph, with microwave dial system. (YSR, 1956.)

Death of Chris Brown, "Chief Le-Mee," of the Miwok, who gave Yosemite Indian demonstration dances, chants and legends at Yosemite Museum for many years. (YSR, 1956.)

Death of Charles Leidig, first white boy born in Yosemite, March 8, 1869. (YSR, 1956.)

1957

California Fish Hatchery at Happy Isles donated to Yosemite and converted to new museum, the Happy Isles Nature Center. (YSR, 1957.)

National Park Service Training Center instituted in Yosemite on a three year trial basis. (YSR, 1957.)

New FM radio system placed in operation. (YSR, 1957.)

Additional Foresta property obtained through cooperation of Yosemite Natural History Association. (YSR, 1957.)

1958

Wawona Covered Bridge rehabilitated following flood damage, to form nucleus of Wawona Pioneer Village. (YSR, 1958.)

Degnan, Donohoe, Inc. Restaurant opens in Yosemite Village. (YSR, 1958.)

Reorganization of Yosemite Protection Division. (YSR, 1958.)

Helicopter used in needleminer control work, Tuolumne Meadows. (YSR, 1958)

MISSION 66 program for Yosemite moves forward with: El Portal property acquired as new administrative site; ten new residences constructed; parking areas at Badger Pass, Washburn and Glacier Points enlarged; campgrounds at Wawona and Bridalveil enlarged and improved; construction of portion of road to replace old 21-mile section of Tioga Road. (YSR, 1958.)

First climb, face of El Capitan. (YSR, 1958.)

Rear projection amphitheater constructed at Camp 7. (YSR, 1958.)

NOTE: *All entries from this point on have been added by the editors.*

1959

The Old Village Store, Degnan's old restaurant and Yosemite Park and Curry Co. maintenance warehouse were demolished and the sites naturalized. Yosemite Park and Curry Co.'s new store and restaurant dedicated May 9. (*Yosemite Sentinel*, May 7, pp. 1-3.)

King Baudoin of Belgium visited park May 22 and 23. (Superintendent's Monthly Report, May, 1959.)

1960

The trailer village portion of the "new town" at El Portal completed and occupied by Yosemite employees. Ultimate population at El Portal of more than 1,000 planned. (*Yosemite Sentinel*, Dec. 2, pp. 1,3 [map].)

1961

Dedication of final park section of "New Tioga Road," June 24. (*Yosemite*, June 24, pp. 31-50; *Fresno Bee*, June 30 and July 2, p. 5-B; *Yosemite Sentinel*, June 30, pp. 1,3; *Yosemite*, Vol. 40, No. 3, pp. 30-59.)

Pioneer Yosemite History Center opened to the public at Wawona. (*Yosemite Sentinel*, July 14, p. 2.) Formal dedication Sept. 11. (*Yosemite Sentinel*, Oct. 2, p. 1; *Yosemite*, Vol. 40, No. 4, pp. 62-104.)

Intensive study by Gibbens and Heady of biological changes in the forests and meadows of Yosemite Valley—changes which may be attributable to human occupation. (University of California Agricultural Experiment Station, Manual 36, 1964, pp. 1-44.)

1962

President John F. Kennedy visited Yosemite Valley, Aug. 17 and 18. (Oakland Tribune, Aug. 18, p. 1-D; San Francisco Chronicle, Aug. 18, "Voice of the West, " p. 1; Yosemite News, Aug. 30, pp. 1-2.)

Yosemite ("Yosemite Nature Notes"), monthly journal of the Yosemite Natural History Association, discontinues publication after 40 years of circulation. (*Yosemite Sentinel*, March 22, p. 4; Yosemite, Vol. 40, No. 6, pp. 122, 145.)

Richard J. Hartesveldt completed studies on "Effect of Human Impact

upon *Sequoia gigantea* and its Environment in the Mariposa Grove." (University of Michigan Ph.D. thesis, mimeo, 310 pp.)

1963

Fourth great flood of recent times hits Yosemite Valley, Jan. 29-Feb. 1. (*Yosemite Sentinel*, Feb. 8, pp. 1-4.)

Work begun on the modernization of Tioga Road from Tioga Pass to Lee Vining. (The history of several contracts in this connection is given in the *San Francisco Chronicle*, Feb. 14, 1966.)

1964

Observance of the Yosemite Centennial, June 26. (*Yosemite Sentinel*, June 12, p. 1, and July 10, pp. 1-2; *Oakland Tribune* [The Knave], June 28, p. 7-FL; *San Francisco Chronicle*, May 30; *Yosemite - Saga of a Century*, YNHA and Sierra Star Press, 1964.)

Yosemite Valley was hit by a flood December 23 and 24, with the Merced River cresting at 13.7 feet. (YSR, 1964.)

1965

Crane Flat Campground, with 160 sites, opened. (YSR, 1965.)

John C. Preston retired, December 30, after 13 years of service as Yosemite Superintendent. John Davis named successor. (YSR, 1965.)

1966

Historic Yosemite Valley Chapel rehabilitated; rededicated May 24. (*Yosemite Sentinel*, May 18.)

Ranger horse patrol restored, June 19. (*Yosemite Sentinel*, July 21.)

Old Yosemite Valley Museum closed and construction begun on modern Visitor's Center. The new center will house museum, auditoriums, and information station. (YSR, 1966.)

National Park Service celebrated 50th anniversary, August 25.

1967

Yosemite received the greatest snowpack ever recorded. Tioga Road was not opened until June 17. (YSR, 1967.)

Carl P. Russell, eminent Yosemite historian and author, Chief Park Naturalist, 1923-1930, Park Superintendent from 1947-1952, died June 20. (*Yosemite Sentinel*, June 29.)

Over two million people visited Yosemite during the year. (YSR, 1967.)

1968

Superintendent John Davis retired January 12, and Lawrence C. Hadley appointed as replacement. (*Yosemite Sentinel*, January 22.)

Historic "Firefall" ordered discontinued by National Park Service Director. Last "Firefall" occurred January 25. (*Yosemite Sentinel*, March 1.)

1969

Record-breaking snowfall in Yosemite. Famous "Wawona Tunnel Tree" in Mariposa Grove fell during winter. (YSR, 1969.)

Historic Mountain House at Glacier Point and Glacier Point Hotel destroyed by fire, August 9. (YSR, 1969.)

1970

Free shuttle bus operation begun in Yosemite Valley, February 9. (USNPS, 1970.)

Mariposa Grove Road closed to private cars. Tram cars available for transportation, May. (YSR, 1970.)

Confrontation in Stoneman Meadow between rangers and about 400 youths, July 4. (USNPS, 1970).

One-way road system instituted in Yosemite Valley, and roads at eastern end of Valley closed to private auto traffic, July 9. Roadways to Happy Isles and Mirror Lake exclusively for shuttle buses, bicyclists, and foot traffic. (YSR, 1970.)

Superintendent Lawrence C. Hadley transferred and replaced by Wayne B. Cone, August. (YSR, 1970.)

Mary Curry Tresidder, Honorary Chairman of the Board, Yosemite Park and Curry Co., died in Yosemite Valley, October 29. (*Yosemite*, Vol. 41 No. 2, Jan., 1971, p. 2.)

United States Natural Resources, Inc., a Menlo Park, CA, based corporation, acquired controlling stock shares of Yosemite Park and Curry Co. (Press Release dated June 26, 1970.)

1971

First bank in Yosemite Valley, a Wells Fargo branch, opened April 16. (YSR, 1971.)

Prescribed burning of selected forest undergrowth begun as technique to decrease danger from fire hazard and to encourage new tree growth. (YSR, 1971.)

Yosemite Guide, informational news sheet, printed and distributed free to park visitors. (YSR, 1971.)

Superintendent Wayne B. Cone, transferred and replaced by Lynn H. Thompson. (YSR, 1971.)

Yosemite Institute founded to provide environmental education for teenage students. 1200 youths participated in pioneering 1971-1972 program. (USNPS, 1971.)

1972

Four of John Muir's grandchildren, along with Horace M. Albright, Dr. Harold C. Bradley, Dr. Carl Sharsmith and others participated in the John Muir Observance, April 21-30. (YSR, 1972.)

Interpretive activities broadened to include ecology float trips, astronomy programs, square dances, night prowls,

bicycle tours, cross-country skiing, snowshoeing and winter camping. (USNPS, 1972.)

National Park Service stables, outbuildings, and seven ranger patrol horses destroyed by fire, July 31. (YSR, 1972.)

National Park Service Director George B. Hartzog, Jr., applied a jackhammer to the parking area opposite the Yosemite Valley Visitor Center, taking the first step in creating a car-free pedestrian "mall" for visitor use, October 4. (YSR, 1972.)

1973

Fire destroyed Camp Curry cafeteria and kitchen, April 22. (YSR, 1973.)

Music Corporation of America purchased the Yosemite Park and Curry Co., taking control August 16 and retaining the established name. (YSR, 1973.)

746 acres within or adjacent to the boundary of Yosemite including the Sierra Club's Soda Springs property at Tuolumne Meadows and the Meyers Ranch in Big Meadow were added to the park. (YSR, 1973.)

Native American interpretive program expanded. 40-foot diameter "round house" constructed at rear of Visitor Center. (USNPS, 1973.)

New wing constructed at Lewis Memorial Hospital. (YSR, 1973.)

1974

Edward C. Hardy began duties as Chief Operating Officer, Yosemite Park and Curry Co., January 1. (YSR, 1974.)

Leslie P. Arnberger became Yosemite's eleventh superintendent succeeding Lynn H. Thompson who was transferred, January 20. (YSR, 1974.)

Degnan's, a concession operation in Yosemite Valley since 1884, sold to Yosemite Park and Curry Co. in March. (YSR, 1974.)

Yosemite Park and Curry Co. observed 75th anniversary, June 1. (*Yosemite Sentinel*, June.)

Big Oak Flat Road 100 years old on July 17.

Coulterville Road still in limited use after 100 years, July 18.

1975

Camp Curry's new cafeteria, replacing the one burned in 1973, opened on May 2. The same night, a fire gutted the Camp's gift shop, built in 1972, and damaged another historic structure adjacent to the new cafeteria. (YSR, 1975.)

Lewis Memorial Hospital, which had operated since 1930, closed because of prohibitive malpractice insurance rates. A clinic run by three resident doctors continued in the building. (YSR, 1975.)

National Park Service discontinued the annual fall horse drive from Wawona to winter pasture near Hornitos. The final drive was held October 8. Horse grazing in the Wawona Meadow was also halted. Both practices had begun more than 100 years previously. (YSR, 1975.)

1976

National Park Service mailed more than 40,000 Master Plan workbooks to the public as step in developing new plan. (YSR, 1976.)

Lightest snow pack on record, 12" to 18" at Tuolumne Meadows, resulted in the earliest opening of the Tioga Road (April 10), after the latest closing on record of December 29, 1975. (*Yosemite Sentinel*, April 9.)

National Park Service's Indian Cultural Museum opened on August 14. (YSR, 1976.)

1977

Badger Pass finally opened with 25" of snow on January 3. (*Yosemite Sentinel*, January.)

The new El Portal Wastewater Treatment Plant put in operation, January. (YSR, 1977.)

Crashed plane, laden with marijuana, found in Lower Merced Pass Lake in late January. One body recovered along with 5,000 pounds of marijuana. Before rangers secured the area, a number of locals and other opportunists removed large quantities of marijuana from the crash site. (*New West,* May 23.)

The Ahwahnee Hotel celebrated 50th anniversary with program and banquet on July 14. (*Yosemite Sentinel,* July.)

Severe drought ended by heavy rains that began in mid-December and continued until June, 1978. (*Yosemite Newsletter,* 1978.)

1978

A draft Master Plan was released by the National Park Service. (*Yosemite Sentinel,* October.)

Yosemite Ski School celebrated its 50th year. (*Yosemite Sentinel,* January, 1979.)

1979

Wawona Hotel's 100th anniversary celebrated with a program, barbecue, and party on the hotel front lawn. (*Yosemite Sentinel,* May.)

Robert O. Binnewies appointed Superintendent of Yosemite National Park, succeeding Leslie P. Arnberger. (*Yosemite Sentinel,* July.)

Revised Draft Master Plan, with emphasis on removal of housing to Wawona, announced by NPS Director William Whalen in Yosemite on November 29 and 30. (Press conference, Yosemite, November 30.)

1980

Nine day January storm caused flooding in Yosemite Valley and evacuation of El Portal trailer park on January 13. All roads to the Park closed because of slides, standing water, and washouts. (*Yosemite Sentinel,* February.)

Long series of earthquakes caused rockslides. Two hikers on Sierra Point trail seriously injured, May 25. (*Mariposa Gazette,* May.)

Yosemite General Management Plan (without Wawona housing proposal) signed by N.P.S. Regional Director, paving the way for final approval, September 17. (YSR, 1980.)

Three hikers killed and six injured in rockslide that destroyed part of trail to upper Yosemite Fall, November 16. (*Mariposa Gazette,* November 22.)

1981

Yosemite General Management Plan (Also known as the Master Plan) officially approved after meeting National Environmental Policy Act requirements. (YSR, 1981.)

1982

Heavy snow storms in January blocked Park roads twice during the month. (YSR, 1982.)

Nearly eight inches of rain fell in three days, February 13-15, and caused minor flooding in Yosemite Valley. (YSR, 1982.)

An enormous rockslide on Highway 140 caused road closure, April 3. The historic Coulterville Road was permanently blocked at its junction with Highway 140. (YSR, 1982.)

Heavy rains melted snow and caused flooding and rockslides. All Park roads closed, guest housing evacuated, and visitors convoyed from Park, April 9-11. The Park was closed until April 14. (YSR, 1982.)

1983

Queen Elizabeth II of England, Prince Philip, and royal party visited Park, March 5-7. (*Yosemite Sentinel,* June.)

Fiftieth anniversary of the dedication of the Wawona Tunnel held on June 10. (YSR, 1983.)

The Tioga Road did not open until June 30, the latest opening on record. (YSR, 1983.)

Wells Fargo Bank closed on September 30 after eleven years of operation. (YSR, 1983.)

1984

January windstorm blew down 150 trees in Yosemite Valley; one employee was killed in Camp 6, eight vehicles were crushed. (YSR, 1984.)

Famed photographer and conservationist Ansel Adams died April 22. (YSR, 1984.)

Yosemite National Park added to coveted World Heritage List, October 31. (YSR, 1984.)

1985

Two hikers were killed and three injured by lightning strike on Half Dome, July 27. (YSR, 1985.)

In August, Yosemite Natural History Association Board of Trustees voted to change organization name to Yosemite Association, effective immediately. (*Yosemite,* Vol. 47 No. 19, Fall, 1985.)

Mt. Ansel Adams dedicated and Yosemite formally recognized as World Heritage Site during August 24 program at Tuolumne Meadows. (YSR, 1985.)

The hydroelectric plant on the Merced River in Yosemite Valley was shut down and its penstock removed, August 26. (YSR, 1985.)

1986

John M. Morehead named Park Superintendent replacing Robert O. Binnewies, February 16. (YSR, 1986.)

Herd of 27 bighorn sheep, last recorded in Yosemite in 1914, reintroduced to Lee Vining Canyon by governmental agencies in March. (YSR, 1986.)

Total visitation for year was 2,982,758 persons, a one percent increase over 1985. (YSR, 1986.)

1987

Horace M. Albright, second Director of the National Park Service, died on March 27 at age 97. *(Los Angeles Times,* March 28.)

Barbara J. Griffin appointed Assistant Superintendent in August, the first woman to fill a high administrative position in the Park. (YSR, 1987.)

Visitation to Yosemite exceeded 3 million persons for the first time in Park history; 80 percent of those visits were made between May and September. (YSR, 1987.)

The abandoned sewage plant was removed from the west end of Yosemite Valley by U.S. Army Engineers, October. (YSR, 1987.)

1988

About 400 persons were evacuated, two were injured, and one child was killed when a tree fell on a Yosemite Lodge cabin during the high winds on February 18. (YSR, 1988.)

Rehabilitated art gallery opened in Yosemite Museum as re-conversion of building to historic use begun, February. (YSR, 1988).

Anniversary of John Muir's 150th birthday celebrated with interpretive events. (YSR, 1988.)

U.S. Postal Service issues "Flag Over Yosemite" 25-cent stamp, May 20. (YSR, 1988.)

Despite a drought, visitation grew to 3,333,927 persons. (YSR, 1988.)

1989

The gathering of firewood in Yosemite Valley was banned on June 1 to reduce smoke from campfires and damage to vegetation. (YSR, 1989.)

Parapalegic climber Mark Wellman and his partner Mike Corbett scaled El Capitan, July 19-26. (YSR, 1989.)

Michael V. Finley replaced John M. Morehead as Yosemite Superintendent, September 25. (YSR, 1989.)

Visitation increased to 3,429,619 persons, a new record. (YSR, 1989.)

1990

LeConte Memorial Lodge designated a National Historic Landmark on June 29. (YSR, 1990.)

Major fires occurred throughout the Park from August 7 to 21. More than 24,000 acres burned. Over 60 homes were destroyed in the community of Foresta. (YSR, 1990.)

Yosemite celebrated its 100th anniversary as a national park on October 1. A special ceremony was held in the Chapel Meadow. *(Fresno Bee,* October 2.)

The Japanese company Matsushita purchased MCA, Inc., owner of the Yosemite Park and Curry Co. MCA announced that the Curry Company would not be part of the deal and would be sold separately. (*Fresno Bee*, November.)

1991

Matsushita Corporation agreed to sell the Yosemite Park and Curry Co. to the National Park Foundation on January 8, with the sale and transfer to become effective in 1993. (YSR, 1991.)

Some Foresta residents were issued permits to begin the process of rebuilding their burnt homes, May 20. (YSR, 1991.)

Mark Wellman and Mike Corbett climbed Half Dome, September 4-16. (YSR, 1991.)

Park visitation reached its highest level ever with 3,547,163 visitors. (*Yosemite*, Vol. 54 No. 1, Winter, 1992.)

BIBLIOGRAPHY

Note: This bibliography, in original form and style, was created by combining the "Cited Publications" and "Additional Bibliography" sections from the 1932 edition of the book with the "Bibliography" from the 1947 edition. Bibliographic references were omitted from later editions.

ADAMS, ANSEL. *Sierra Nevada: The John Muir Trail* ["Transmission of emotional experience"] (Berkeley, 1938), 50 plates.

ADAMS, VIRGINIA and ANSEL ADAMS. *Illustrated Guide to Yosemite Valley* (San Francisco, 1940), 128 pp., illus., maps.

ADJUTANT GENERAL. Records in Adjutant General's Office. Memo re Lieut. T. Moore in Sierras, 1852. Prepared for F. P. Farquhar.

ALBRIGHT, HORACE M. "How the National Park Service Came into Being: A Reminiscence," *American Civic Annual*, 1929, pp. 9-12.

—. "Yosemite on the Way to Protection," *American Civic Annual*, 1929, pp. 23-25.

American Motorist. "Yosemite Motor-Conquered," September, 1916, p. 37.

AMERICAN PLANNING AND CIVIC ASSOCIATION. Portfolio on the national park and monument system (Washington, D.C., n.d.), four booklets, 32 pp. each.

ANONYMOUS. *Mono County* (F. W. McIntosh, Reno, 1908), 96 pp., illus.

—. Standard Oil Bulletin, September, 1926.

ARCHIBALD, J. F. "A Cavalry March to the Yosemite," *Illustrated American*, November, 1896.

AYRES, THOMAS A. Original pencil drawings made in Yosemite Valley, 1855 and 1856 (Yosemite Museum).

BADÈ, WILLIAM FREDERIC. "The Hetch Hetchy Situation [editorial]," *Sierra Club Bulletin*, 9 (1914): 3, 174-176.

—. "John Muir in Yosemite," *Natural History*, March-April, 1920.

—. *The Life and Letters of John Muir*. 2 vols. (Boston and New York, 1924).

BAILEY, C. A. "Unfrequented Paths of Yosemite," *Overland Monthly*, 2d series, Vol. VIII (July, 1886), pp. 88-92.

—. "The Vantage Point of Yosemite," *Sunset*, April, 1899.

BANCROFT, HUBERT HOWE. *History of California*, I, 1542-1800 (San Francisco, 1884), 744 pp.; III, 1825-1840 (1885), 792 pp.; IV, 1840-1845 (1886).

—. *Tourists' Guide*, 1871.

BARRUS, C. "In the Yosemite with John Muir," *The Craftsman*, December, 1912.

BARTLET, L. "By Rail to the Yosemite," *Pacific Monthly*, Vol. XVII (June, 1907), pp. 730-738.

BEADLE, J. H. *The Undeveloped West*, (Philadelphia, 1873), 824 pp., illus.

BEATTY, M. E. "Bears of Yosemite," *Yosemite Nature Notes*, 1943, pp. 1-16.

—. "A Brief Story of the Geology of Yosemite Valley," *Yosemite Nature Notes*, 1943, pp. 33-40.

—. "C. E. Watkins, One of the Early Photographers of Yosemite Valley," *Yosemite Nature Notes*, 1936, pp. 17-18.

—. "Glaciers of Yosemite," *Yosemite Nature Notes*, 1934, pp. 44-46.

—. "History of the Firefall," *Yosemite Nature Notes*, 1934, pp. 41-43.

BEATTY, M. E. and C. A. HARWELL. "Birds of Yosemite," *Yosemite Nature Notes*, 1938, pp. 1-36.

BELDEN, C. J. "The Tioga Road across the Sierra Nevada," *The Geographical Review*, June, 1919.

BELL, MAJOR HORACE. *Reminiscences of a Ranger* (Santa Barbara, 1927), 500 pp., illus.

BIDWELL, JOHN. "First Emigrant Train to California," *Century Magazine*, November,1890.

—. *John Bidwell's Trip to California, 1841* (St. Louis, 1842), 32 pp.

BLACKWELDER, ELIOT. "Pleistocene Glaciation in the Sierra Nevada and Basin Ranges," *Bull. Geol. Soc. Amer.*, 42 (1931), 865-922.

BLAKE, MARY E. *On the Wing* (Boston, 1883), 236 pp.

BODDAM-WHETHAM, J. W. *Western Wanderings* (London, 1874), 364 pp., illus.

Bodie Daily Free Press, November 3, 1879; January 26, 1884.

Bodie Standard, November 7, 1877; June 6, 1881.

BOLING, CAPTAIN JOHN. "Letter from Camp on Fresno River," *Alta California*, June 14, 1851.

—. "Letter from Yosemite Valley," *Alta California*, June 12, 1851.

BOLLES, IDA SAVAGE. "Sidelights on Major James Savage," *Yosemite Nature Notes*, 1929, pp. 15-16.

BORELL, ADREY E. "History of Fishing in Yosemite," *Yosemite Nature Notes*, 1934, pp. 57-60.

BOWLES, SAMUEL. *Our New West* (New York, 1869), 524 pp., illus.

BRACE, CHARLES LORING. *The New West*, (New York, 1869), 374 pp.

BRANSON, I. R. *Yosemite against Corporation Greed* (Aurora, Neb., 1909), 39 pp.

BREITENSTEIN, A. J. "The Park-to-Park Highway," *New West*, May, 1917, pp. 17-20.

BREWER, WILLIAM H. *Up and Down California in 1860-1864* (Yale University Press, New Haven, 1930).

BREWSTER, E. T. *Life and Letters of J. D. Whitney* (Boston, 1909), 411 pp.

BROCKMAN, C. FRANK. "Administrative Officers of Yosemite," *Yosemite Nature Notes*, 1944, pp. 53-57.

—. "Broadleaved Trees of Yosemite National Park," *Yosemite Nature Notes*, 1947, pp. 1-40.

—. "Contributions of the Naturalist to Winter Recreation," *Proceedings, Second Park Naturalist Conference* (Washington, D.C.), pp. 74-80.

—. "Development of Transportation to Yosemite," *Yosemite Nature Notes*, 1943, pp. 49-63, 69-72, 76-79, 81-86, 91-96, 101-103.

—. "The Great Sierra Snow Survey," *Natural History*, March, 1946, pp. 105-109.
—. "Introduced Trees in Yosemite National Park," [Landmarks of pioneer activities], *Yosemite Nature Notes*, 1947, pp. 1-40.
—. "Little Change in Yosemite's Glaciers," *Yosemite Nature Notes*, 1942, pp. 89-91.
—. "Principal Administrative Officers of Yosemite: Frederick Law Olmsted," *Yosemite Nature Notes*, 1946, pp. 106-110.
—. "Principal Waterfalls of the World and Their Relation to Those in Yosemite National Park," *Yosemite Nature Notes*, 1945, pp. 1-32.
—. "The 'Why' of Snow Surveys," *Yosemite Nature Notes*, 1946, 57-61.
—. "Yosemite and the Mother Lode Country," *Yosemite Nature Notes*, 1946, pp. 81-85.
BROMLEY, I. H. "The Big Trees and the Yosemite," *Scribner's Monthly*, January, 1872.
BROWER, DAVID R. "Beyond the Skiways," *Sierra Club Bulletin*, 23 (1938): 2, 40-45.
—. "Lost Arrow," *Sierra Club Bulletin*, 31 (1946): 6, 121-122.
—. "Skiing the Sky-Land," *American Ski Annual*, 1947, pp. 49-59.
—. "Winter Sports Dilemma," *Sierra Club Bulletin*, 31 (1946): 5, 6-7.
BROWER, DAVID R. with RICHARD M. LEONARD. "A Climber's Guide to the High Sierra: Part IV, Yosemite Valley," *Sierra Club Bulletin*, 25 (1940): 1, 41-63.
BRYANT, HAROLD C. "A Nature Preserve for Yosemite," *Yosemite Nature Notes*, 1927, pp. 46-48.
—. "Recollections," *Yosemite Nature Notes*, 1932.
—. "A School for Nature Guides," *Yosemite Nature Notes*, 1925, pp. 9-10, 16.
—. "Trails and Trail Use," *Proceedings of Eighth Appalachian Trail Conference*, 1938, pp. 26-30.
BRYANT, HAROLD C. and WALLACE W. ATWOOD, JR. *Research and Education in the National Parks* (Washington, D.C., 1932), pp. 1-66.
BRYCE, JAMES. *National Parks — The Need of the Future*. University and historical addresses, 1913, 433 pp.
BUCKLEY, J. M. *Two Weeks in the Yosemite and Vicinity* (New York, 1884), 36 pp.
BUNNELL, L. H. "The Date of Discovery of the Yosemite," *Century Magazine*, September, 1890.
—. *Discovery of the Yosemite* (Chicago, 1880), 332 pp., portrait, map.
BURNS, J. "Yosemite," in T. Cook's *Letters from the Sea and Foreign Lands* (1873), 124 pp.
BURNS, NED J. *Field Manual for Museums* (National Park Service, Washington, D.C., 1941), xii + 426 pp.
BURROUGHS, JOHN. "The Spell of the Yosemite," *Century Magazine*, N.S., Vol. LIX (November, 1910), pp. 47-53.

CALIFORNIA ALPINE CLUB. *Trails*, (San Francisco, 1920 to date).
CALIFORNIA FISH AND GAME COMMISSION. *California Fish and Game*, (Sacramento, 1914 to date).
CALIFORNIA LEGISLATURE. *Investigations of Yosemite Commissioners; Assembly*

Hearings, 1889, 430 pp.

CALIFORNIA STATE BOARD OF TRADE. *Yosemite Valley: History, Description and Statement of Conditions Relative to the Proposed Recession to the National Government*, Circular 13 (Sacramento, 1904), 34 pp., map.

CALIFORNIA STATE MINERALOGIST. *Report, 1888*, pp. 367-371.

California, Statutes of, chap. dxxxvi, 1865-66.

CALIFORNIA SUPREME COURT. Frémont Decision (Burnett). Case of *Biddle Boggs* vs. *Merced Mining Company, 14th California Report*, January term, 1858.

Century Magazine. Editorial, "Amateur Management of the Yosemite Scenery," September, 1890.

—. Editorial, "The Care of the Yosemite Valley," January, 1890.

CHAMBERLAIN, A. "Scenery as a National Asset," *Outlook*, Vol. XCV, May 28, 1910, pp. 157-169.

CHAMBERLAIN, NEWELL D. *The Call of Gold: True Tales of the Gold Rush to Yosemite* (Mariposa, 1936), 184 pp., illustrations, maps.

CHAPMAN, C. E. *History of California, The Spanish Period* (New York, 1921), 528 pp., illus.

CHASE, J. S. *Yosemite Trails* (Boston and New York, 1911), 354 pp., illus.

CHURCHILL, C. M. *Over the Purple Hills* (Denver, 1876), 336 pp., illus.

CLARK, GALEN. *The Big Trees of California* (Redondo Beach, 1907), 104 pp., illus.

—. *Indians of the Yosemite Valley and Vicinity* (Yosemite, 1904), 110 pp., illus.

—. "Yosemite: Past and Present," *Sunset*, Vol. XXII, April, 1909, pp. 394-396.

—. *The Yosemite Valley: Its History, Characteristic Features, and the Theories Regarding Its Origin* (Yosemite Valley [Nelson L. Salter], 1910), 108 pp., illus.

CLARK, W. A. "Automobiling in Yosemite Valley," *Overland Monthly*, 2d ser., Vol. XL (August, 1902), pp. 104-110.

CLARKE, CLINTON C. *The Pacific Crest Trailway* (Pasadena: Pacific Crest Trail System Conference, 1945), 126 pp., maps

—. "Story of Building the Pacific Crest Trailway, 1932-1942," bulletin of the Pacific Crest Trail System Conference, Pasadena, Calif., 1942, pp. 1-6.

CLELAND, R. G. *Pathfinders*, of the series "California" (Los Angeles, 1929), 452 pp., illus.

CLEMENS, SAMUEL L. *Roughing It* (Hartford, 1872), 592 pp., illus.

CLOOS, ERNST. "Structure of the Sierra Nevada Batholith," in *Guidebook 16*, International Geological Congress (Washington, D.C., 1932), pp. 40-45, map, bibliog.

COFFMAN, JOHN D. "How Much and What Kind of Forest Land Should Be Devoted Exclusively to Recreation and Aesthetics?" *Journal of Forestry* (February, 1937), pp. 210-214.

COLBY, WILLIAM E. "The Completed LeConte Memorial Lodge," *Sierra Club Bulletin*, 5 (1904): 1,66-69, illus.

—. "The John Muir Trail," *Sierra Club Bulletin*, 10 (1916): 1, 86-92.

—. "The Sierra Club," *Forestry and Irrigation*, August, 1905, pp. 391-393.

—. "The Soda Springs Purchase," *Sierra Club Bulletin*, 8 (1912): 4, 272-274.

—. "Yosemite and the Sierra Club," *Sierra Club Bulletin*, 23 (1938): 2, 11-19.

—. "Yosemite's Fatal Beauty," *National Parks Magazine* (January-March, 1947), pp. 4-11.

COLE, JAMES E. "Museum [Yosemite] Scientific Collections," *Yosemite Nature Notes*, 1936, pp. 27-32, 37-40.

—. "Origin of the Name, 'Yosemite,'" *Yosemite Nature Notes*, 1936, pp. 49-54.

COMMONWEALTH CLUB OF CALIFORNIA. "Should We Stop Building New Roads into California's High Mountains?" *The Commonwealth* 12 (June 2, 1936): 22, 325-386, illus.

CONE, MARY. *Two Years in California* (1876), 238 pp., illus.

CONWAY, JOHN. Time Book, Glacier Point Road Construction (Yosemite Museum).

COOK, LAWRENCE F. "Forest Fire Prevention," *Yosemite Nature Notes*, 1945, pp. 57-61.

—. *The Giant Sequoias of California* (Washington, D.C., 1942), 28 pp., illus.

CORCORAN, MAY STANISLAS. "Wilderness Odds," *Oakland Tribune*, Magazine Section, July 5, 1925.

Cornhill Magazine, "Early Spring in California," April, 1883.

COSMOPOLITAN HOUSE. Grand Register, 1873. [A massive record of visitors during the stagecoach days in the Yosemite Museum.]

Country Gentleman, October 9, 1856.

COY, O. C. *California County Boundaries*, (Sacramento, 1923), 336 pp., maps.

—. *Gold Days*, of the series "California" (Los Angeles, 1929), 382 pp., illus.

CRAMTON, LOUIS C. "The National Parks under Stephen T. Mather," *American Civic*, 1929, pp. 13-16.

CRANE, AGNES. "Staging to the Yosemite," *Leisure Hour*, August, 1883.

CROCKER, H. S., & CO. *Yosemite Illustrated in Colors* (San Francisco, 1890).

CROFUTT, G. A. *New Overland Tourist and Pacific Coast Guide* (1878), 322 pp., illus.

—. *Transcontinental Tourists' Guide* (New York, 1872), 224 pp.

CURTIS, W. B. "Our National Parks and Reservations," *Annals, American Academy of Political and Social Science*, March, 1910, pp. 15-24.

DALE, H. C. *The Ashley-Smith Explorations, 1822-1829* (A. H. Clark Co., 1918), 352 pp., 3 plates.

DANIELS, M. "The National Parks of California," *California's Magazine*, July, 1915.

DAVIDSON, G. "The Occupation of Mount Conness," *Overland Monthly*, February, 1892.

DEGNAN, MARY ELLEN. "Early Day Experiences in Yosemite" (MS [1941] in Yosemite Museum).

DE QUILLE, DAN. "The Perils of the High Sierras," *Overland Monthly*, March, 1887, pp. 311-322.

DICKENSEN, LUELLA. *Reminiscences of a Trip Across the Plains in 1846, and Early Days in California* [Yosemite Valley in 1854] (San Francisco, 1904), 118 pp.

DIXON, JOSEPH S. "A Study of the Life History and Food Habits of Mule Deer in California," *California Fish and Game*, 20 (1934): pp. 181-282, 315-354.

DOERR, JOHN E. "An Appraisal of the Winter Use in Snow Areas of the National Park Service," MS, pp. 1-10, with tabular summary of character of areas, extent of use, accommodations, and installations of winter sports facilities, pp. 1-8 [Yosemite, pp. 8-10 of "Appraisal," and p. 8 of Summary], 1946.

DRURY, AUBREY. *California: An Intimate Guide* (New York, 1935) [Yosemite region, pp. 408-418, 445-478].

DRURY, NEWTON B. "Half a Century and the National Parks," *Park Service Bulletin* (September-October, 1940), pp. 1-6.

—. "National Park Service Grazing Policy," *National Parks Magazine* (July-September. 1944), pp. 16-17.

—. "The National Park Service: The First Thirty Years," *American Planning and Civic Annual* (1945), pp. 29-37.

—. "The National Parks in Wartime" (Chicago: National Park Service, 1943; included with "Justifications for Appropriations for the Fiscal Year Ending June 30, 1944"),pp. 1-14, mimeographed [see also *American Forests* (August, 1943, pp. 374-378, 411, for another article, same title].

—. "Policy of the National Park Service Regarding Winter Use," Memo. of March 21, 1946, mimeographed, pp. 1-3.

—. "Preserving the Native Landscape in California," *National Parks Bulletin*, 15 (1940): 68, 11-15.

—. "What the War Is Doing to National Parks and Where They Will Be at Its Close," *Living Wilderness*, 9 (1944): pp. 11-15.

DUDLEY, W. R. "Report on the Big Trees of California," U.S. Dept. of Agriculture, Div. of Forestry, Bulletin 28, 1900, pp. 1-30, illus., maps.

DUMBELL, K. E. M. *Seeing the West* (New York, 1920), 206 pp., illus.

ELLIOTT, WALLACE W. *History of Fresno County, California* (W. W. Elliott & Co., San Francisco, 1881), 246 pp., illus.

ELLSWORTH, RODNEY SYDES. *The Giant Sequoia* (J. D. Berger, Oakland, California, 1924), 168 pp., illus.

ERNST, EMIL F. "The Cause of Ghost Forests in Yosemite," *Yosemite Nature Notes*, 1936, pp. 25-27.

EVANS, WILLIS A. "Fishes of Yosemite National Park," *Yosemite Nature Notes*, 1944, pp. 1-20.

FARQUHAR, FRANCIS P. "Colonel Benson," *Sierra Club Bulletin*, 12 (1925): 2, 175-179.

—. "Exploration of the Sierra Nevada," *Quarterly of California Historical Society*, March, 1925.

—. "Frémont in the Sierra Nevada," *Sierra Club Bulletin*, February, 1930, pp. 73-95.

—. "Jedediah Smith and the First Crossing of the Sierra Nevada," *Sierra Club Bulletin*, 28 (1943): 3, 35-52.

—. "Northward over the John Muir Trail," *Sierra Club Bulletin*, 11 (1920): 1, 34-38.

—. *Place Names of the High Sierra* (San Francisco, 1926), 128 pp.

—. "Spanish Discovery of the Sierra Nevada," *Sierra Club Bulletin*, Vol. XIII, No. 1 (Feb., 1928), pp. 54-61.

—. "Walker's Discovery of Yosemite," *Sierra Club Bulletin*, 27 (1942): 4, pp. 35-49.

FINCK, H. T. *The Pacific Coast Scenic Tour* (1890), 310 pp., illus.

FOLEY, D. J. *Foley's Yosemite Souvenir and Guide*, (Galen Clark's description of exploration of Mariposa Grove) (1915), 116 pp., illus.

FONT, PEDRO. Mapa del Viage que Hizo el P. F. Font a Monterey, y puerto de San Francisco; y del Viage que Hizo el P. F. Francisco Garces por El Rio Colorado hasta su Desemboque, y para arrira Hasta P.F. Petrus Font fecit Tubutama anno 1770. (Original in Seville; copy in Yosemite Museum.)

FOUNTAIN, PAUL. *The Eleven Eaglets of the West* (New York, 1906), 362 pp.

FRY, WALTER, and JOHN R. WHITE. *Big Trees* (Stanford University Press, 1930), 114 pp., illus.

FRYXELL, F. M. "A Painter of Yosemite [Chris Jorgensen]," *The American Scandinavian Review*, winter, 1939, pp. 329-333, illus.

—. "The Thomas Moran Art Collection of the National Parks," *Yosemite Nature Notes*, 1936, pp. 57-60.

GARFIELD, J. R. Decision of Secretary of Interior Garfield, May 11, 1908, approving the application of San Francisco for the Hetch Hetchy reservoir site, *in* Proceedings before the Secretary of the Interior in re Use of Hetch Hetchy Reservoir Site in Yosemite National Park by the City of San Francisco (Washington, D.C., 1910), pp. 1-6.

GLASS, ALFRED. "Brief History of the Village Chapel," *Yosemite Nature Notes*, 1945, pp. 114-118.

GLASSFORD, W. A. "Climate of California and Nevada," 51st U.S. Congress, 2d Session, Ex. Doc. 287, Appendix 67 (Washington, D.C., 1891), pp. 333-356.

GLEADELL, W. H. "Yosemite Memories," *Electric Magazine*, December, 1896.

GODFREY, ELIZABETH H. "Chronicles of Cosie Hutchings Mills" (1941 MS in Yosemite Museum), pp. 1-14.

—. "Joseph N. LeConte," *Yosemite Nature Notes*, 1946, pp. 66-69.

—. "Thumbnail Sketches of Yosemite Artists" [T.A. Ayres, Thomas Hill, Charles D. Robinson, Albert Bierstadt, Thomas Moran, William Keith, Chris Jorgensen, Gunnar M. Widforss, Harry C. Best, Ferdinand Burgdorff], *Yosemite Nature Notes*, 1944, pp. 21-97, *passim*; 1945, pp. 37-76, *passim*.

—. "Yosemite Indians Yesterday and Today," *Yosemite Nature Notes*, 1941, pp. 49-72.

GODFREY, WILLIAM C. "Among the Big Trees in the Mariposa Grove," *Yosemite*

Nature Notes, 1929, pp. 37-50 [illus. with 15 original pen and ink drawings].

GOETHE, C. M. "Nature Guides," *Survey*, 44 (April, 1920): 145.

—. "Yosemite Nature Guides," *Sierra Club Bulletin*, 11 (1921): 2, 167-170.

GOMPERTZ, H. M. "A Closer Acquaintance with Yosemite," *Sunset*, 1900.

GORDON-CUMMING, CONSTANCE F. *Granite Crags of California* (Edinburgh, 1886), 374 pp., illus.

GRAVES, J. A. *California Memories* (Los Angeles, 1930), 330 pp., illus.

GREELEY, HORACE. *Recollections of a Busy Life* (New York, 1868), 624 pp.

GREENWOOD, GRACE. *New Life in New Lands* (New York, 1873), 414 pp.

GRINNELL, JOSEPH and TRACY IRWIN STORER. *Animal Life in the Yosemite* (University of California Press, 1924), xviii+752 pp., map and illus.

GUNNISON, A. *Rambles Overland* (1884), 246 pp.

HALL, ANSEL F. "The Early Days in Yosemite," *California Historical Society Quarterly*, January, 1923.

—. "Educational Activities in National Parks," *Proc. First Pan Pacific Conf.* (Washington, D.C., 1927), pp. 397-413.

—. "The Educational Development of Yosemite National Park," *Sierra Club Bulletin*, 11 (1923): 4, 411-416.

—. *Guide to Yosemite* (1921), 98 pp.

—. *Handbook of Yosemite National Park* (1921), 347 pp., illus.

—. Letter, 1930, to C. P. Russell re Yosemite Museum history (in Yosemite Museum).

—. *Yosemite Valley: An Intimate Guide* (Berkeley, 1929), 80 pp.

HALL, HARVEY N. and CARLOTTA C. HALL. *A Yosemite Flora* (San Francisco, 1912), pp. 282

HAMILTON, E. H. "The New Yosemite Railroad," *Cosmopolitan Magazine*, September, 1907.

HAMLIN, CHAUNCEY J. "Studying Nature in Place," *Proc. First Pan Pacific Conf.* (Washington, D.C., 1927), pp.435-443.

—. "Yosemite Museum Formally Presented to Park Service," *Yosemite Nature Notes*, 1926, p. 95.

HANNA, PHIL TOWNSEND. "Yosemite Re-born," *Touring Topics*, July, 1926, pp. 16-19.

Harper's Magazine. "The Yosemite Valley," May, 1886, pp. 697-708, illus., map.

HARRIS YOSEMITE CAMP GROUNDS, Register of Yosemite Campers, 1878.

HARWELL, C. A. "Beginning of Nature Guiding," *Yosemite Nature Notes*, 1932, pp. 2-3.

—. "The Stephen Tyng Mather Appreciation Memorial Plaque Dedication," *Yosemite Nature Notes*, 1932, p. 1.

HILDEBRAND, JOEL H. "A Nation of Onlookers?" [Advocates that skiers get away from "the merry-go-round of packed slope and ski tow."] *American Ski Annual*, 1945-46, pp. 145-150.

HILL, H. A. "A Trip to Yosemite Valley," *Penny Monthly*, July, 1871.

HITTELL, J. S. *Bancroft's Pacific Guide Book* (San Francisco, 1882), 270 pp., illus.
—. *Hittell's Handbook of Pacific Coast Travel* (San Francisco, 1887), 264 pp., illus.
—. *The Resources of California* (San Francisco, 1867), 462 pp.
HITTELL, T. H. *Adventures of James Capen Adams* (San Francisco, 1860), 378 pp., illus.
—. *History of California*, Vol. III (San Francisco, 1897), 982 pp.
HODGDON, T. J. Manuscript by C. P. Russell on interview with Mr. Hodgdon [in Yosemite Museum].
HOFFMANN, C. F. Notes on Hetch Hetchy Valley, *California Academy of Natural Sciences, Proceedings*, Vol. III, Part V (1868), pp. 368-370.
HOLDER, C. F. "Famous Basaltic Columns," *Scientific American*, February 2, 1901.
HOLMES, A. E. Letter to J. V. Lloyd (in Yosemite Museum).
Homer Mining Index (Lundy), June 12, 1880; July 22, 1882.
HOWARD OF GLOSSOP, WINIFRED MARY (DE LISLE) HOWARD. *Journal of a Tour in the United States, Canada, and Mexico* (London, 1897), 356 pp., illus.
HUBER, WALTER L. "The John Muir Trail," *Sierra Club Bulletin*, 15 (1930): 1, 37-46.
HUDSON, T. S. *A Scamper through America* (New York, 1882), 289 pp.
HUNTINGTON, E. *The Secret of the Big Trees* (1913), 24 pp., illus.
HUSSEY, JOHN A. "Discovery of the Tuolumne Grove of Big Trees," *Yosemite Nature Notes*, 1937, pp. 60-63.
HUTCHINGS, J. M. *In the Heart of the Sierras* (Oakland, 1886), 496 pp., illus.
—. *Scenes of Wonder and Curiosity in California* (San Francisco, 1862), 268 pp., illus.
—. *Souvenir of California* (San Francisco, 1894), 102 pp., illus.
HUTCHINSON, J.S. "A New Link in the John Muir Trail," *Sierra Club Bulletin*, 11 (1923): 4,357-367.
HUTH, HANS. "The Evolution of Preservationism in Europe," *Journal of the American Society of Architectural Historians* (July-October, 1941), pp. 5-13 [Yosemite on pp. 5, 12].

INGRAM, K. C. Letter to C. P. Russell (in Yosemite Museum) regarding Southern Pacific records of railroad building.
IRVING, WASHINGTON. *The Rocky Mountains* (Philadelphia, 1837). Two vols., frontis., map.

JACKSON, HELEN HUNT. *Bits of Travel at Home* (Boston, 1878), 414 pp.
JAMES, HARLEAN. *Romance of the National Parks* (New York, 1939), xiv+240 pp., illus.
JEFFERS, L. R. *The Call of the Mountains* (1922).
—. "Memories of the Mountains of California," *Scribner's Magazine*, May, 1919.
JOHNSON, CLIFTON. *Highways and Byways of the Pacific Coast* (1907), 324 pp., illus.
JOHNSON, ROBERT U. *Remembered Yesterdays* (Boston, 1923), 624 pp., illus.
JOHNSTONE, E. McD. *West by South, Half South* (Buffalo, 1890), 98 pp., illus.
JONES, FANNIE CRIPPEN. "The Barnards of Yosemite" (MS in Yosemite Museum).

KING, CLARENCE. *Mountaineering in the Sierra Nevada* (1872), 292 pp. [Several subsequent eds., the latest edited by F. P. Farquhar (New York, 1935, 2d printing, 1946), 320 pp., illus.]

KITTREDGE, FRANK A. "Death of Maggie Howard, 'Tabuce,' Participant in Yosemite Indian Demonstration, Yosemite Interpretive Program," Memo., Superintendent to Director, January 29, 1947, 2 pp.

—. "His [Col. C. G. Thomson's] Contribution to the National Parks," *Yosemite Nature Notes*, 1937, pp. 37-38.

—. "The National Park Service: The Thirtieth Anniversary," *Yosemite Nature Notes*, 1946, pp. 86-88.

—. "Trails of the National Parks," *American Civic Annual*, 1931, pp. 18-22.

—. "Yosemite During the War Years," *Yosemite Nature Notes*, 1946, pp. 73-77.

KNEELAND, SAMUEL. *The Wonders of the Yosemite Valley* (1872), 98 pp., illus.

KNOWLTON, E. "Yosemite on Foot," *Overland Monthly*, Vol. V, July, 1870, pp. 84-89.

KROEBER, A. L. "California Place Names of Indian Origin," *University of California Publications in American Ethnology*, 12 (1916): 2, 31-69.

—. "Handbook of the Indians of California," Bulletin 78, Bureau American Ethnology (Washington, D.C., 1925).

—. "Indians of Yosemite," in *Handbook of Yosemite National Park* (Ansel F. Hall, ed.; New York, 1921), pp. 49-73.

KUYKENDALL, R. S. *Early History of Yosemite Valley* (Washington, D.C., 1919).

KYLE, C. W. *Yosemite: The World's Wonderland* (1915).

LAIDLAW, WALTER. "A Camping Tour to Yosemite," *Outlook*, June 5, 1897, pp. 319-324.

LAYTON, G. I. *Two Years in the Life of the Felon, Grovenor I. Layton, Lynched at Sonora, 1852* (A. R. Orton, 1852), 40 pp., illus.

LeCONTE, J. N. *Alpina Americana, No. I: The High Sierra of California* (American Alpine Club, New York, 1907).

—. "The Soda Springs Property in the Tuolumne Meadows," *Sierra Club Bulletin*, 9 (1913): 1, 36-39.

LeCONTE, JOSEPH. *The Autobiography of Joseph LeConte* (1903), 337 pp., plates, portraits.

—. *A Journal of Ramblings through the High Sierras of California by the "University Excursion Party"* (San Francisco, 1875). [Reprinted, *Sierra Club Bulletin*, 3 (1900): 1, 1-107. New ed., San Francisco, The Sierra Club, 1930, xviii+152 pp., illus.]

—. "Rough Notes of a Yosemite Camping Trip," *Overland Monthly*, 2d ser., Vol. VIII, October, November, December, 1885.

—. "Yosemite," *Sunset*, 2 (1899): 119-190, illus.

LEIDIG, CHARLES T. "The Leidig Family in California" (MS).

—. "President Roosevelt's Visit to Yosemite in May, 1903," [a report by the President's guide and cook] 4 pp., 1941, typed MS in Yosemite Museum.

LEONARD, RICHARD M. "Piton Technique on the Cathedral Spires," *Appalachia*, December, 1934, p. 178.

—. "Rock Climbing in Yosemite, *Sierra Club Bulletin*, 23 (1938): 2, 116-119.

—. "Use of Wilderness Areas," *American Civic and Planning Annual*, 1939, pp. 227-231.

LEONARD, RICHARD M. and DAVID R. BROWER. "A Climber's Guide to the HighSierra: Part IV, Yosemite Valley," *Sierra Club Bulletin*, 25 (1940): 1, 41-63.

LEONARD, RICHARD M., et al. *Mountain Records of the Sierra Nevada* (Sierra Club, San Francisco, 1937), 118 pp. (mimeo.).

LEONARD, ZENAS. *Leonard's Narrative, 1831-1836* (Cleveland, 1904), 317 pp., illus.

LESTER, JOHN ERASTUS. *The Atlantic to the Pacific* (Boston, 1873), 366 pp.

—. *The Yo-Semite* (an address, Providence, 1873), 40 pp.

LEWIS, RALPH H. "Park Museums - State and Local" [Part I, Trailside Museums; Part II, Historic House Museums; Part III, Museums in the Survey], *Museum News*, 19 (1941): 10, 7-12; 11, 7-12.

—. "A Survey of National Park Service Museums," *Museum News*, 19 (1941): 7, 10-12.

LEWIS, W. B. "Yosemite as a Playground," *California Forestry* (June, 1917), pp. 12-13.

—. "Yosemite Timber Lands Saved," *American Civic Annual*, 2 (1930), 7-9.

Littell's Living Age, "The Yo-Hamite Valley of California," January, 1860.

LLOYD, JAMES D. "The Removal of the Old Yosemite Village," *Yosemite Nature Notes*, 1926, pp. 26-31.

LOCKWOOD, J. A. "Uncle Sam's Troopers in the National Parks of California," *Overland Monthly* (March, 1889), pp. 356-368.

LOGAN, OLIVE. "Does It Pay to Visit Yosemite?" *Galaxy*, October, 1870.

LUDLOW, F. H. "Seven Weeks in the Great Yosemite," *Atlantic Monthly*, June, 1864.

McCLELLAN, R. GUY. *The Golden State* (1874).

MAIER, HERBERT. "The Purpose of the Museum in the National Parks," *Yosemite Nature Notes*, 1926, pp. 37-40.

Mammoth City Herald, July 9, 1879 - February 12, 1881.

MARIPOSA COUNTY. Minutes of Board of County Supervisors (Mariposa Courthouse).

Mariposa Gazette, "'Old Timers' Convention in Yosemite," June 24 and July 1, 1943.

MARSHALL, W. G. *Through America* (1881), 424 pp.

MARVIN, JOHN G. "Account of the Yosemite Expedition," *Alta California*, April 23, 1851.

MATHER, STEPHEN T. "Administration of the National Parks of the United States," *Proc. First Pan Pacific Conference* (Washington, D.C., 1927), pp. 427-452.

—. "The New Yosemite," *California Forestry*, September, 1917, pp. 38-39.

MATTHES, FRANÇOIS E. *Geologic History of the Yosemite Valley*, U.S.G.S. Prof. Paper 160, Washington, 1930, pp. 1-137, illus.

—. "John Muir and the Glacial Theory of Yosemite," *Sierra Club Bulletin*, 23 (1938): 2, 9-10.

—. "Studying the Yosemite Problem," *Sierra Club Bulletin*, 9 (1914): 3, 136-147.

MATTHEWS, ALBERT. "The Word Park in the United States," Publications of the Colonial Society of Massachusetts, 8 (1906): 373-399 [development of the Yosemite Park idea, pp. 382-387].

MAULDING, MRS. J. ATWOOD. Letter to William E. Colby from Director of Personnel, Department of Interior, October 19, 1940, copy in National Park Service files.

MEINECKE, E. P. "The Skier and His Government" [in minutes, Section on Forests and Recreation, Commonwealth Club, June 25, 1941], pp. 1-5, mimeo.

MERRIAM, C. HART. *The Dawn of the World: Myths and Weird Tales Told by the Mewan Indians of California* (Cleveland, 1910), 274 pp., illus., bibliog.

—. "Indian Village and Camp Sites in Yosemite Valley," *Sierra Club Bulletin*, 10 (1917): 2, [202]-209.

—. "Route of Jedediah S. Smith in 1826," *California Historical Society Quarterly*, October, 1923, pp. 228-236.

MERRILL, GEORGE P. *The First One Hundred Years of American Geology* (Yale University Press, 1924), 774 pp.

MICHAEL, ENID. "The Common Nesting Birds of Yosemite Valley," *Yosemite Nature Notes*, 1930, pp. 41-64.

—. "A Distributional List of Yosemite Birds," Bulletin 2, Yosemite Natural History Association, 1927, pp. 1-15.

—. "Nature Garden a New Feature of Yosemite Museum," *Yosemite Nature Notes*, 1932, pp. 4-5.

MILLER, G. C. "A Pioneer of the Yosemite," *Overland Monthly*, 2d. ser. Vol. LV (April, 1910), pp. 390-394.

MILLS, COSIE HUTCHINGS [MRS. GERTRUDE HUTCHINGS MILLS]. Letter to Mrs. Elizabeth Godfrey: reminiscences of pioneer days in Yosemite Valley. (MS in Yosemite Museum.)

MILLS, E. A. "Touring in Our National Parks," *Country Life in America*, January, 1913, pp. 33-36.

MINTURN, WILLIAM. *Travels West* (London, 1877), 396 pp.

MOFFITT, JAMES. "History of the Yosemite Elk Herd," *California Fish and Game*, 20 (1934): 37-51.

MORRIS, MRS. J. E. *A Pacific Coast Vacation* (New York, 1901), 256 pp., illus.

MORRIS, PAUL. "Big Oak Flat Road - Historic," *San Francisco Examiner*, April 19, 1925, p. A-15.

Motor West. "The Motor Conquest of Yosemite National Park," September 15, 1916.

MUIR, JOHN. "The Creation of Yosemite National Park: Letters of John Muir to Robert Underwood Johnson," *Sierra Club Bulletin*, 29 (1944): 5, 49-60 [with notes by Wm. E. Colby].

—. "The Endangered Valley: The Hetch Hetchy Valley in Yosemite National Park," *Century Magazine*, January, 1909, pp. 464-469, illus. [Reprinted in *Scribner's Magazine*, November, 1909, and *Sierra Club Bulletin*, January, 1916.]

—. "Features of Proposed Yosemite National Park," *Century Magazine*, September, 1890, pp. 656-667.
—. "Galen Clark," *Sierra Club Bulletin*, 7 (1910): 4, 215-220, illus.
—. *Letters to a Friend, 1866-1879* (Boston, 1915), 194 pp.
—. *The Mountains of California* (1894), 382 pp., illus.
—. *My First Summer in the Sierra* (1911), 354 pp.
—. *Our National Parks* (1909), 382 pp., illus.
—. *Picturesque California* 1881-1891, 10 vols., illus.
—. "Studies in the Sierra," *Sierra Club Bulletin*, 9-11 (1915-1921).
—. "The Treasures of the Yosemite," *Century Magazine*, August, 1890, pp. 483-500, illus., maps.
—. *The Yosemite* (1912), 284 pp., illus.
—. "The Yosemite National Park," *Atlantic Monthly*, August, 1899, pp. 145-152.
MURPHY, T. D. *Three Wonderlands of the American West* (1912), 180 pp., illus.

Nation Magazine. "Preservation of the Yosemite Valley," February 6, 1890.
—. "The Yosemite Recession," April 27, 1905.
NATIONAL PARKS ASSOCIATION. "Newton B. Drury is New Director of the National Park Service [Editorial]," *National Parks Bulletin*, 15 (1940): 68, 16.
NICHOLS, GRACE. "Pioneer Shrines in Yosemite," *Yosemite Nature Notes*, 1934, pp. 22-24, 29-32, 37-40, illus.

OLMSTED, FREDERICK LAW. "Government Preservation of Natural Scenery," Brookline, Mass., March 8, 1890 [a leaflet; reprinted, *Sierra Club Bulletin*, 29 (1944): 5, 61-66].
Out West Magazine. Editorial, "The Big Trees," 1904.
—. Editorial, "Yosemite for the People," August, 1902.
Outlook. "A National Park Service," Vol. C, February 3, 1912, p. 246.

PATTERSON, J. E. "Life History of *Recurvia milleri*, the Lodgepole Pine Needle-Miner, in the Yosemite National Park, California," *Journal of Agricultural Research*, 21 (1921): 3, 127-143.
PECK, J. K. *The Seven Wonders of the New World* (1885), 320 pp.
Peregoy Hotel Register, 1871-1875 (in Yosemite Museum).
PERRY, H. E. "Museum Guests Recall History of Yosemite Valley," *Yosemite Nature Notes*, 1930, pp. 1-3.
PIERREPONT, EDWARD. *Fifth Avenue to Alaska* (1884), 329 pp.
PORTER, T. C. *Impressions of America* (1899), 241 pp., illus.
PRESNALL, C. C. "Indian Picture Writing in Yosemite," *Yosemite Nature Notes*, 1930, p. 94.

—. "Indian Rancherias Found," *Yosemite Nature Notes*, 1930, pp. 107-108.

—. "The Lost Arrow Nature Trail," *Yosemite Nature Notes*, 1929, pp. 109-112.

—. "Translating the Autobiography of a Big Tree," *Yosemite Nature Notes*, 1933, pp. 5-7.

PROCTOR, A. PHIMISTER. *An Ascent of Half Dome in 1884*. Grabhorn Press, San Francisco, 1945, 20 pp. [reprinted in *Sierra Club Bulletin*, 31 (1946): 6, 1-9].

RADCLIFFE, CORWIN. "Rad's Ramblings," *Merced Sun-Star*, June 14, 15, 18, and 19, 1926.

RAYMOND, I. W. Letter of February 20, 1864, to Senator John Conness, Records of United States Public Land Office, National Archives, Washington, D.C.

RENSCH, H. E. and ETHEL G. RENSCH. *Historic Spots in California, I: The Southern Counties*, Stanford University Press, 1933, xxii+598 pp.

REYNOLDS, G. E. *Guardians of Our National Parks*, compiled from *Stockton Record*, 1923-24.

RHODA, J. "Uncle Sam in the Yosemite," *Overland Monthly*, N.S. Vol. LXI, June, 1918, pp. 590-594.

RICHARDSON, A. D. *Beyond the Mississippi* (1867), 572 pp., illus.

RICHMAN, I. B. *California under Spain and Mexico, 1535-1847* (Boston and New York, 1911), 542 pp., illus., maps, plans, charts.

RIDER, FREMONT. *Rider's California* (1925), 668 pp., illus.

ROBINSON, C. D. "Painting a Yosemite Panorama," *Overland Monthly*, 2d. ser., Vol. XXII, September, 1893, pp. 243-256.

ROBINSON, L. N. R. *Our Trip to the Yosemite Valley* (London, 1883), 38 pp.

ROBINSON, ROBERT C. "A Nation-wide Public Naturalist Survey," *Proceedings Second Park Naturalist Conference, National Park Service* (Washington, D.C., 1940), pp. 25-33 (mimeo.).

ROORBACK, E. J. "Night on Glacier Point," *Overland Monthly*, 2d. ser., Vol. XLVIII, October, 1906, pp. 207-11.

RUSSELL, CARL P. "Dr. Herman Carey Bumpus, 1862-1943," *Yosemite Nature Notes*, 1943, pp. 97-101.

—. "Early Years in Yosemite," *California Historical Society Quarterly*, Vol. V., No. 4, 1926.

—. "H. C. Bumpus Inspects the Yosemite Educational Project," *Yosemite Nature Notes*, 1928, pp. 21-23, illus.

—. "Hiker's Camps of Yosemite National Park," *Yosemite Natural History Association, Bulletin I* (1925), 12 pp., maps.

—. "The History and Status of Interpretive Work in National Parks," *Regional Review*, July, 1939, pp. 7-14.

—. *One Hundred Years in Yosemite: The Romantic Story of Early Human Affairs in the Central Sierra Nevada*, Stanford University Press, 1931, 242 pp., illus.

—. "Seasonal Migration of Mule Deer," *Ecological Monographs*, 2 (1932): 1-46.

—. "Sierra Nevada Winter Journeys [cross-country skiing]," *Sunset*, January, 1928.

—. "Tribute to G. E. Reynolds of the Stockton Record," *Yosemite Nature Notes*, 1928, pp. 64-65.

—. "Two Interviews with Maria Lebrado, Last of the Original Yosemite Indians" (1929), (MS in Region Four Headquarters, National Park Service, San Francisco).

—. "Yosemite Discoverers Immortalized," *Yosemite Nature Notes*, 1925, pp. 43-45, illus.

RUSSELL, ISRAEL C. *Glaciers of North America* (Boston, 1897) [glaciers of the Sierra Nevada, pp. 37-54].

RUSSELL, R. E. Letter from Headquarters, Camp Fresno, May 17, 1851, *Alta California*, June 12, 1851.

San Francisco Examiner, May 30, 1925.

SAWYER, MRS. W. C. "A Camping Trip to the Yosemite Valley," *Chautauqua*, August, 1893.

SCHLAGINTWEIT, R. VON. *Californien: Land und Leute* (1871), 386 pp., illus.

SCHMECKEBIER, L. F. "The National Parks from the Scientific and Educational Side," *Popular Science Monthly*, Vol. LXXX, June, 1912, pp. 531-547.

SENN, NICHOLAS. *Our National Recreation Parks* (1904), 148 pp., illus.

SEXTON, LUCY FOSTER. *The Foster Family*, (1925).

SEYD, ERNEST. *California and Its Resources* (London, 1858).

SHARSMITH, CARL W. "Environmental Adaptations of Some Yosemite Plants," *Yosemite Nature Notes*, 1943, pp. 17-21, 27-30.

—. "Recent Botanical Collections [in Yosemite National Park]," *Yosemite Nature Notes*, 1944, p. 100.

SHAY, JOHN C. *Twenty Years in the Backwoods of California* (Boston, 1923), 142 pp.

SHINN, CHARLES HOWARD. *Mining Camps, American Frontier Government* (New York, 1885), 316 pp.

SHIRLEY, JAMES C. *The Redwoods of Coast and Sierra* (University of California Press, 1937; 4th ed., 1947), 84 pp., illus.

Sierra Club Bulletin (San Francisco, 1893 to date).

—. "John Muir Memorial Number," 10 (1916): 1, 134 pp., illus.

—. "The Sierra Club and Yosemite," 10 (1917): 2, 135-145.

SMITH, BERTHA H. *Yosemite Legends* (1904), 64 pp.

SMITH, GRANT H. "Bodie, the Last of the Old-Time Mining Camps," *California Historical Society Quarterly*, March, 1925, pp. 64-80, illus.

—. "More Notes on Tioga Mining History: A Visit to Tioga Mine," *Yosemite Nature Notes*, 1929, pp. 25-27.

SOLOMONS, THEODORE S. "After Forty Years," *Sierra Club Bulletin*, 18 (1933): 1, 20-23.

—. "The Beginnings of the John Muir Trail," *Sierra Club Bulletin*, 25 (1940): 1, 28-40.

SOVULEWSKI, GABRIEL. "The Story of Campgrounds in Yosemite Valley," *Yosemite Nature Notes*, 1937, pp. 81-84.

—. "The Story of Trail Building in Yosemite National Park," *Yosemite Nature Notes*, 1928, pp. 25-28.

SPENCER, JEANNETTE DYER (ed.). *Ahwahnee, Yosemite National Park, Calif.* [An account of the history and furnishings of the Ahwahnee Hotel.] (San Francisco, 1935), 32 pp., illus.

STARR, WALTER A., JR. *Guide to the John Muir Trail and the High Sierra Region* (Sierra Club, San Francisco, 1934), ix+146 pp., map [2d ed., 2d printing, 1946].

STEWARD, JULIAN H. *Indian Tribes of Sequoia National Park Region* (National Park Service, Berkeley, 1935), 30 pp. (mimeo.).

Stockton Record. 1924 to date, "Out-o'-Doors Section."

STODDARD, C. A. *Beyond the Rockies* (1894), 214 pp., illus.

STODDARD, C. W. "In Yosemite Shadows," *Overland Monthly*, Vol. III (August, 1869), pp. 105-112.

STORNOWAY, LEWIS. *Yosemite: Where to Go and What to Do* (1888).

STORY, ISABELLE F. "Plans for Memorials to Stephen T. Mather," *American Civic Annual*, 1931, pp. 44-46.

STROTHER, F. "The Yosemite in Winter," *Country Life in America*, January, 1909, pp. 262-264.

SUMNER, E. LOWELL. "The Biology of Wilderness Protection," *Sierra Club Bulletin*, 27 (1942): 4, 14-21.

TAYLOR, BENJAMIN F. *Between the Gates* (S. C. Griggs & Co., Chicago, 1878, 1883, 1886), 292 pp., illus.

TAYLOR, F. J. *The Yosemite Trip Book* (1926).

TAYLOR, MRS. H. J. "The Cemetery in Yosemite Valley," *Yosemite Nature Notes*, 1932, pp. 1-4, illus.

—. "Construction of Coulterville Road Recalled by V. Bruschi," *Yosemite Nature Notes*, 1930, pp. 73-74.

—. "The Death of the Last Survivor," *University of California Chronicle*, January, 1932, pp. 51-55.

—. "Hetch Hetchy Water Flows into San Francisco," *Yosemite Nature Notes*, 1934, pp. 89-91.

—. "The Return of the Last Survivor," *University of California Chronicle*, January, 1931, pp. 85-89.

TAYLOR, KATHERINE AMES. *Lights and Shadows of Yosemite* (1926).

—. *Yosemite Tales and Trails* (San Francisco, 1934), 78 pp., illus.

TAYLOR, RAY W. *Hetch Hetchy: The Story of San Francisco's Struggle to Provide a Water Supply* (1926).

THAYER, JAMES B. *A Western Journey with Mr. Emerson* (1884), 142 pp.

THOMSON, CHARLES G. "Conservation in the National Parks," *Yosemite Nature Notes*, 1935, pp. 1-5.

—. "Ecology of the Wawona Road," *Yosemite Nature Notes*, 1937, pp. 38-39.

—. "Hiding Yosemite's Visitors," *American Civic Annual*, 1932, pp. 26-30.

—. "The Place of National Parks in the State Plan," *American Planning and Civic Annual*, 1937, pp. 240-243.

TILESTON, JOHN BOIES. *Letters of John Boies Tileston* (privately printed, Boston, 1922), 138 pp.

TINKHAM, GEORGE H. *California Men and Events, 1769-1890* (Stockton, 1915), plates.

TISSANDIER, A. *Six mois aux Etats Unis* (1886), 298 pp.

TOLSON, HILLORY A. (Comp.). *Laws Relating to the National Park Service, the National Parks and Monuments* (Washington, D.C., 1933), 318 pp.

TOMLINSON, E. T. *Four Boys in the Yosemite* (1911), 406 pp.

TORREY, BRADFORD. "On Foot in the Yosemite," *Atlantic Monthly*, August, 1910, pp. 228-237.

TRESIDDER, DONALD BERTRAM. "The National Parks: A Public Health Problem" (MS in Yosemite Museum).

TRESIDDER, MARY CURRY. "D. A. Curry" (MS in Yosemite Museum).

—. *The Trees of Yosemite* (Stanford University Press, 1932), 134 pp.

TRIPP, STEPHEN T. "Memorandum Regarding Churches in Yosemite," 1941, pp. 1-3, MS in Yosemite Museum.

TRUMAN, BEN C. *Tourists' Illustrated Guide, California* (1883), maps, illus.

Tuolumne County, History of (1882)

TURRILL, CHARLES B. *California Notes* (1876), 232 pp., illus.

UNITED STATES CONGRESS. Chap. clxxxvi of the statutes at large, passed at 30th Congress, Session I, 1864.

—. [The Yosemite Reservation and the Yellowstone National Park Act], *Congressional Globe* (June 30, 1872), p. 697.

UNITED STATES DEPARTMENT OF THE INTERIOR. "Decision of the Secretary of the Interior [on Lake Eleanor and Hetch Hetchy Valley reservoir sites]," *Sierra Club Bulletin*, 6 (1908): 4, 321-329.

—. "Hetch Hetchy Valley, Yosemite National Park," in *Annual Report* [1913] (Washington, D.C., 1914), 1: 90-93.

—. *National Parks Portfolio* (1917), 260 pp., illus.

—. *Proceedings before the Secretary of the Interior in re Use of Hetch Hetchy Reservoir Site* (Washington, 1910).

UNITED STATES GEOLOGICAL SURVEY. *Fifth Annual Report* (1883-84), pp. 31-32, 302-328.

—. *Eighth Annual Report*, I (1886-87), 261-394.

UNITED STATES NATIONAL PARK SERVICE. *Annual Reports*, 1916 - 1932 (Washington, D.C.); 1933 to date, in Annual Report of Secretary of the Interior.

—. *A Bibliography of National Parks and Monuments West of the Mississippi River*, Vol. I (Western Museum Laboratories, Berkeley, 1941, mimeo.).

—. "Interpretive Plan, Yosemite," in Yosemite National Park Master Plan, Development

Outline, sheets 1-5, map (1942).

—. "Interview with John Degnan, December 13, 1941" (MS in Yosemite Museum), 8 pp.

—. Proceedings Second Park Naturalists Conference (Washington, D.C., 1940), 368 pp. (mimeo.).

—. "Superintendent Thomson Succumbs," *Park Service Bulletin,* 7 (1937): 1-3.

—. Yosemite National Park Master Plan [A "conservative device" for regulating physical developments. It is kept up to date. Copies are filed in the park, in the Region Four Office, San Francisco, and in the office of the Director, National Park Service.]

UNITED STATES SENATE. *Report of Commission on Roads in Yosemite National Park, 1899, Senate Document No. 155,* 56th Congress, 1900.

UNITED STATES WAR DEPARTMENT. *Annual Report of the Chief of Engineers, 1879.* Appendix OO, pp. 2144-2210, 2233-2238.

VAN NAME, W. G. *The Yosemite National Park - How Its Boundaries Have Been Trimmed* (privately printed, January, 1924), 8 pp., maps.

VINT, THOMAS C. "Post War Possibilities for the Sierra Slope Parks: Yosemite, Kings Canyon, Sequoia" [a proposal to view as one problem the national parks of the Sierra Nevada]. Report submitted to the Director, April 13, 1945,14 pp., map.

VISCHER, EDWARD. *Vischer's Views of California* (1862), 12 plates with 25 engravings.

VIVIAN, A. P. *Wanderings in the Western Land* (London, 1879), 426 pp., illus.

WALKER, MYRL V. "Oyster Shell Scale in Yosemite National Park [a scale insect introduced by pioneers]," *Yosemite Nature Notes,* 1945, pp. 81-85.

—. "Reptiles and Amphibians of Yosemite National Park," *Yosemite Nature Notes,* 1946, pp. 1-48.

—. "Yosemite: Type Locality for Amphibians and Reptiles," *Yosemite Nature Notes,* 1944, p. 108.

—. "Yosemite: Type Locality for Recent Mammals," *Yosemite Nature Notes,* 1945, p. 52.

WASSON, JOSEPH. *Account of the Important Revival of Mining Interests in Bodie and Esmeralda Districts* (Spaulding, Barto & Co., San Francisco, 1878), 60 pp., maps and sketches.

WATSON, DOUGLAS S. *West Wind: The Life Story of Joseph Reddeford Walker* (privately printed, Percy H. Booth, Los Angeles, 1934), 112 pp., map.

WEBB, WILLIAM SEWARD. *California and Alaska* (1891), 268 pp., illus.

WEGNER, J. H. "Evidence of an Old Indian Trail Located," *Yosemite Nature Notes,* 1930, p. 67.

WESTERGREEN, E. E. "Cutting Corners to the Coast (Tioga Road)," *Motor,* October, 1915.

WHITNEY, H. A. "Mineral Resources of Mono County," in *Report of State Mineralogist, 1888.*

WHITNEY, J. D. *Geological Survey of California, Vol. I: Geology* (1865).

——. *The Yosemite Guide-Book* (1869, 1870; pocket eds., 1872, 1874), 134 pp., maps.

WILBUR, RAY LYMAN. "What the National Parks Mean to the People of the United States," *American Civic Annual*, 1929, pp. 5-8.

WILEY, W. H. and S. K. *The Yosemite, Alaska, and the Yellowstone* (1893), 230 pp., illus.

WILLARD, E. P. "In Camp at Yosemite," *Western Monthly*, October, 1869.

WILLIAMS, JOHN A. *Yosemite and Its High Sierra* (Tacoma and San Francisco, 1914), 146 pp, illus., maps.

WINEMAN, MODE. "Camera Studies of California National Parks," *Yosemite Nature Notes*, 1927, pp. 9-12 [the author's work in Yosemite, 1902. Representative prints and enlargements of the Wineman photographs are preserved in the Yosemite Museum].

WISELEY, J. L. "The Yosemite Valley," *Harper's Magazine*, May, 1866.

WOLFE, LINNIE MARSH (ed.). *John of the Mountains* (Boston, 1938), xxii+458 pp.

——. *Son of the Wilderness: The Life of John Muir* (New York, 1945), xvii+364 pp.

WOODS, DANIEL B. "Southern Mines [Mariposa and Tuolumne counties]," in *Sixteen Months at the Gold Diggings* (New York, 1851), pp. 77-166.

WRIGHT, GEORGE M., JOSEPH S. DIXON, and BEN W. THOMPSON. *Fauna of the National Parks of the United States: A Preliminary Survey of Faunal Relations in National Parks* (Washington, 1933), 158 pp., illus.

YARD, ROBERT STERLING. "Director of the Nation's Playgrounds," *Sunset*, September, 1916, p. 27, illus.

——. *The John Muir Trail: A Brief Account of the Mather Mountain Party's Outing of 1916* (Washington, D.C., 1918), 94 pp. (mimeo.), 46 photographic prints.

——. "The Unforgotten Story of Hetch Hetchy," *American Forests*, December, 1934, pp. 567-569, illus.

YEAGER, DORR G. *Your Western National Parks* (New York, 1947), illus., maps.

YOSEMITE NATURAL HISTORY ASSOCIATION. *Yosemite Nature Notes* (Yosemite, July, 1922, to date).

YOSEMITE NATIONAL PARK. *Report of the Acting Superintendent*, 1892-1914, and *Report of the Superintendent*, 1916 to date.

YOSEMITE PARK AND CURRY COMPANY. "The Firefall: Explanation and History" (pamphlet printed in Yosemite, 1940), 6 pp.

——. *History of the United States Naval Special Hospital* (Yosemite National Park, 1946), 76 pp.

YOSEMITE PARK COMMISSION. *Report, Revision of Park Boundaries*, 1904.

YOSEMITE PARK NATURALIST. *Monthly Reports*, July, 1921, to date.

Yosemite Tourist [D. J. Foley's newspaper], "Highway Robbery on Chowchilla Mountain," July 10, 1906.

YOSEMITE VALLEY COMMISSIONERS. *Biennial Report*, 1867-1904.

INDEX

One Hundred Years in Yosemite
A Printing History
Compiled by Hank Johnston

A. *One Hundred Years in Yosemite: The Romantic Story of Early Human Affairs in the Central Sierra Nevada*. By Carl Parcher Russell, Field Naturalist, National Park Service. Foreword by Horace M. Albright, Director, National Park Service. Stanford University Press, April, 1932. Pp. xvi+242. Forty-three photographs. Appendix includes nine documents, chronology, bibliography, and index. Hardcover, 6" x 9"with dust jacket.

B. *One Hundred Years in Yosemite: The Story of a Great Park and Its Friends*. By Carl Parcher Russell, Chief Naturalist, United States National Park Service. Foreword by Newton B. Drury, Director, National Park Service. University of California Press, 1947. Text revised from item "A." Pp. xviii+226. Fifty-one photographs, one foldout map. Appendix includes chronology, bibliography, and index. Hardcover, 5 1/2" x 8 1/2"with dust jacket.

C. *One Hundred Years in Yosemite: The Story of a Great Park and Its Friends*. By Carl Parcher Russell. Yosemite Natural History Association, 1957. Pp. xiv+206. No foreword. New preface. Forty-two photographs. Text revised from item "B." No bibliography. Appendix includes chronology and index. Softcover, 5 3/4" x 8 3/4".

D. *One Hundred Years in Yosemite: The Story of a Great Park and Its Friends*. By Carl Parcher Russell. Yosemite Natural History Association, 1959. Basically a second printing of item "C" except text slightly revised and chronology updated.

E. *One Hundred Years in Yosemite: The Story of a Great Park and Its Friends*. By Carl Parcher Russell. Yosemite Natural History Association, 1968. Basically a third printing of item "C" except text slightly revised and chronology updated.

F. *One Hundred Years in Yosemite: The Story of a Great Park and Its Friends*. By Carl Parcher Russell. Yosemite Natural History Association, 1976. Pp. xiv+210. Basically a fourth printing of item "C" except text revised, and new page added. Chronology updated to 1974. Printing date shown as 1968, but book actually issued in 1976. Bicentennial logo added to front cover.

ONE HUNDRED YEARS IN YOSEMITE

This reprint was prepared for publication by the
Yosemite Association using OmniPro OCR software.
Editorial duties were shared by
Mary Vocelka and Steven P. Medley.

Designed by Michael Osborne Design, San Francisco, CA.
Type compostion in Cochin.
Printed on Mustang Vellum Offset 60# text and
bound in Speckletone Cream 80# cover by
Delta Lithograph Co., Valencia, CA.